MEMPHIS MEMOIRS

Memphis Memoirs

Paul R. Coppock

Memphis State University Press

Manufactured in the United States of America

Library of Congress Cataloging in Publication Data

Coppock, Paul.
    Memphis memoirs.

    Fifty-eight sketches originally published in the Commercial Appeal.
    Includes index.
    1. Memphis—History—Collected works. 2. Tennessee—History,
Local—Collected works. I. Title.
F444.M545C66   976.8'19   80-24019
ISBN 0-87870-110-9

Within

1   Way Back

2   As It Was

3   Blood, Et Cetera

4   For Profit

5   Some of Our Best

6   Hospital Heroes

MEMPHIS MEMOIRS

1
Way Back

Memphis on the Nile

The oldest works of mankind in Memphis are two engraved stones from a temple that stood in ancient Memphis on the Nile. These stones are the first things seen in the lobby of City Hall, an appropriate link to the original Memphis. The stones were brought to Memphis in 1917 by Robert Galloway, chairman of the Memphis Park Commission. Galloway had found them in Memphis, Egypt, in 1913, but it took him four years to get approval to remove them from the country. They were first housed in the Overton Park Zoo, and later were moved to the new City Hall when it opened.

Old Memphis is gone now. Its temples and other massive buildings were handy sources of stone when Cairo was being built on the other side of the Nile and slightly downstream. But enough fragments remain for the site to be marked on maps. Much more often seen are photographs of the great pyramids, which are gigantic monuments in the royal graveyard of pharoahs who ruled at Memphis.

There are some similarities between modern Memphis and the great city of the thousands of years of Egyptian power. But they were dissimilar in important ways. One of the most striking differences, which gets very little comment, was the way the old Egyptians reacted to the flooding of their big river. The higher the flood on the Nile the

Temple Stones in City Hall (from *The Commercial Appeal* files).

greater the prosperity. They looked forward to the flood and helped it spread over as many acres as possible. They let nature fertilize their fields with sediment from the floods. Their crops stopped where the water stopped. A less-than-normal flood meant a smaller crop. We can only speculate how the old Egyptians would have reacted if they had rich rain-watered fields miles from the river, as we do, but levees to keep the water away would have been strange to them.

There is another contrast between the two cities that gets little attention. Old Memphis got along without lawyers. Each citizen presented his case and questioned his witnesses. Trials were conducted by a panel of judges who came to a temple door to listen. It takes thirty columns of yellow pages to list the lawyers in modern Memphis. Of course residents of old Memphis might have preferred the lawyers, juries, and appeals method. Justice on the Nile was pretty rough, especially for tax offenders. If they failed to pay on time they were beaten, one stroke for each day of delinquency. If they were caught cheating on taxes the penalty could be having the nose cut off. If it was a bad case the ears could be lopped off, too. If it was very bad the eyes were gouged out. A government official caught out of line might be exiled to distant mines for life.

Probably the greatest difference was the stability of occupational assignments in the community. The carpenter was the son, the grandson and the great-grandson of carpenters. He worked with the same kinds of tools his ancestors had used, sometimes with the very tools. And he expected to need similar tools in his life after death. It was the same with potters, stone masons, and artists. Jewelry was a specialty of old Memphis, made by a tribe of dwarfs who had short arms and legs but normal torsos.

We all know about dozens of men who have, within one generation, moved out of poverty to become millionaires, and sons of men who punched timeclocks by the hour who have moved into the professions. But the Egyptian boy took up his father's work. There was one exception. A few boys were taken into the temples where priests taught them to write. The scribes were needed by everyone else and advancements to better jobs were open to them. It was the beginning of many centuries of high standing for the learned man. It was, at the same time, a very limited ''school'' system.

In farming, Egyptians were the experts of the ancient world. Like the United States, Egypt raised more food than it needed. We sell it to other nations as surplus. In the old days other peoples fled from famine to

Egypt, as the Old Testament tells. The Egyptians were good at it because they had been farming longer than anyone else. It is customary to trace our manner of living back through Europe to Rome and then to Greece. But part of the roots of classical Greece were in Egypt. The tribes that developed Greek civilization were still learning how to farm when the Egyptians were growing such big crops that part of them could leave the land, go to the city and buy their food from earnings as craftsmen in making tools, construction of buildings, and even decorating finer structures.

This ability of part of the people to grow enough food for all is a mark of the dividing line between primitive man and civilization. It allowed the other men to develop other skills and it allowed them to live closer together in cities. Part of the Greek roots go back to a similar change in the region drained by the Tigris and Euphrates, but it was Memphis on the Nile that was the great city in the area where Greece grew.

Old Memphis distributed part of the food through municipal breweries. But the word "beer" is misleading for modern readers if used for the brew of old Memphis. Residents of the first Memphis drank it flat and warm. The cold glass of suds was unknown.

The two cities of Memphis were similar in that both had famous doctors to whom the ill came from great distances. They went to old Memphis even when they had to hazard the dangers of travel in small boats across the Mediterranean. Doctors of old Memphis knew about illness from disorders within the body, while the rest of the world was blaming demons and evil spirits. Doctors in old Memphis were especially skilled in some kinds of surgery. They also knew something about preventive medicine. Egyptians, at least in the upper classes, knew about hygiene and were noted for frequency of bathing.

Aside from its doctors, old Memphis was notable for its engineers. They designed the pyramids, devised methods of mining huge blocks of stone, and organized methods to move them long distances and then lift them up the sloping sides. They did it all so well that the pyramids still stand while the other six "wonders of the world" are gone.

The engineers were also good at building canals to spread the floods over more acres, and to drain them, according to need. They had a river broader than the Mississippi at Memphis and they bridged it. Their bridge floated up and down with the river stage because it rested on ninety pontoon barges. As Memphis has a West Memphis, old Memphis had an "East Memphis," another city on the other bank of the river, joined to it by a reliable span.

Crude foreigners arrived in Memphis wearing cloaks of wool, to find the privileged Memphians wearing cool linens, woven of Egyptian flax. While others were still making records on clay tablets, the Egyptians invented light and easily carried paper. Our 365-day year is based on the Egyptian calculations of when the Nile would flood and recede.

This was the city of Memphis, which shows up in the Bible as Noph (Isaiah 19:13, Jeremiah 2:16, Ezekiel 30:13 and 16), as well as "Memphis" in Hosea 9:6, and sometimes "Moph" in Hebrew records, or "Men-nifer" in Greek, or "Menf" among the Arabs. It was the city of the first king in the history of the world, Menes, and he called it "The White City." Even when the center of government was moved upriver to Thebes, the importance of Memphis continued high for many centuries, until the Mohammedan army swept over Egypt in 638.

The extreme age of Memphis on the Nile is almost impossible to understand for residents of the United States, who are so often reminded that our nation has been independent for 200 years. We think the temple stones brought to our City Hall represent great age. That seems so because the history in which we are interested concerns events since then. Alexander conquered the world including Egypt and left Macedonians on the throne, including Cleopatra. Jesus lived. Rome fell. Charlemagne rose to European power. Columbus sailed to the New World. England spread her flag around the globe. These and many other events that have shaped modern man have occurred since those decorative stones were added to the temple in Memphis.

But consider how long the Egyptian story is before Amasis put his touch on the temple. Moses was reared in the royal court at Memphis and led the famous exodus about 800 years before Amasis. It had been about 1,200 years since Joseph and his brothers made history in Memphis. The chronicles of Memphis ran back 2,700 years before Amasis.

In the temple to which he gàve two new doorways, the most extraordinary sight, to this generation, would have been a bull named Apis. This bull was considered to be the living representative of Ptah. The bull lived the pampered life of divinity and crowds of people came to admire him. When he died the bull was mummified and put in a sarcophagus, with mummies of his predecessors. His records showed dates of his birth, his recognition as a god, his "enthronement," and his death. After proper mourning, another bull was chosen.

The cult of the bull seems foolish now but it was in line with other cities, where other animals were honored. More distinctive of Egypt was history's first doctrine of one god. A pharoah more than 800 years before Amasis had insisted on abolition of all gods except one, the disk of the sun. But his reform was quickly abandoned after his death and Egypt returned to honoring many gods of unequal power. Highest eminence among the gods of Egypt was given to Ptah. He was the builder of cities, the god of civilization. He was the guardian of artists. He carried the symbols of life, strength and stability. Ptah was the father of lesser gods and of men. He was the shaper of the world.

The Great Temple of Ptah at Memphis was a place of high distinction to Egyptians for many centuries. It is a distinction unparalleled among American cities for Memphis to have two stones from that temple.

Tishomingo

Tishomingo is a favorite among Indian names retained in the area once occupied by the Chickasaws. When Mississippi organized government in the former Indian land a huge Tishomingo County was set up to manage local government in the area now divided between Alcorn, Prentiss, and Tishomingo counties. It was so large it often was called "The Great State of Tishomingo," and the county seat, Cincinnati, later Jacinto, seemed to be on its way to becoming a major city. Tishomingo Creek played a part in the famous Civil War battle at Brice's Crossroads. Tishomingo is a Memphis street name. Tishomingo is the Johnston County seat in Oklahoma, second home of the Southern tribes.

So, who was this famous Chickasaw? "Mingo" is the word for chief and is added to the names of several individuals. It sometimes is written "Miko." The "Tisho" is written sometimes as "Tishu." He lived in Lee County, in the area now known as the Bethany Community. But he also lived in Union County, in the neighborhood once known as Ellistown, his home in old age.

As a young warrior he fought beside the colonists in the Revolution, serving under General Anthony Wayne. Tishomingo was also an admirer of George Washington. In the War of 1812 he served under General Andrew Jackson. His war record includes nine battles and he was paid a veteran's pension.

In tribal management Tishomingo was more secretary of state than president or top man. The big chief was Ishtehotopah, and Tishomingo was his chief counsellor. There were other counsellors but his opinion was extraordinarily persuasive. There is an old account of other counsellors going silent when Tishomingo announced his decision. Each of the others rushed to say, "That's just what I thought." They adopted the Tishomingo idea with unanimous consent and the chief, having said little, accepted it.

Tishomingo thought of himself as the successor to Piomingo, as a full-blooded Chickasaw who was guiding the nation. But historians say that, without Tishomingo seeing what was happening, management was sliding into the hands of half-breeds.

James Logan Colbert, a Scot who had settled among the Chickasaws, admired them so much he married three sisters, who filled his home with sons. His oldest son was named William, but his mother gave him the name of Chooshemataha. He was the leader of the Chickasaw band that fought in the War of 1812. He helped Jackson fight the Creeks. Everyone going up or down the Natchez Trace had to pay a high fee for crossing the Tennessee River on Colbert's Ferry, owned by another son, George, whose Indian name was Tootemastubbe. He was against teachers, saloon keepers, and missionaries, but he dressed like a white man while building a fortune in horses, slaves, and land. Another son, James, had a tavern on the Natchez Trace and had an education which enabled him to be the usual interpreter and letter-writer. Most influential of the sons was Levi, whose Indian name was Itawamba. He acquired a standing in his later years that allowed him to speak for the whole Chickasaw Nation.

It was the half-breed Colberts whom the English-speaking settlers had to convince when Chickasaw treaties were being discussed, even though the names of Tishomingo and others appeared on the documents. But it was Tishomingo who undertook to enforce one of those treaties. There was a treaty in 1816, signed by Andrew Jackson, Tishomingo, and others, by which traders were shut out of the Chickasaw Nation because of disputes and frauds. This treaty made it the law of the United States that any white person "who shall bring goods and sell them in the nation" was to forfeit all of his goods, the proceeds of their disposal going half to the Chickasaws and half to the United States.

This had been the law for years while traders took their chances by making forays into the nation, and stirring up more of the troubles which had caused them to be outlawed. Bureaucrats from Washington had turned a blind eye. Eventually Tishomingo acted. He was old and in poor health but he was the highest chief in that part of the country. So when Marshall Goodman and John Walker showed up with a stock of trade goods, Tishomingo took possession and turned the merchandise over to John L. Allen, assistant Indian agent for the United States. The traders were expelled. Allen sold the goods and split the proceeds according to the law.

But the traders sued the Indian chief and the assistant agent for $2,000. A federal law had been violated, but the traders got into the state court in Monroe County. A jury ruled for the traders and gave a judgment of $593.09 against Tishomingo and Allen. Proof clearly showed that the goods had been brought into the Chickasaw country for sale, but the jury was impressed by the lack of evidence of a sale being completed. The Circuit Court had acted in 1832. There was an appeal in which Mississippi's High Court of Errors and Appeals approved the judgment. The poor old chief was unable to pay, of course, and eventually was jailed. The jail that held him was only four miles from land still owned by the Chickasaw Nation.

In one view of the situation, the chief was fortunate. The Mississippi Legislature in 1829 and 1830 had adopted laws abolishing Chickasaw jurisdiction. There was a fine of $1,000 and imprisonment up to a year for exercising the office of chief, mingo, head man or other post of Indian power. If Mississippi had used that law on Tishomingo he would have been more severely punished than he was when he tried to enforce a federal law.

Because of the trial and jailing of Tishomingo and the Mississippi laws of 1829 and 1830, the Chickasaws wanted a new treaty, and the Pontotoc Treaty of 1832 was adopted. It says on its face: "Being ignorant of the language and laws of the white man, they (Chickasaws) cannot understand or obey them. Rather than submit to this great evil, they prefer to seek a home in the West, where they may live and be governed by their own laws."

In this treaty Tishomingo, recently jailed under Mississippi law, was restored to his place as chief by the federal government. He signed the document and accepted, as a treaty clause, a pension of $100 a month. The government was undertaking little additional expense since Tishomingo was very old.

The treaty of 1832 provided for the Chickasaws to give up the last fragment of their land, 6,422,400 acres in North Mississippi, for $3 million. It was never paid. The government slipped out by saying the thirty-year-old overdue account was forfeited when the Indians sent their braves into the Civil War on the side of the South. The Chickasaws were to be undisturbed in their Mississippi homes until land acceptable to them, and west of the Mississippi River, was found. But the government fell down on that promise, too, while settlers rushed into the Indian country. The Chickasaw Nation had to solve that one in 1837 by paying the Choctaws $530,000 for the western part of their assigned territory in what is now Oklahoma.

Chickasaw removal had only a few similarities to the "Trail of Tears" of the Cherokees. The Chickasaws were wealthy compared with other tribes. They had adopted the farming methods of their white neighbors and had done very well, especially in raising cotton and horses. When several families decided it was time to move they formed a group and came into Memphis riding good horses beside trains of wagons stacked with plows, harrows and other implements, with other wagons bearing chests of drawers, beds and tables, and leading strings of slaves and horses. Here they boarded boats and rode to Fort Smith. They preferred to move themselves, especially when it was found that government transportation had a limit of thirty pounds on boat luggage, while Congress debated whether that was too generous.

There were wealthy Chickasaws, including several families of Colberts, but of course, there were some poor Indians who had a rough trip and bad food, acceptable to government inspectors. The Indians of all tribes were a minority and they lacked the salaried men and women who spend all year organizing modern protests. The Chickasaws moved gradually for years, while Tishomingo lingered behind on his land near Elliston. In 1836, the same year the huge county was created and given his name, he prepared for the journey by selling his acreage for $2,400. A few months later almost half of it was stolen, allegedly by a neighbor, Benjamin Ellis. Court records still show Ellis indicted for larceny. The indictment of 9 May 1837 shows Ellis accused of using arms to get forty-five $20 bank notes and one $100 bill. Ellis was released under $2,000 bond and his trial was set for 16 May 1837. But the record of the trial outcome is missing. Whether justice or injustice held sway in this case, the old chief set out for the territory where his relatives had gone. He almost made it.

His days ran out on 5 May 1841, when he got to Fort Coffee, on the south bank of the Arkansas River near modern Spiro, Oklahoma. He had attained 100 years, perhaps 104. Scant as his belongings were, he held fast to his Army commission signed by George Washington. And his last words were: "When I am gone beat the drum and fire the guns." The garrison rolled out full military honors for the wrinkled relic of a long past of service to the Chickasaw Nation and to the United States.

Isaac Shelby

In 1817 President Monroe asked Isaac Shelby to become Secretary of War, but Shelby turned down the place in the presidential cabinet, saying he was too old. He was sixty-six and he had been aged by three wars, by the tribulations of being the first governor of Kentucky and by numerous other public offices. But the next year he was asked to represent the United States, with Andrew Jackson, in obtaining West Tennessee and West Kentucky from the Chickasaws by treaty. He accepted and a treaty that opened for settlement the whole country west of the Tennessee River was signed.

Isaac Shelby was a contrast to Andrew Jackson and many others who lifted themselves in one lifetime out of obscurity to great distinction. Shelby inherited prominence and leadership, although he made the name more illustrious than it had ever been before. His grandfather, Evan Shelby, acquired thousands of acres in Maryland, where he prospered in the raising of cattle and sheep, in the Indian fur trade, and as a surveyor. He was a county judge and a militia captain. His father, also Evan, built a fort and a store in Virginia, which became the strategic location where immigrants left the westward route to turn north on Boone's Wilderness Road. The part of Virginia to the north was later separated as the new state of Kentucky. A survey showed that Shelby's Fort was on the line separating Virginia and North Carolina and the settlement around the fort grew into Bristol, Virginia, and Bristol, Tennessee.

During the Revolution, Isaac's father was in command of all garrisons maintained by Virginia along its 300-mile border with North Carolina. In the militia organization, Major Evan Shelby was in command, with two sons, Isaac and James, as captains, and another son, Evan Shelby III, a lieutenant.

The father was named a commissioner to negotiate for Virginia with the Cherokees. When the survey showed his fort and store were in North Carolina, he was elected to the North Carolina Senate. Carolina made him brigadier general of the Washington District, the top commander of a huge area. North Carolina also named him to negotiate with the insurgent State of Franklin. The people of the short-lived state then elected him governor, but Evan Shelby declined.

This was the background of Isaac Shelby. He was born 11 December 1750, and was a sheriff in Maryland before he was twenty. Isaac went into battle for the first time at twenty-three, under command of his father. In his first war he fought for the British. The Earl of Dunmore,

Isaac Shelby

governor of Virginia, attacked the Shawnee, who lived on the north side
of the Ohio River but hunted on the south side and attempted to shut out
hunters from the English colonies. Lord Dunmore's War was a one-
battle conflict, yet it had considerable meaning. For the Shawnee,
having lost the battle at Point Pleasant, agreed to allow white hunters in
the region that later became Kentucky, and to allow white travelers on
the Ohio River.

On the battlefield, the English built Fort Blair, with Isaac Shelby
second in command of the garrison while still only twenty-three. He
became a surveyor for Richard Henderson, the big operator in frontier
land claims, and while marking the Henderson lands he looked over the
country on his own account.

In 1775 he found some secluded land that seemed to be the fairest he
had seen in all his travels and he put his mark on 1,400 acres. He was
twenty-five and unmarried but he pitched his tent there. He came back
many times and eventually built his fine home, Traveler's Rest, there.
For the rest of his life it was where he wanted to be, although his
responsibilities carried him many miles away from the Danville,
Kentucky, region and the family that followed his marriage.

In the early stages of the American Revolution, the fighting in the West was a matter of holding off Indians incited by the British. Virginia included many millions of acres west of the mountains, and the war Virginia fought and financed was of high meaning to the other colonies in revolt.

Isaac Shelby was named commissary general by Virginia, and assigned to buy supplies for the western campaigns. He had the experience of his father's store. He also had the wealth and credit to keep on buying when money from Williamsburg was slow in coming. When Lieutenant Colonel George Rogers Clark pursued the troublesome Indians into the region that later became Indiana, it was Shelby who supplied him. There also was Indian fighting to do in the hills that later became East Tennessee, and Isaac Shelby was in the thick of it.

Isaac Shelby was, in addition, a criminal court judge. He was a delegate to the Virginia Legislature in 1777. Later that year surveyors said the Shelby fort was in North Carolina. So Shelby was sent to the North Carolina Legislature in 1781 and again in 1782. And all the time he was earning his living raising cattle on the farm, and working in the store.

By the time Shelby got to the North Carolina Legislature, he was a very famous man. He had organized and led into battle one of the units of frontier riflemen who soundly defeated the British at King's Mountain on 7 October 1780. It was a turning point in the Revolution and Shelby was honored by formal resolutions from both the North Carolina Legislature and the Continental Congress.

In the western country, King's Mountain was a proud story for many years, and men who had been there were special heroes. Shelby was often called "Old King's Mountain." Only the Battle of New Orleans took its place in the pride of the people and that was nearly thirty-five years later.

Aside from the military accomplishment, Shelby was in the center of the story because Major Patrick Ferguson, having swept through Georgia and endangered the North Carolina and Virginia settlements west of the mountains, sent a special messenger to Shelby. Ferguson demanded that the mountain officers stop resisting the British army and announced that if opposition continued, he would lead his army over the mountains, hang the leaders, and destroy the countryside with torch and sword. It was this message that caused Shelby and John Sevier to gather up the riflemen and go after Ferguson.

As the war wound down toward the peace treaty of 1783, Shelby was able to return to a more normal life. He took part in surveying for North Carolina in 1782 some land where Nashville was being established. The same year he went back to his land near Danville and built a cabin where he had slept in a tent years before. In 1783, when he was thirty-two, he married Susannah Hart, nineteen-year-old daughter of a long-time friend of the family. He then began to build the fine home he called Traveler's Rest. It was of stone, often said (in error) to be Kentucky's first stone building.

Shelby liked to farm and was good at it. He had a large place on which he raised cattle, sheep, horses, mules, and hogs, keeping blood-line records and sending livestock to market frequently. He also kept a herd of deer for the meat. His farm also produced grains, fruits, hemp, tobacco, cider, apple brandy, and whisky. In a time of barter trading, the produce of Traveler's Rest was considered superior, especially the whisky. When wealth was largely in land, he accumulated more than 6,000 acres in several counties.

More than that, he was an earnest advocate of improved farming methods. He organized the Kentucky Society for Promoting Useful Arts, became its first president and was active in the agricultural work for many years. He also was a founder of the Kentucky Bible Society and became vice president of the American Bible Society. He was a Presbyterian, but was indifferent as one of the original trustees of Transylvania Seminary. He corrected himself somewhat by his later services as a trustee of Centre College. He was also the sheriff of Lincoln County for years.

Soon after he moved to the Danville region the big question before the public was what to do about Virginia's government. It was many miles away over the mountains and there was little understanding of western needs. For instance, the local militia could only act when attacked and only within its own district. If the Virginia militia was needed, it was necessary to send a messenger to Williamsburg and wait for him to get back.

Late in 1784 delegates from the people of the West met to consider what to do. Shelby was chairman. The First Kentucky Convention was replaced by the second and others, down through the tenth, with Shelby's hands gradually molding a new state government. The First Congress of the United States under the new Constitution finally authorized admittance of Kentucky.

The day of admission, 4 June 1792, was also Shelby's inaguration day as the first governor of the new state. He was forty-one. At six feet he was somewhat above the average height of his generation. He was well muscled and able to continue to march or work far beyond the limits of the ordinary man. He was known to everyone as a soldier and his record was very good. There was never a breath of scandal around him. Everyone knew he was a straight talker, meaning precisely what he said. There was never serious consideration of anyone else as first governor. However, he doubted that he was qualified and wanted to turn it down. And when the four years were over he flatly refused a second term, went back to Traveler's Rest, and enjoyed the happiest years of his life.

But when war clouds rolled, Shelby took up the cares of office again. Less than a month after war was declared in 1812, he announced for governor. The election was only a month away but he was swept into office. Failures and rising fears of Indian disorders came, with good reason. The governor put on the ceremonial sword from his King's Mountain triumph and led 3,500 mounted Kentuckians toward war in the Detroit region. At the Battle of the Thames, 5 October 1813, the British were thoroughly defeated and the Indian confederation was broken up.

Shelby accepted only one more call to major public service. The Chickasaws held the river ends of Tennessee and Kentucky as hunting grounds, the last large piece of Indian land in the region. Shelby was a veteran in dealing with Indians in war, in treaty making, and in friendship. He had for years recommended purchase of those lands by the United States. So he agreed to go with Jackson to seek a treaty and purchase. He was sixty-eight, which was old in those days. His legs had almost given out, and on the way south he sometimes had to get out of the saddle and walk to get the blood flowing.

Whatever patience he had wore thin. There came a day when the Chickasaw chiefs wanted to nudge up the price another notch and General Jackson agreed. General Shelby ordered his horse and started home, but his son got him to come back and compromise. The offer of $240,000 in twelve years had been moved up to $300,000 in fifteen annual payments. That was for 4,600 square miles, which, with the Indian title extinguished, probably was worth $10 million. The treaty date was 19 October 1818. Slightly more than a year later, 24 November 1819, Tennessee legislators set up Shelby County, which now has more acres, more people, and more wealth than any other county in the state. (Nine states have counties named for Shelby and seven have Shelbyvilles, but Shelby, Mississippi, is named for M. D. Shelby.)

Shelby lived on until 18 July 1826. There were eleven children, more than sixty grandchildren and numerous nephews to carry on the name. The *Dictionary of American Biography* still uses 4½ columns to record his life. A book-length biography appeared in 1972, *Isaac Shelby, Kentucky's First Governor and Hero of Three Wars*, by Sylvia Wrobel and Geroge Grider. Thomas D. Clark, the Ole Miss graduate who became the outstanding writer of Kentucky history books, said in his *Kentucky: Land of Contrast:* "Kentuckians are still looking for a governor who can do better than their first."

Isaac Shelby's fame was as a war hero and governor yet biographers say Shelby considered everything else interruptions in his chosen life on the farm. There even came times when he refused to stay at his capitol desk. On such occasions a person had to leave the city, journey to Danville, get out to the farm, and trudge through the fields if they really had to see the governor.

Judge Overton

John Overton was a patient man. In 1794, when he was a young lawyer in the new town of Nashville, he paid $500 for a doubtful claim to 5,000 acres of forest owned by the Chickasaw Indians. It was twenty-four years before the Chickasaws sold out by treaty, but Overton held on. The 5,000 acre parcel included a good landing for Mississippi River flatboats at the mouth of Wolf River, and it included part of the bluff looking down on the big river—but high above the broadest floods ever known.

Overton foresaw a metropolis in some hazy future when the Indian title had been cleared away, when the Tennessee country had become a state, and when the people who had been trickling over the mountains sent back word of the rich lands of the West. It was twenty-five years after Overton's purchase when surveyors laid off streets and parks for the town of Memphis, Town government was formed by election of seven aldermen on 26 April 1827, which was thirty-three years after the purchase, with only a few settlers willing and able to pay as much as $100 for a Main Street lot. But the metropolis came true and today the Overton acres are the portion of Memphis roughly between Union and Vollintine, from the river to East Parkway.

Another indication of John Overton's patience was his marriage. He waited and he waited some more, while building a home, Traveller's Rest, on the outskirts of Nashville. He was fifty-four when he chose a doctor's widow, Mrs. Francis May, the former Mary McConnell White.

John Overton

Patience and persistent effort were also characteristic of the Overton campaigning that lifted Andrew Jackson to the White House. He first proposed Jackson for the presidency in 1815. It was about 1820, the year Monroe was reelected, that Overton began the organized push for Jackson. In 1821 Overton was one of three men who formed an informal committee of close friends to advocate the Jackson cause and to answer quickly the Jackson detractors.

In 1824 the Overton organization was so strong that Jackson received the largest number of votes, and won more states than any of his three rivals, although he lost the presidency when the decision was thrown to the House of Representatives. The campaigning for Jackson went on and in 1828 Jackson was elected to head the nation.

It was a most remarkable victory. All previous presidents had come from seaboard states, while Jackson was a Westerner. All other presidents had been aristocrats, while Jackson was considered a man of the people in national politics, even though he was associated with the wealthy class in Tennessee politics. It was the beginning of the end of "King Caucus," by which members of the House controlled presidential nominations. Jackson represented a new age of politics.

Displacing the old men and the old methods was a formidable task, but the Jackson margin was clear in 1828. He was elected again in 1832, and his longtime associate, Martin Van Buren, was elected in 1836. There was more to victory, of course, than committee work, letter writing and political schemes. Jackson was a spectacular figure, a giant among war heroes. He and his friends took popular stands that divided the voters of an expanding nation.

Perhaps one of Overton's most unusual accomplishments was remaining Jackson's friend, partner, and confidant as long as he lived. Other men were at Jackson's side only temporarily.

The two men had appeared in Nashville during the same month, young and poor lawyers in search of a future. The year was 1789, and Overton was twenty-three, Jackson a year younger. Overton had come from Virginia, where he taught several years to help his brothers and sisters stay in school, and for two years had studied law in Kentucky. They immediately became mutual admirers, partly because they were so different. Overton was a student, a man who acquired books until he had the biggest library in Tennessee, a methodical person who made complete notes on everything he did, kept his letters and legal papers on file, and was an expert on land values. In his later years he owned more land than anyone else in the state, and sometimes was called the richest man in Tennessee.

Jackson was a man of action, a stormy personality, and sometimes shy of cash. This pair of lawyers soon shared the same office, and the same room as boarders at the home of John Donelson's widow. They almost lived out of the same purse, for it was their custom, whenever one of them bought property, to put half of it in the name of the other, and whenever one was away, for the other to act in his name. When separated both wrote frequently, and continuously, although both married and each built big homes on opposite sides of town. Jackson was often away at war or in Washington as a representative, a senator, and then as president.

Overton was first known in Nashville as supervisor of federal revenue for Washington County, North Carolina, appointed by President Washington. (Washington County later became the state of Tennessee.) It was a position that left him with plenty of time for the practice of law, which he did with enthusiasm.

Overton made himself a specialist on land titles. Land ownership was a briar patch of legal thorns in which thousands of settlers were uneasy about whether another man could successfully claim their fields. English judicial precedents were of little help because legal titles in the

West had so little in common with old England. Sometimes there were Indian titles, legal though often ignored. Tennessee judges departed from the methods of Virginia, which were used in Kentucky. North Carolina ideas about land titles sometimes were of more value, but there had also been four years of the State of Franklin, there had been a period as a territory of the United States, and, after 1796, there been a Tennessee state government.

Overton had to whittle out his own model. He did it so well the Tennessee legislators sent him to North Carolina to get a compromise on questions of title between the two states. In 1804 he was made a member of the Superior Court of Tennessee. When that court was replaced in 1811 he was named to the state's Supreme Court. He wrote two volumes of Tennessee Reports, recounting cases before the high court from 1791 to 1816. As a lawyer and a judge he had been the strongest influence in the formation of the state's land law. He was commonly accepted as the authority.

Overton resigned from the bench in 1816. He was fifty and had so much property that he needed to look after it. He returned to the courts sometimes in big cases. One parcel of property he attended to during the years after he left the bench and before the Jackson presidential campaigning was on the Fourth Chickasaw Bluff. On the day in 1794 after he got title, he transferred half of it to Jackson. The record shows Jackson paid $100, although he may have paid nothing under their standing partnership arrangement.

Overton held his half. Jackson got into a financial bind in 1797 and sold half of his part to the Winchesters. Just after he, as a representative of the United States government, had talked the Indians into selling West Tennessee, Jackson sold half of what he had left to the Winchesters. So, when Memphis was established, Jackson only had one–eighth, the Winchesters had three–eighths, and Overton had a half of the land.

In 1823 Jackson sold his eighth to John Christmas McLemore. Sales were slow and prices low, and when the Overton-Winchester-McLemore agreement ran out in 1829 each took his share of the land. The Winchesters stayed in Middle Tennessee, except for young Marcus, who was sent to the bluff to manage the development for the owner-partners. Jackson sold out early. Overton came to the site of the real estate promotion to get things started, then returned to Nashville and kept his finger on the pulse by mail. His was the dominant personality among the founders, both by ownership of the largest share and because of the time and effort he put into the town.

His influence as an attorney and a judge was pervasive in the formative years of Tennessee law. He was the winning advocate of Jackson in national politics. And through all his long years of prominence there was never a hint of a question about his honesty.

Yet nature gave John Overton a bad deal in the appearance of success that often comes with wealth and power. He was small, bald and sickly. He was known as a penny-pincher, even though he also was known as a good host in his six-room bachelor home (expanded to fourteen rooms after his marriage). He was especially known for the expensive cognac he served. In Overton's later years a visitor found him in Jackson's home. Overton was sitting in the family circle but the little man (5'3") with a bandana thrown over his baldness, his nose and chin almost meeting, was unsuccessful in trying to get into the conversation.

Overton lived to be sixty-seven and to see Jackson begin his second term. He died on 12 April 1833, a time when Memphis was a muddy-dusty settlement with an impressive name and bright dreams, but hardly any residents. He held his land and so did his family. When population boomed and real estate prices climbed some of them sold but fragments were still held by heirs, some of them named Overton, more than a century later.

His daughter, Ann (Mrs. R. C. Brinkley), lived here and her family has been prominent ever since. His grandson, John Overton, was president of the taxing district (with duties of mayor) from 1881 to 1883. His real estate firm, Overton and Overton, was said to be Tennessee's largest. He was also a director of the Bank of Commerce.

Another grandson, Overton Lea of Nashville, held a plot of woods until the city bought it in 1901. Lea's Wood was renamed East Park. The people chose, in a newspaper coupon contest, to honor the founder by changing it to Overton Park. Watkins Overton was mayor in 1928–40 and in 1949–53, which was longer than any mayor in the history of Memphis. He was the great-great-grandson of John Overton, whose patient development of plans for the city began more than 180 years ago.

General Winchester

James Winchester, the man who named Memphis, liked history. He had read about the biggest city of the ancient civilization in the valley of the Nile. His knowledge of the distant past was also plain in the naming of his sons. They were Marcus Brutus, Lucilius and Valerius Publicola. Shifting to another era of history, he named another son Napoleon. He passed up Egypt, Rome, and France to go to Mount Parnassus in old

James Winchester (from *Old Summer* by Walter T. Durham).

Greece for the name of Castalian Springs, which became the nearest town to his home.

Aside from scholarship, James Winchester is known as chief of the surveying party which put Winchester Road on the modern map of Memphis. He had a fine surveyor to read the instruments but it was his name that goes with the drawing of the line that separated land kept by the Chickasaws from land sold to the United States. One side of the line became Mississippi and the other Tennessee.

The treaty was signed in October 1818. Winchester came to the bluff on which Memphis was about to be built and went overland to the Tennessee River, where the surveyors began a line of trees blazed with "U.S." which ran to the Mississippi River. They arrived at the big river in early July 1819. It was a fast job but even faster was another survey of the lots about to be sold in Memphis, which had begun in April.

Unfortunately the Winchester survey made a slight error while still in the hills. By the time the line was completed (about the lower edge of Chucalissa) the mistake had widened to a strip of land nearly four miles wide, which had to be moved into Tennessee when more accurate surveys were made in 1837.

Two other surveys had agreed with the Winchester line and the revised markers of 1837 show an agreement between the two states, rather than where the line was intended to be, about a half mile north. Still, because of this mistake, some settlers, who thought they were clearing farms in Mississippi suddenly had to do their voting in Tennessee. Another result is that the south part of Shelby County, below Winchester Road, has roads on the grid lines of Mississippi, while in the rest of the county the roads wander in curves and bends.

Survey stakes on the bluff where Memphis grew came late in the life of Winchester and many miles from his home in Sumner County. He called it Cragfont. The house stood on a hill, taller than the trees around it, dominating the hilltop as well as the valley spread out below. It was a broad building having, on the lower floor, two windows of twenty-four panes each, on each side of a double front door. Details of cornices, eaves, and windows equaled anything in Annapolis, an old center of wealth and fine homes when Cragfont was completed in 1802.

There was a splendid garden attached, with roses, jonquils, two pear trees for their blossoms, lilacs, thyme, sage, strawberries and other varieties of vegetable, herbs and flowers. A deep lake, spring-fed, was near. It was a magnificent home secluded from the main roads, and it still is magnificent and secluded. It has been preserved without alterations to its original dimensions. It is one of the great houses of Tennessee.

It was even more remarkable when it was newer, for it was an accomplishment of grandeur on the frontier. The property was on the true frontier when James Winchester and his brother, George, arrived in 1785. They settled on it and in 1793 they chose the Cragfont name. In 1794 a fight with Indians took place in which the brother was killed and scalped.

At Cragfont the Winchesters skipped the slow years of progress through lean-to, one-room log cabin, two-room cabin with a dogtrot between them, a second floor with stairway and hall between the upper rooms, and finally, a clapboard covering for the logs. The Winchester method avoided all that. They must have sent back east for workmen and materials to put an Atlantic seaboard dwelling in the Indian hunting grounds.

The Winchesters lived there until the Yankees drove them out during the Civil War. One of the proud accomplishments of the Association for Preservation of Tennessee Antiquities has been restoration of the house, which began in 1956.

James Winchester built a fine home where the Indians still resisted.

He was born in Maryland (6 February 1752) and was twenty-four when he, with his younger brother, enlisted in the Flying Camp to fight the Revolution. Both won battlefield promotions for bravery. At Staten Island he was wounded and taken prisoner. He was in prison a year before being exchanged. He was again captured at Charleston but was released in time to fight under General Nathaniel Greene on the southern front. James was a captain and George a lieutenant when they saw the triumph at Yorktown.

It was only four years later that they departed Maryland for the Mero District of North Carolina. George held several local offices and operated a mill, while James became a prosperous planter and merchant. Although James was a businessman on his way to wealth, he was known as a veteran of the Revolution who became famous locally as an Indian fighter. In the Mero District militia he was a captain, then a colonel, and a brigadier general.

North Carolina made him one of the three commissioners who established Sumner County, which included his property, in 1777. In 1778 he was a member of the North Carolina Constitutional Convention. When the region in which he lived was separated from Carolina as the state of Tennessee in 1796, he was elected to the state senate and was its first speaker. The capital was then at Knoxville and the white population of the state numbered about 78,000. Governor John Sevier continued his appointment for Tennessee as a brigadier general.

At Cairo, Tennessee, Winchester and his associates had a large and diverse business. They sold the land on which the town was built. They had a large store, a cotton gin and a cotton spinning factory, as well as a blacksmith shop, and a shoemaker's shop. They sometimes went to wholesalers in Baltimore and Philadelphia, but their main connection was in New Orleans. For the downriver trade they developed such a big keelboat and barge shipping business that a large warehouse was built, and eventually they had the first boat built, in Pittsburgh, for the Cairo trade.

The New Orleans business, both selling the produce of Sumner County and buying merchandise for the neighbors, became so large that a commission house was established in the Crescent City, with Winchester's son-in-law, James W. Breedlove, as manager. Cairo, three miles from Cragfont, was a bustling center of business and population as long as the general lived.

The General was drawn away from business by the war of 1812. He was a brigadier and commander of the Army of the Northwest. Under his supervision a huge fort, enclosing more than three acres, was built on the Maumee River in the northwestern corner of Ohio. A two-story blockhouse stood at each of the four corners, and a sentinel house over each of four gates. A tunnel was excavated from inside the fort to the river, to assure water in case of seige. When completed it was named Fort Winchester by his superiors.

But his superiors failed to supply either winter clothing or food with the result that the troops were afflicted by death and sickness. A great deal of mismanagement characterized the American war effort. For Winchester there was the added difficulty of rivalry with General William Henry Harrison, who maneuvered himself into command. Winchester was unpopular, since he was older and had a reputation for strict discipline.

Winchester was in command of forces defeated disastrously at the River Raisin, on 22 January 1813. He was accused of gross negligence, which he denied vigorously in print, but he was never able to get an official inquiry in a contest with General Harrison that continued for years. In 1814 General Andrew Jackson made him commander of a large Gulf Coast area, with headquarters at Mobile. In 1815 Winchester surrendered Fort Bowyer on Mobile Bay. Great Britain won the fort although the British had lost the war weeks before. News moved so slowly that they fought in overtime on the coast.

Winchester was sixty-three when he took off his uniform again and went back to his business at Cairo, and his life of ease at Cragfont. He had a secretary, Charles Cassedy, to write his letters and compose his defense in the River Raisin case. Cassedy was a writer of talent under his own name, the county's most outstanding writer of that period, according to Walter T. Durham writing in *Old Sumner,* a storehouse of Winchester information.

The old veteran also took time to be a trustee for Cumberland College in Nashville, and Transmontania Academy in Gallatin. He lived on until 26 July 1826, and in this later stage of his life, became a founder of Memphis. John Overton had, in 1794, bought for $500 the John Rice claim to 5,000 acres on the bluff where Memphis was built later. He transferred half ownership to Andrew Jackson.

Overton was on his way to great wealth, but Jackson ran up on a financial sandbar in 1797 and sold half of his half to Stephen and Richard Winchester for $625. They promptly sold their interest to their brothers, James, the wealthy businessman of Cairo, Tennessee, and William, a Baltimore bank president and merchant. James had an eighth of the claim and William, who died in 1812 leaving several heirs, had an eighth.

All of this had only speculative value as long as the North Carolina titles were overlaid by ownership and possession by the Indians. The Chickasaws gave up by treaty in November 1818. Next month Jackson sold an eighth, which was half of what he had left, to James Winchester, who paid $5,000.

As Memphis was founded, Winchester thus owned a fourth interest in the 5,000-acre partnership and held power of attorney over another eighth belonging to the William Winchester family.

Memphis was 350 miles across the wooded hills from Cragfont, and even farther by boat, but Winchester used far more effort on behalf of the new town than Jackson. The hero of New Orleans almost ignored Memphis until he sold his remaining share in 1824 to John Christmas McLemore, another Nashville man, but the first of the owning partners to move to Memphis.

Until then, the owners had been represented on the bluff by Marcus Winchester, the general's oldest son. He was sent from the elegance of Cragfont and the companionship of a family of fourteen children into the rough frontier. Marcus because a member of the original Shelby County Court, operator of the first store (and for many years the biggest), first postmaster, first mayor, first man to serve some of the activities of a banker, and builder of the finest house in town.

Jacinto Days

When the Chickasaws yielded to the pressure of squatters by giving up their land by treaties in 1832 and 1837, the State of Mississippi established a huge county in the northeastern corner. It was so big it was called "The Great State of Tishomingo," and it occupied the area now divided between the counties of Alcorn, Prentiss, and Tishomingo.

The county seat was a new town, first called Cincinnati, at the middle of the vast acreage of forested hills. That was in 1836, while the Indians were still searching for a new homeland in the West. A frame building served as county offices during the several years that groups of Chickasaw families migrated across the river.

While the new town was flourishing, young men returned from the war in Mexico (1846–48) proud of their military records. Another form of pride filled residents of Cincinnati, Mississippi, with assurance of such a large town that there would be confusion about two "great cities"

Tishomingo County Courthouse

with the same name. So the town name was changed to Jacinto, recalling
the battle of San Jacinto. The Spanish say "jacinto" when we say
"hyacinth." The Spanish sounds like "hah-THEEN-tow," which the
Mississippians translated into "jay-CIN-ta."

In 1854, with the Indians gone, Jacinto acquired a courthouse in
keeping with the vast county. It is a two-story structure of red brick, with
a courtroom and two jury rooms on the upper level. It is fifty-six by forty
feet and has walls eighteen inches thick, with a twelve-foot ceiling in the
first-floor rooms. The contractor was paid $6,798.

In the 1850s a telegraph line was built in connection with the laying of
the Mobile & Ohio rails, and the forward-looking people of Jacinto got
the amazingly fast message service extended to their town. But the next
summer, a disastrous drouth destroyed crops, and the humming wires
were suspected of messing up the weather. So, according to the folklore,
angry farmers chopped down the telegraph poles.

Jacinto had an advantage over other towns with a stagecoach line to
La Grange, Tennessee, a center of trade and culture. It expected to be

the largest town in the region and was well along the way to that goal, rivaled only by Eastport, the Tennessee River shipping point for the whole region.

There were two newspapers, the *Jacinto Democrat* and the *North Mississippi Union*. A copy of the *Union* has been reproduced and sold for years as a memento for visitors to the town. This copy shows that the Jacinto newspaper attracted advertising from numerous merchants in Eastport, which was about twenty miles away as the crow flies, a long journey in the days of horses and winding roads over high hills. There also was advertising from the medical and legal schools of the Memphis Institute. Another offered Hayes & Craig hats and caps at Louisville, Kentucky.

It was this Jacinto newspaper that was chosen for the swan song of Jacob Thompson's congressional career. He was leaving Washington by choice of the voters after 12 years in the House, and he used 7½ columns for a resume of his work. He went on to a considerable career afterward and later moved to Memphis, where he stood high among his contemporaries.

In those prosperous years of the '50s, the town was favored with two good academies. One of them went on to years of fame under the leadership of E. W. Carmack. When he was only twenty, he founded Euclid Academy on the family homestead. That was at Mackey's Creek, and the year was 1848. It was one of the very first academies in that part of the state. When his father died in 1851, Carmack moved the school to Jacinto. This was the school often called "Jacinto College." Carmack had some income as clerk of probate court for fourteen years and held other positions of trust, as well as operating Euclid Academy.

The other academy appeared in 1856 under the leadership of John F. Arnold as the Jacinto Male Academy. It offered Greek and Latin to the older boys. Its later years were obscure, but Arnold's school probably went under as the Civil War started.

A few years before the war, Jacinto lost its hope of being a major city and began to lose its people. The Memphis & Charleston Railroad was built through Corinth. Then the Mobile & Ohio was built through Rienzi, which is even closer to Jacinto.

Roads to Jacinto were deplorable, which made little difference when all roads were bad, but the cars ran on the rails every day, rain or shine. That was a tremendous advantage to railroad towns. There was a similar advantage for railroad towns compared to communities on tributary rivers, because boats were stopped by low water and boiler explosions.

Residents of Jacinto moved to Iuka, Corinth, and Rienzi, leaving the fine courthouse to slumber in the sun.

In 1865, with the war over, Carmack moved his academy into the courthouse. In 1870 the legislature split up big Tishomingo into three counties with three county seats, none of them Jacinto. The new Tishomingo county seat was Iuka. Alcorn County was set up, with Corinth as the courthouse town, Prentiss County had Booneville.

A remarkable deal was made. Carmack was hired to copy by hand a set of the county records for the new county officials at Iuka and another for officials at Booneville. The originals were transferred to Corinth. In payment, Carmack was given the courthouse.

The academy in the old courthouse became a widely known school. It probably never had more than fifty pupils (and they were of assorted ages). The older boys were offered Hebrew as well as Latin and Greek. Carmack was a good teacher, and his associates were W. I. Gibson, "Toke" Reynolds, Will Polk and J. O. Looney, all remembered with favor by their pupils. Gibson had been taught by Carmack, gone on to Virginia, taken his degree and returned to help Carmack. He could speak fluent Latin and was capable of holding the interest of other teachers attending a teachers institute through five consecutive days of lectures.

When Peabody was established in Nashville, a large part of the Jacinto boys took their degrees there. Others went to Ole Miss, where an admission officer is supposed to have said that Jacinto boys were as well prepared as applicants from any school. Carmack died in 1882, and his associate, Looney, took over, continuing the school until 1895. In an extraordinary act of admiration, the Carmack students made up a fund and put a fine monument on his grave at Jacinto.

Carmack also is remembered because his son, Frank, went on from the academy to study medicine. He was a physician for many years at Iuka and, at various times, mayor, newspaper editor, school superintendent, and the early authority on geology of the area.

He is even better remembered for his connection with Edward Ward Carmack, his nephew, who was editor of *The Commercial Appeal*, a U.S. senator, champion of the antisaloon forces in Tennessee, and Nashville editor. Senator Carmack, who was shot and killed on the street, lived most of his life in Tennessee, but during his formative years (from about 2½ until he was about 7), he was under the daily influence of his teacher-uncle in the Jacinto home. His widowed mother had moved in with her three small children during the Civil War.

With the school closed, little Jacinto withered away even more. When Dunbar Rowland published his two volumes on Mississippi in 1907, he used only one paragraph for the town. He said: "It lies in a hilly country, and has a church and an academy." It also had a post office, but the academy was long gone and the nearest bank was in Rienzi. The 1900 census takers had found just eighty-nine residents, Rowland said. When the Works Progress Administration (WPA) brought out the American Guide Series book on Mississippi in 1938, the town was left out entirely.

The old bricks quietly became a century old. On a Sunday in summer, some students or former residents with happy memories of Jacinto came back for a reunion and dinner on the grounds. The Methodist congregation moved into the dusty courtroom, and the preacher spoke from the judge's bench each Sunday. The Methodists disbanded in 1961. Population went down to about twenty-three.

The quiet was broken suddenly in 1964. The Methodist bishop had sold the old courthouse to a wrecker, whose workers showed up on Sunday to lay out the work for the next day. Joe Smith, who had gone to school there and who lived next door, telephoned Mrs. Fayette Williams at Corinth. She enlisted her husband and O. T. Holder in spreading the alarm, which reached newspapers and became a running story that went on for years.

There seemed to be a providential intervention when a hard rain fell on Monday and continued, for five days in a row. It was difficult to keep the crowbar crew out long enough for the preservationists to organize.

The church had once been offered $800 for the old bricks, and there had been a futile try for state historic funds. The price went down to $600, which was the selling price to a wrecker who calculated he could get more than $3,000 for the handmade bricks. But a committee got him to agree to $2,500. Dr. Joe Stevens of West Point, Mississippi, wrote out a $2,000 check, which was accepted. Protectors of the old courthouse organized the Jacinto Foundation, Inc., and invested $6,000 into fresh mortar and shutters. Brick flooring was used on the lower level where countless shoes had worn deep hollows.

This is an extraordinary restoration for it has local tax money. People of the three counties who attended court at Jacinto tax themselves a quarter mill ($2.50 for each $1,000 of assessed valuation). This is a steady flow of maintenance money. Then there was $15,000 in Bicentennial money and $132,000 in state money to match a federal grant.

Joe Smith, who has guided thousands of visitors without pay, is now an official guide with a small salary. Mississippi tourist officials frequently feature this unusual sight in publications that bring visitors from forty-nine states.

The Jacinto Foundation operates a country store year 'round, and it has a twenty-six-acre park, including camp grounds. A pioneer doctor's office is awaiting restoration. The intention now is to restore the whole town. Betsy Whitehurst (2135 Hickory Road, Corinth, Miss. 38834), executive secretary, has plans for representatives of the foundation to visit Salem, Illinois, in preparing a schedule. Whatever else is added and however long it takes, the central attraction is an original example of the "Federal" style of architecture, the only one in the region and a sharp contrast to the columned mansions of white in the "Greek Revival" style which were built during the same decade.

Prophet's Vision

One of the most influential men in enlarging the importance of Memphis—and one of the least known—was Edmund Pendleton Gaines. He was the general who planned the nation's defense and who saw how big railroads would be when the first locomotives were still chuffing along a few miles of track on the eastern seaboard. In this planning ahead General Gaines saw how the Memphis bluff would become the terminal for roads and rails and the river crossing to new states of the western future.

General Gaines moved army headquarters for the whole West to Memphis in 1831. He chose Memphis for his home in the 1830s when this town had lots of mud, mosquitoes, and magnificent hopes, but very few people. During this time he was closely associated with Marcus Winchester, the first mayor, who spoke for the proprietors in disputes with settlers.

He was exceptional in another way. Others who lived here during the first twenty years of the town rarely wrote anything. They left a skimpy record of letters, diaries, pamphlets or books. But General Gaines was required to do lots of writing for the military bureaucracy, and he campaigned for his ideas with letters and pamphlets.

He lived from 1777 to 1849, was slight of person but stood so straight he seemed tall. He was a man of reserved dignity, urbanity and courtesy. Gaines was a veteran of the battlefield and was long accustomed to high position before his interest in Memphis developed. In 1814, when he was thirty-seven, he had been promoted to brigadier general and a few

Edmund Pendleton Gaines (from *Edmund Pendle-ton Gaines* by James W. Silver).

months later had become a national hero by repulsing the British siege of Fort Erie.

His family had moved to the east end of Tennessee when he was twelve. At eighteen he was a lieutenant in a volunteer rifle company. He was later appointed an ensign in the regular army and then advanced up the steps to brevet major general.

When he was only twenty-four he had been chosen to make the original Natchez Trace survey. When Shelby County government was established in 1820, General Gaines was in command of the southeastern border of the United States, against the uneasy Indians, Spanish, and English.

With the Southeast quieted by annexation, Gaines was made commander of the army's Western Department. It was a vast responsibility. It was the Army that chose locations for new forts along the advancing frontier, built the forts, explored the territory, made the maps, surveyed some important roads, made Indian treaties, paid government money to the chiefs, put the lid on wars between tribes, protected settlers, and managed movement of Indians across the river to their new land. The

Army then had an East–West command arrangement, under which Gaines also had some alternate experience in managing the other half from New York headquarters.

Out of these experiences came the Gaines objective of designing fast movement for a small army. His great fear was a third war with England and the invasion of coastal cities. The situation seemed to him to demand a development of floating batteries, to be towed into position for protection of the ports. On the interior he wanted roads over which troops could be shifted rapidly. As soon as the railroad proved its practical usefulness he became an earnest advocate of rails for even faster movement.

It was superiority of the Memphis position on the bluff for steamboats and for steam railroads that made Gaines the champion of this city when it was nothing but a village with dreams. It was General Gaines who proposed for defense purposes a road through the wilderness from Memphis to Little Rock. This became the famous Military Road, started by the Army in 1826. This is the route serving the same purposes as the Broadway of America highway for tourists many years later, Federal Highway 70, and Interstate 40, part of a giant expense authorized by Congress in 1956 in the name of defense. As the Military Road this route helped settlers move westward, as many as twelve hundred of them in the single month of September 1837. It was also the way used by many Indians to get to their new homes across the river.

General Gaines is credited with stimulating Matthew Maury to campaign for the building of the Memphis Navy Yard. This was followed by plans for a federal armory, which proceeded as far as naming boundary streets for military heroes. Streets such as Wellington and Orleans are still on the modern map of the city.

It was 1834 when General Gaines proposed a railroad from Memphis to Little Rock. It took until 1871 to complete these rails. He began advocating rails from Charleston to Memphis in 1831. It took until 1857 to complete the iron link between the Atlantic ports and rails of the East, but that line was built. It was the city's first railroad. It was the first line of rails across the South. It was paramount in building prestige of Memphis, and it probably was the greatest Gaines contribution to Memphis, although his fundamental interest was in transportation for the Army.

The general obtained from Washington the services of Colonel Stephen H. Long, of the topographical bureau. Long found that Memphis would be the best place for the rail terminal and surveyed three routes to the sea, by way of Knoxville, Charleston, and Savannah. He found the Charleston way would be the best and much the cheapest. Some public figures in Nashville and Jackson, Tennessee, however, were of the opinion that the mouth of the Hatchie was a better site for the rail terminal than the mouth of the Wolf, which would have boosted Fulton or Randolph, rival towns, over little Memphis. But Gaines, well aware of mercantile as well as military services, was a strong believer in Memphis as the position ''destined to become the seaport and principal commercial emporium of the state.''

In 1833 Gaines presided at a public meeting to consider Shelby County seeking cooperation of neighboring counties in organizing a railroad to the interior of Tennessee. It was followed by a meeting at Bolivar and one at Jackson, with delegations from north Alabama invited. The original plan was financing of the Western Rail Road Company, to connect Memphis and Jackson. It was superseded by the Atlantic and Mississippi Railroad, which grew into the Memphis & Charleston line, now the Southern Railway.

In 1838, long before any of them had been built, General Gaines had a detailed plan, with maps for five interior railroads, three of them terminating in Memphis. One would go through Tennessee to Virginia, and on to New England connections. Another would go to Savannah (or Charleston). The third would cross the big river here on its way to the Arkansas, the Red, and Sabine rivers. In 1845, Gaines was pushing the presidential cabinet for rails from Memphis to Charleston, with branches to the Gulf at Mobile and Pensacola. He also advocated rails from Memphis to Texas. The price tag on the Gaines rails was less than $46 million.

It seems almost impossible that a man of such strong hands in forming young Memphis and the young U.S. Army should have such a low profile in the modern city, or should be better memorialized in Florida than here. But there are reasons. He was only twelve when his family moved to Tennessee, which took him into the frontier experience with unfriendly Indians and the tradition of quick reaction. Thus it seemed normal to him to act without waiting for the upper level of command to approve, modify, or instruct. This one element in his personality put him into frequent disfavor among Washington officials, who were more available to newspapermen and other opinion makers than the commander on the edge of civilization.

There was also a feud that went on for years with General Winfield Scott. They had both been promoted to major, to lieutenant colonel, to colonel, and to brigadier general on precisely the same days. But Scott was brevetted major general twenty-one days before Gaines. The feeling became so intense that Scott challenged Gaines to a duel. Another time Gaines sent back unopened a letter from Scott. In addition, a letter 150 pages long about Gaines's faults was written and circulated by Scott.

Army officers educated at West Point, which opened in 1802, developed doubts about officers who had not gone to the Point. Gaines had, of course, learned on the job of fighting. He had also developed a specific plan for another method of training officers, of good character but without the income or political connections to enter the Point.

He planned six major Army posts from the western end of Lake Superior to the junction of the Canadian River with the Arkansas, in modern Oklahoma. Each of these posts was to be an academy of practical military training. Grounds of thirty-six square miles would surround each fort-academy to control the surroundings and especially to keep away whisky sellers. Cadets were to be prohibited from drinking "julaps," smoking cigars, chewing tobacco, or gambling. The general dreamed of an army with higher pay to attract men from other trades in numbers that would replace the drunks who infested the ranks and frequently deserted. He thought liquor was the usual cause of desertion, a grave crime. He wrote that the only punishment that would produce the terror that would stop desertion was shooting.

Another plan of his was destined to meet with opposition. The floating batteries he was so sure were necessary for defense of port cities would have been manned by the Army, which reduced his chances for support from admirals.

In other words, General Gaines was faulty in public relations, indifferent to politics and politicians, and a visionary years before the nation was ready for him. His neglect by regional writers has been monumental, even though his Memphis neighbors knew his visions, as noted by James D. Davis, the first writer about the village days, and despite recognition from a convention here in 1845. He has had more recognition since publication of a book about him in 1949, *Edmund Pendleton Gaines: Frontier General* by James W. Silver. Perhaps it helped when another book was published, *The Famous Case of Myra Clark Gaines* by Nolan B. Harmon Jr., (1946). It tells of the marriage contract between General and Mrs. Gaines, immense wealth, a lost will probated forty years late, forgery, bribery, Spanish law, the Louisiana code, and an estate contest heard by thirty Supreme Court justices. The general and his petite wife "won," forty-two years after his death, and six years after hers.

The Silver biography says Gaines was "one of the nation's prophets of the age of the steel rail. . . . His enthusiastic propounding of the gospel of the iron rail was probably Gaines' least-known and most signal contribution to the development of his country." Many of his undertakings were delayed but they were accomplished. He was a man who was building up Memphis in the 1830s before many other persons had chosen to settle on the bluff. He ought to be better know by his beneficiaries.

2
As It Was

Archibald Yell

Newcomers to Arkansas are likely to be curious about a county named "Yell" and a town named "Yellville" in another county. Questions will turn up the answer that there was once a prominent Arkansan named "Yell," and perhaps that his first name was "Archibald" but little else.

He was of high importance when Arkansas was a new state. He was the first member of the House of Representatives, when population was so small there was only one. He was elected in August of 1836, reelected the next year and again in 1844. During the gap in years he was governor, 1840–1844.

Yell was born at Salisbury, North Carolina, (9 August 1797) into a family that moved to Tennessee about 1809. He first came to public notice as a soldier under Andrew Jackson, whom he greatly admired. They met in preparation for the campaign against the Creeks. Yell was underage but the captain of a company of volunteers, the Jackson Guards.

The general saw Yell perform with gallant courage at Talladega and Horseshoe Bend. Yell again was conspicuous at New Orleans and in the Seminole War.

Yell was without formal education but he read some law and attained local prominence as an attorney with offices in Shelbyville and

Archibald Yell (from *History of Arkansas* by John
Hallum).

Fayetteville. He also attained recognition among Masons, by being
elected grand master of the Tennessee lodge directly from the floor
without serving the usual progression of preliminary offices. He had
entered politics because a committee of Masons asked him to. They had
expelled a man for misbehavior and he had become a candidate for
reelection to the legislature on an anti-Mason platform, with vile things
to say about the fraternal order. Yell responded, became a candidate,
defeated the troublemaker and served in the General Assembly, representing Bedford County in the house in 1827–1829.

He was a Tennessee lawyer when Jackson became president. In 1831
Yell received the presidential appointment to manage the land office in
Little Rock. After a few months Yell resigned and went back to the law
in Tennessee. Jackson came back to him in 1832, offering Yell a choice
of becoming the territorial governor of Florida or territorial judge of
Arkansas. He chose Arkansas and the man who had a law office in
Fayetteville, Tennessee, set up his court in Fayetteville, Arkansas.

He was a handsome man of thirty-five, with 150 pounds well distributed over a frame of 5'10" under a thatch of red hair and piercing blue

eyes. He was full of humor and good cheer. His personality drew men of assorted temperaments, each of whom was convinced that Yell was their best friend. They kept on feeling that way through the years of office building.

He also was courageous beyond reason. There was a time when a sheriff told the judge the accused was absent from court because everyone was afraid to join the posse to bring him in. It developed that the wild man was just then holding a wild party in a saloon. Judge Yell went in after him by himself, threw shouted curses in his face, seized him by the throat and demanded that he come to court. The judge walked out, with the culprit meekly following to the courtroom.

Judge Yell wanted to be the first governor and he probably would have been elected easily. But he declined to become a delegate to the convention that wrote the state Constitution because that might have interfered with his judicial obligations. He stayed on the bench and rival politicians slipped in a clause requiring governors to be four-year residents, just a mite longer than Yell had been there.

So he became Representative Yell, taking his seat 5 December 1836. He was reelected for the term that expired 3 March 1839. He was the sole voice of Arkansas in the House at a time when Tennessee had thirteen representatives.

He got to the governor's chair the next year. The new state had set up two banks, with seven branches, backed by the state's taxing power. They were badly mismanaged. In a notable instance $500,000 in bonds was issued to secure a loan of $250,000 from a New York bank, but only $122,000 got to Arkansas, while the bonds were sold in London for $325,000. Yell made the banks a campaign issue and launched an investigation when he was elected.

Investigators found fraud as well as amateur mismanagement. Paper money issued by the state banks was only worth thirty cents on the dollar in 1839. By 1844 both Arkansas banks had been shut down.

Governor Yell was caught between his obligation to preserve the state's credit and his disinclination to tax the people of Arkansas to redeem bonds issued in fraud and sold illegally. His answer was to be expected when the question came to involve a class issue in which the bondowners were seen as monopolistic and aristocratic owners of big acres.

One of the results was that in 1846 the state constitution was enlarged by an amendment prohibiting the chartering of a lending institution of any kind. For lack of banks, Arkansas farmers had to accept the terms of credit offered by their suppliers and brokers, which reduced the chances of a profitable crop. It was still a state without banks when Civil War troubles were added.

Archibald Yell was a man of broad interests. He proposed more and better schools. He especially wanted schools, helped by federal money, to teach agriculture. He proposed a state board to foster internal improvements. He once vetoed a law that would have allowed a wife to control her own property because the proposed wording would have left her husband liable for her debts.

Already a notable Mason because of his Tennessee record, he made a bigger place in the fraternal order by establishing the first Masonic lodge in Arkansas. He had such a pleasant personality that after his first two wives died and he was a widower with five children, he won a third wife. He outlived her, too.

It may be that his highest skill was as a campaigner. It was so impressive that the Democrats sent a delegation to ask him to step down as governor in order to run for Congress again in 1840. The Whigs had assembled their strength and obtained strong candidates. On this campaign the candidates, traveling together, came upon a frontier gambling event in which a beef was the prize of a shooting match. The sharpshooters bought tickets for a chance to compete. Yell introduced himself to every man and boy in the crowd, bought a chance, fired the most accurate shot, won the beef, asked if there was a widow nearby who needed it, sent it to her, and then bought a jug of whisky, which he shared with everyone.

His adversary stood above the gambling and drinking. But on down the road it seemed that dignity would have its day at a rural revival meeting. It was a vain hope. The campaigners had hardly arrived when Yell took a place in the "Amen Corner" and enthusiastically led the singing. The Whig candidate was a thoroughly worthy person of excellent standing, a friend and neighbor of Yell, but hopeless in competition for votes against the Yell personality.

Back in Congress in 1845, Yell was strongly for the Oregon expansion policy, for a bigger army, and the annexation of Texas. When the Texas situation developed into war, Yell felt so strongly that he left Washington, 1 July 1846, and returned to the soldier's life as colonel of the First Arkansas Volunteer Cavalry. He left without resigning his seat in Congress. Arkansas elected a replacement but Yell remained technically in office, while Congress waited for war news.

The Arkansas outfit commanded by Yell had some good men as well as some brave ones. But it also had some rough characters from the backwoods, untrained but overconfident, and strangers to discipline. Although history books tell of a United States victory at Buena Vista, the Arkansas battle in that front was a disaster. When cavalrymen with swords attacked horseback soldiers with long spears, odds were in favor of the longer reach of the spearmen. In this instance the defenders also outnumbered the men with sabers five to one. Yell got out in front of his men on 22 February 1847, galloped into the massed enemy, and died on a Mexican lance.

Lean Jimmy

His name was James Chamberlain Jones. During part of his life he was "Governor Jones," as head of the Tennessee government. During another part he was "Senator Jones" in Washington. But sometimes he was called "Lean Jimmy." For he was very lean, more than six feet tall and weighing only 125 pounds when his health was good. His leanness was accentuated by an unusually large nose and small eyes, overhung by massive brows.

His gaunt frame was even more conspicuous because he often confronted on campaign platforms his long-time opponent who was sometimes called "Little Jimmy." His rival, however, became better known, and is still known, as President James K. Polk. "Little Jimmy" was shorter than normal and was robust in appearance, although his health was weak.

Polk was a powerful man in politics. He had found the real levers of strength as clerk to the state senate during four legislative sessions in 1818–1822. He was elected to the state House of Representatives in 1823, and went to Congress in 1825. Polk was reelected continuously and rose to be Speaker of the House, a leading figure in Washington, and an outstanding Democrat nationally. He was associated with Andrew Jackson.

Although the family had known frontier poverty, Polk's father became wealthy and powerful in Maury County (Columbia). Polk was a graduate of the University of North Carolina, and the top student of his class, with campus standing as a debater. He quickly became a Nashville lawyer with a good income. Polk left Congress only because his party needed him badly as a candidate for governor. He won in 1839.

In 1841 Polk was forty-six, a veteran of political wars. He was governor and running for reelection. That was the year he was chal-

James C. Jones

lenged by Jones, who was a mere thirty-two, with only the political experience of one term in the lower house of the legislature. He had only a slim claim to education.

Yet Jones climbed up on the same stumps from which Polk had come down. Frequently one candidate spoke for two hours, followed by his rival for the same length of time, with each coming back for a half-hour rebuttal. There were eight months of this campaigning. The candidates were offering a big entertainment event in times of few amusements. Polk was an excellent speaker who made a clear presentation of issues with an adequate supply of stories and humor, and he was backed up by abundant experience in government.

But Jones was his superior in funny stories, mimicry, homely illustrations and burlesque. Jones was also a likeable person, with a strong appeal as he mingled with the crowds face to face. One of his assets was an ability to get the folks who lived way back in the coves and hollows to come out on election days.

"Lean Jimmy" and "Little Jimmy" were utter contrasts in Whig-Democrat politics as well as in appearance, and even in attitudes. There were times when Polk had concluded a sound and solid address only to have Jones get slowly to his feet, pull a coonskin from his pocket, gently stroke the pelt and open by saying, "Did you ever see such fine fur?" When he had finished, his foes were baffled to find what his position was so they could attack. Sometimes his friends were puzzled, too, but whatever he meant to say, they liked the way he said it.

Writers have been puzzled ever since by how he did it but he drove Polk out of the governor's chair. The figures are clear—53,000 for Jones to 50,000 for Polk. Jones was the first Tennessee governor born in this state.

It was a time of change, with old parties splitting and new political forces being organized. In Tennessee it was a period of almost even strength for Democrats and Whigs. In the legislature the Whigs had a majority in the lower house and the Democrats in the senate. The senate then had twenty-five members and they were split thirteen to twelve. They even had a thirteen to twelve vote on whether to go to lunch.

This one-vote Democratic majority in the senate was determined to prevent the Whig house majority of three in the membership of seventy-five from naming a new U.S. senator. So the two houses never got together while the voice of Tennessee in the Senate at Washington was silent. For almost two years in 1842 and 1843 both Tennessee seats in the United States Senate were vacant.

Governor Jones rode out the storm and in 1843 went up against Polk again and beat him again. This time the margin was 58,000 to 54,000. It was a peculiar fact that Polk got more votes than when he had won in 1839, and more than Jones got in winning in 1841, but he still lost in 1843.

The second inauguration of Governor Jones was marked by his appearance in a suit made of Tennessee silk. There were extensive efforts to add silk growing and manufacturing to Tennessee's business and to jobs available for women. The state had a special school to teach the growing of mulberry trees and silk worms, with tax money offered in bounties of ten cents a pound for cocoons, and fifty cents a pound for reeled silk.

Whig strength at the ballot box grew until they won majorities in both houses of the legislature. In 1851 the legislators sent Jones to the U.S. Senate.

Meantime, Polk, twice defeated by Jones for the governor's office, had become president. He was the first "dark horse" candidate to win. His edge in the nationwide vote was very thin, and he went to the White

House without having won his home state. But Polk was president from 1845 to 1849. He had announced in advance he would serve only one term. He also announced the main things he hoped to accomplish, and he did them in a way that has won higher marks from modern historians than he got during the years of his presidency. He wore out what remained of his health under the responsibilities of office. Polk came back to Tennessee expecting death, which came 15 June 1849, scarcely three months later.

Jones, whose winning of the governor's office in 1841 and 1843 is a special chapter in Tennessee politics, made another deep mark in the record as a U.S. senator. In 1856 he stood on the floor of the Senate chamber and renounced the Whigs whose banner he had carried throughout his years of high offices. He also sent a fourteen-page pamphlet to his public, explaining what he had done. ''The Democratic Party affords the best, if not the last hope of safety and security to the South,'' he told the senators. His term ran out a few months later and he retired from partisan politics. Railroad building had become his chief interest.

He had moved to Memphis and become a man of primary importance in the development of this city. Jones had been born in Wilson County in the Nashville area. About 1850, which was after he was governor but before he became a senator, he moved to a farm near Memphis. Jones had become associated with Robertson Topp of the Town of South Memphis, and R. C. Brinkley and Sam Tate of Memphis, in the effort to get a railroad for the bluff.

The Memphis & Charleston Railroad had been chartered in 1846. In 1849 Jones and Topp represented Memphis at the Atlantic and Pacific Convention at Holly Springs, Mississippi, and Jones became convention chairman. Resolutions at this convention largely shaped the route to be followed by the Charleston rails.

Jones and Topp then went to the Memphis and Charleston convention at Huntsville, Alabama. There they sold $300,000 in stock in the Charleston company in two days, which later grew to $706,000 in stock subscriptions in north Alabama, plus $1,500,000 in aid from Alabama state funds. Stockholders, meeting at Huntsville, made Jones president of the railroad on 30 April 1850. He thus was president of the railroad at the same time he was senator from Tennessee. Being in Congress then was considered a part-time job, and members were more likely to share a boarding house with other congressmen during winter sessions than to have a Washington home.

Back on the bluff, Topp, the leading figure in South Memphis, campaigned for unification of the two towns, which was accomplished on 1 January 1850. A few months later citizens of the enlarged Memphis voted to add city tax money to the railroad financing. It was Jones who was president of the railroad when it bought fourteen acres in March of 1851 for the terminal yards and headquarters building which became the depot on Charleston (later renamed Lauderdale and much later Danny Thomas). The first four miles of track were completed in June of 1852. The tracks reached Germantown in August that year, with cars running and making money between Memphis and the end of the line where construction was going on.

For all of the Jones skill in dealing with legislators, there was trouble in Mississippi. The railroad wanted to barely cross the tip of the state on the way to Muscle Shoals. But Holly Springs was determined to have the tracks come that way, as the stage coach route did. Mississippi finally issued a charter to the Charleston line in a settlement that resulted in the Mississippi Central rails being built from Canton, through Holly Springs, to Grand Junction and the M&C tracks, then on northward to Jackson, Tennessee. Meantime other construction crews were building toward Memphis from Stevenson, Alabama. It was Senator Jones who swung the sledge hammer for last spike ceremonies on 28 March 1857.

Contrary to the stories of many other railroads, the M&C made money from the opening on tracks still being built. For the twelve months beginning in mid-1858 it cleared 12½ percent of the full cost of construction, with a gross of more than $1.3 million. There were 271 miles of track from Memphis to Stevenson, and it carried the load with 30 locomotives, 454 freight cars, 38 passenger cars and 14 for baggage.

This was a railroad that had had nothing but six miles of long abandoned track when James Jones became president eight years earlier. Hardly anything in Memphis history can be compared with this railroad in building up the city and its business. "Lean Jimmy" Jones died the next year, on 29 October 1859, and is buried in Elmwood Cemetery. His was a spectacular career as governor, senator and railroad builder, even though he gets small space in Memphis histories and none at all in histories of the nation.

Delta Whig

James Lusk Alcorn was a leader in Mississippi politics most of his life. His greatest accomplishment was winning state tax money for the levees designed to hold high water out of the Delta fields. Individual plantation owners had tried to build their flood barriers and county tax money had been brought in, but the financing was too feeble for the size of the levee system necessary.

It turned out that federal taxes were needed years later, but the state financing was a great gain for its day and a great political victory for the Whigs over the Democrats of that time, who held for strict interpretation of the Constitution and a heavy lid on spending by state governments, as well as federal budgets.

With the help of a big flood in the spring of 1858, Alcorn led the way to creation (2 December 1858) of a levee commission with broad powers in the Delta. At its first meeting Alcorn was elected president, with an annual salary of $6,000 in state tax money, higher than any other state official. However, he is far more likely to be remembered as governor in 1870–1871 and senator in 1871–1877. He is even more likely to be recalled as the moderate Republican who was defeated by a radical Republican for governor in 1873.

Alcorn was born in Illinois, went to school and entered politics in Kentucky, before moving on south on a flatboat. He tied up on the river bank in 1844, when settlers were still moving into the Delta lands. Alcorn was twenty-eight. He had a college degree and the experience of being a deputy sheriff and a member of the Kentucky Legislature. He became a lawyer in Panola County during the year of his arrival. His farming in the Moon Lake country prospered, and so did his law practice.

In 1846, two years after his arrival, he was a member of the Mississippi legislature and he was there until 1857. He lost a bid for Congress in 1856 and declined a nomination for governor in 1857. In the prewar era Alcorn was in tune with his neighbors. He was a Whig and so were most of the large planters and the merchants of Memphis. He was distinguished as an advocate of staying in the Union as the best hope of preserving slavery. With war near, Coahoma County elected him to the "secession convention" in Jackson. Pro-Union delegates accompanied him from every county in the river area. But they were a minority and eventually they joined the majority for secession.

Alcorn and other Whigs went to war promptly with commissions in

James Lusk Alcorn (from *James Lusk Alcorn* by Lillian A. Pereyra).

the state armies. But when the Confederate command was formed, officer commissions arrived for others, leaving out Alcorn. He had tangled with Jefferson Davis, a Democrat, for years, had a low regard for him as a president, and early in the war went home.

While battle lines were distant, he raised cotton and sold it to smugglers. Whenever he could he bought with Confederate money but sold for gold, a profitable method used by others. When the blue army arrived, Alcorn refused to take the loyalty oath and the federals counted him a secessionist.

Long after the war, Alcorn flatly declared his belief in racial inferiority. Yet he supported the idea of ballots for Negroes and hoped racial politics could be avoided by Negro membership in both parties.

He was especially conspicuous for his strong belief in schools supported by taxes. In a general way they were new to Mississippi after the war, although there were exceptions. Columbus had had free schools for years, but a statewide effort in 1848 resulted in townships in charge and only two of them had free schools. There were none for black children, although some families taught their house servants. It was the "Black and Tan Convention" of 1868 that really got the schools started as a statewide system.

The theory of everyone paying school taxes was unpopular. In counties with many Negro children but few Negro taxpayers, there were protests. Objections were especially strong, to the point of forceful resistance, in the hill counties. Violence appeared, usually blamed on the Ku Klux Klan. Alcorn obtained from the legislature a law forbidding masks and disguises, and a special fund with which he could hire secret investigators. This was in 1870.

In 1871 there was terrorism in the counties of Lowndes, Monroe, Noxubee, Oktibbeha, Choctaw, Winston, Kemper, Itawamba, Alcorn, Tishomingo, Prentiss, Pontotoc, Lee, Leake, Tippah, Union, Chickasaw and Lauderdale. There were murders in Lauderdale, Lowndes, Noxubee and Meridian counties. Buildings in which schools for Negroes had been started were burned, even though they were churches or rented structures. Threats to teachers came by letter and by visitors in the night. Sometimes teachers were whipped. The superintendent of schools in Monroe County was badly beaten and forced to leave the county.

The peak of violence came in Meridian. Armed white men from Alabama often came into Meridian after Negroes who had run away from work contracts. A committee of Negroes went to the governor to complain. They returned and were reporting to a meeting when fire broke out. Several were arrested. At their trial two days later (6 March 1871), there was a riot in which the Negroes on trial were killed. So was the judge. Then a committee took the mayor to the county line and convinced him he should stay away. The next night three prominent Negroes in jail for protection were removed and killed.

Although worse outbursts of violence probably had taken place under other governors, Alcorn's name was blackened with the Meridian riot. The legislature refused him additional tools for cutting down the violence. He was caught in crossfire from conservatives who were outraged by the speed with which he had moved into the new era of free schools, and from radicals who would rather have had the Yankee army in charge than for Alcorn to prove the state could manage its own affairs.

It probably is impossible for those who have known free public schools all their lives to realize what a struggle it was to get them started in this part of the country. The conflict in 1870 in North Carolina was over the question of compelling school attendance, a theory opposed by

The Memphis Daily Appeal. The Memphis newspaper, while Alcorn's school troubles were mounting, editorialized on ''the humbug that agitates the fanatics of North Carolina'' and saw ''no necessity for running down and forcing into the schoolrooms mackerels who will not absorb an education.'' A few days later the newspaper attacked again, saying that a state that could force children into school also could ''force them to attend Sunday School and it can force their parents to attend church.''

In the fall of 1871 there was an abrupt decline of violence. Support of public education by the white population became common. But Alcorn ·was left in the middle. At a time of high importance of the Negro vote, black leaders turned toward Republicans who promised more, while radical Republicans attacked him for his ineffective efforts to restrain the Klan. He was almost alone among Mississippi Whigs in accepting the Republican label.

The Mississippi Legislature sent him to the United States Senate in 1865 but senators turned him back at the door. In 1869 he was elected governor, and while governor the legislature again elected him to the Senate. This time he held back and remained governor until after the 1871 elections. He then went to Washington, serving from 1 December 1871, until 3 March 1877. But his day was over long before his term expired. He had been defeated as a candidate for governor in 1873 by the radical Adelbert Ames, a former Yankee general who went back to Massachusetts when his term was over.

Alcorn went back to his fine plantation, ''Eagles Nest,'' in Coahoma County, practiced law at Friars Point and lived on until 19 December 1894. He came back into public life as a member of the constitutional convention of 1890, and his name is well preserved because of the name of the county formed while he was governor, and by the name of Alcorn College.

Editor, Senator, Martyr

When the words *The Commercial Appeal* were first combined on the pages of that newspaper, on 1 July 1894, the editor was Edward Ward Carmack, one of the most controversial personalities in the story of Tennessee. He was tall and red-haired. He was a writer with a huge stock of words and an ability to use barbed expressions, tipped with vitriol. He could attract both unlimited admiration and violent dislike. He probably was even stronger on the platform than at the writing desk.

Edward Ward Carmack   Malcolm Patterson

He was a poor boy from near Castalian Springs (Sumner County), the son of a Campbellite preacher who had died without worldly goods while the boy was small. He was a juvenile worker on farms and in a brickyard until friends helped him get to the famous Webb School.

Carmack became a lawyer at Columbia, Tennessee. He soon entered politics as a member of the lower house in Nashville in 1885, representing Maury and Williamson counties. He then turned to newspapering, becoming editor of the *Columbia Herald* and, in 1888, of the *Nashville American*. He was brought to Memphis as editor of the *Memphis Daily Commercial* in 1892. Carmack was already known across the state for colorful phrasing of editorials, caustic words, and the ability to speak as well as to write. His talents were quickly applied to local politics.

A judge had been accused of accepting bribes from gamblers. The judge was supported by *The Appeal-Avalanche* and its owner, W. A. Collier. *The Commercial* took the other side with a "Law and Order League," which was attempting to sweep crime out of Memphis and bring in prohibition of liquor sales.

A personal battle between Carmack and Collier developed. Collier's paper called *The Commercial* "a hired assassin of character." It said *The Commercial* was the "kind of newspaper that goes about begging for alms one day and burning barns the next." It said Carmack was "a common blackguard from the hill country." So Carmack replied in *The*

Commercial with an editorial saying Collier had debauched *The Appeal* "to the level of a night-strolling trollop plying its trade in the back alleys of the town, dealing in shame for a morsel of bread, selling its soul to whomever may buy."

The next confrontation seemed to be a duel, but friends kept them apart. The judge was convicted and Carmack and Collier went right back to war in a city election, lost by the Carmack side. Then Collier lost his editorial voice. He was operating on credit when the panic of 1893 struck, *The Appeal* was thrown into receivership and *The Commercial* owners bought it. The consolidation resulted in the appearance of *The Commercial Appeal*. Before *The Commercial Appeal* was well launched on its expanded career Carmack was gone. The overriding issue of the times was the demand for coinage of silver to increase the money supply. The South, farmers of the West, and Populist politicians were sure the panic and depression were artificially caused by the gold dollar.

In 1894 the Tennessee Democrats attempted to straddle, with a silver platform and a conservative candidate for governor. It was a compromise in which Carmack took a hand at the convention. But plans went awry when the Republican candidate came in slightly ahead. That had to be doctored by the legislature with a recount that gave the Democrat enough edge to become governor.

Elections for Congress that year went badly for the Democrats; so poorly that a headline in *The Commercial Appeal* said, "Heaven and Mississippi Still Remain True to the Grand Old Democratic Party. Pretty Near Everything Else Seems to Have Gone Over to the Republicans."

The Carmack answer to this situation was for the silver coinage advocates to take over the Democratic Party. He believed in silver and he feared that former Democrats would vote for Populist candidates, whom he said were anarchistic, violent, and vicious. Carmack was most conspicuous in the silver campaigning. He was chairman of a silver meeting in Memphis and introduced the famous speaker, William Jennings Bryan. He accompanied Bryan to another meeting in Jackson, Tennessee. In an editorial he welcomed more than two thousand Democrats to a three-day convention. The Memphis meeting was in many ways the trial run of the tactics and oratory with which the silver men took over the Democratic convention of 1896 and made Bryan the presidential candidate.

But Carmack was only the editor hired by the five men who owned the newspaper, and three of them held firm to the gold standard. They were

West Crawford, a cotton broker, W. B. Mallory, his partner in the cotton business; and Luke Wright, a lawyer of great prominence. While Carmack, the editor, was leading the silver parade, Crawford, the owner, was organizing a Southwide sound money convention, also held in Memphis.

On the silver side of the split in ownership of the newspaper were John Overton Jr., grandson of one of the founders of Memphis and head of a bank and an insurance company; and Gilbert Raine, head of a large insurance firm.

Carmack was safely in control of the editorial page, with a five-year contract, but the hard feelings between the gold men and the silver advocates were so intense that in a newspaper board meeting in April 1896 a "gold bug" director said that Carmack would have been fired except for the contract. So Carmack produced the contract, tore it up and announced, "I have resigned." The only account of this scene that has been preserved was written by a young lawyer, Kenneth McKellar, who later became a senator. He told of Carmack coming to the McKellar office to borrow money immediately after the resignation. It was announced on 28 April 1896.

The Commercial Appeal, having taken up the silver cause under Carmack, continued in that policy under a new editor and campaigned for the Democratic platform and for Bryan.

While the story of Carmack giving up his job rather than his principles is long established, some political ambition was also involved. Dr. Thomas Harrison Baker, whose history of *The Commercial Appeal* was published in 1971, discusses this motive at some length.

There had been talk of Carmack as a candidate for Congress in 1896. He had been unable to displace Josiah Patterson in 1894. But the three gold bug owners of *The Commercial Appeal* and their political associates controlled the Shelby County party machinery. They demanded and got the local Democratic convention to renominate Patterson for a fourth term in the House. Carmack resigned from *The Commercial Appeal* the day the Patterson nomination was sewed up.

Tennessee's silver Democrats withdrew from the party, held another convention in August and nominated Carmack. The contest took top position that year. Among other things, it included all five owners of *The Commercial Appeal* taking conspicuous parts in campaigning, three against Carmack and two for him. The editorial page took both sides, backing a silver man for president and a gold man for Congress.

The vote count put Carmack in Washington, but the Patterson contest was fast and strong, and it was two years before the Carmack win was confirmed. McKellar was his attorney. This was also the beginning of long and exceedingly bitter conflicts between Carmack and Malcolm Patterson, son of Josiah, who had managed the campaign.

In the election of 1898, Carmack was sent back to Congress. In the election of 1900, he was promoted to the Senate. While Carmack was in the Senate the Memphis seat in the House was won by Malcolm Patterson, who served three terms, from 1901 to 1906, and then resigned to become governor. Carmack lost his bid for a second Senate term in 1906 and returned to Nashville as a lawyer. In 1908, when Patterson ran for a second term as governor, Carmack undertook to defeat him in one of the most spectacular political wars of Tennessee history.

Prohibition was the great issue and it split the public so badly that the Democrats took the unusual step of holding a primary election for the gubernatorial nomination. Carmack was an ardent dry and Patterson championed the wet side. It was also a contest of country (Carmack) against city (Patterson).

Both were orators of the first class and both were already known to the public. When they spoke from the same stage in Memphis, 8,000 persons turned out. *The Commercial Appeal* took the Patterson side. Public feeling ran high, but it is probable that few opinions were changed by the speeches since a large part of the state had both a local option prohibition and plenty of illegal liquor.

The result was a kind of draw. Patterson and the wets won the governor's chair but the drys won the legislature. Carmack turned away from the law and politics again to become an editor once more, this time of *The Tennessean* in Nashville. He continued his attacks on Patterson and his supporters, especially Duncan Cooper. Two years before, Cooper had been active in defeating Carmack. On 8 November 1908 he accused Cooper of bringing about a sinister alliance between Patterson and a former governor, John Cox. The next afternoon Cooper and his son, Robin, found Carmack on the street. Both had pistols. So did Carmack, who may have fired first. His pistol had two empty shells. Robin Cooper's had three empties. Three bullets hit Carmack and he fell dead in the gutter.

A few weeks later the legislature adopted a statewide prohibition law. Patterson vetoed it. The legislature overrode him. But that also was a kind of draw. The drys got the law but big cities kept the liquor. It was five years before the law got to Memphis.

Both Coopers were found guilty of second degree murder, with twenty-year sentences. The state Supreme Court sent the Robin Cooper case back for a retrial, which was never held. Robin came back into the news years later. Two men took him from his home late on the night of 10 August 1919. He was found in his parked automobile, mysteriously beaten to death. The high court affirmed the conviction of the older Cooper. Less than two hours after the ruling Governor Patterson pardoned him.

The uproar was deafening but Patterson defended his action and went back to the practice of law in Memphis when his term ended. In 1915 he lost an attempt to go to the Senate. He was a Circuit Court judge from 1923 to 1934, and wrote a daily column for the editorial page of *The Commercial Appeal*. In 1932 he lost as a candidate for the nomination for governor.

Carmack was considered a martyr to the cause of outlawing the saloon. The Anti-Saloon league obtained from the first legislature after his death authority to put his statue on the steps of the Capitol. It took them years to raise the money, but the statue was unveiled in 1925. Only three others are honored on the Capitol grounds, President Jackson, President Polk, and Sam Davis, boy spy for the Confederates.

On the Carmack statue base the Women's Christian Temperance Union placed a plaque with his "Pledge to the South." It is:

> The South is a land that has known sorrows: it is a land that has broken the ashen crust and moistened it with tears; a land scarred and riven by the plowshares of war and billowed with the graves of her dead; but a land of legend, a land of song, a land of hallowed and heroic memories.
>
> To that land every drop of my blood, every fibre of my being, every pulsation of my heart, is consecrated forever.
>
> I was born of her womb; I was nurtured at her breast; and when my last hour shall come, I pray God that I may be pillowed on her bosom and rocked to sleep within her tender and encircling arms.

Redneck Leader

James Kimble Vardaman lived in North Mississippi and, in the early years of the century, ran for office again and again. He was a candidate for governor in 1895 and lost. He was a candidate for governor in 1899 and lost. He tried to go to the U.S. Senate in 1907, and 1910, and 1918, and 1922, and he lost each time. He got to the Governor's office once, in the voting of 1930, and he went to the Senate once, after the 1911 campaign.

James Kimble Vardaman

The Vardaman campaigning was a powerful force in Mississippi politics when he lost as well as when he won, for he could make his ideas heard as editor of the *Winona Advance* in the 1880s, as publisher of the *Greenwood Enterprise* from 1890 to 1895 and of the *Greenwood Commonwealth* from 1896 to 1903, and publisher of the *Issue,* a Jackson weekly (1908-1912) with the sole purpose of keeping his name before the public while out of office. He also had *Vardaman's Weekly* from 1919 to 1922.

Away from Mississippi the Vardaman name means only the man who replaced Le Roy Percy in the Senate. His son, William Alexander Percy, has thousands of admirers for his writing skill, especially in *Lanterns on the Levee.* One chapter in this book tells of his father being accused of being "a prosperous plantation owner, a corporation lawyer and unmistakably a gentleman." The Will Percy words for Vardaman include: "a kindly, vain demogogue unable to think," "overdressed," looking like a "top-notch medicine man," "an exhibitionist playing with fire." His oratory was called "bastard emotionalism and raven-tressed rant."

Seeking more information on a man who drew such scorn from Will Percy leads to a large number of Mississippians who felt the same way and to another large number of persons to whom Vardaman was the living exemplar of all that is good. Some of his followers compared Vardaman to Moses and Jeremiah, and even to Jesus.

He had very black hair which he wore at shoulder length, and often showcased against a white suit. He was the "Great White Chief." He was the leader of the rednecks. The word had been thrown at one of his followers by an opposing speaker. It was intended to silence the heckling. Instead it pleased the Vardaman folks. They enjoyed it, used it to describe themselves and, during at least one campaign, had a cheer that went, "We are the low brows! We are the rednecks! Rah for Vardaman!" The Vardamanites liked to parade in red neckties with "redneck" placards.

Vardaman came into politics through the law. His only school was one room, built of logs. He read the books in the law offices of his uncle, Pierson Money at Carrollton, and greatly admired his cousin, Hernando DeSoto Money, who was in Congress. As was typical of his later career, he lost when he first sought office. He wanted to go to the legislature in 1885. But he won in 1889, when he was twenty-nine years old. He was in the House at Jackson, representing Leflore County, for six years, and was speaker in 1894. He had become one of the "Bourbons" in control of the state's politics, strange as that may seem to those who know only of his later years.

On his way to the governor's chair he became widely known for his attitude toward Negroes. He was interviewed by *The Commercial Appeal* in April of 1903 when he came to the Hotel Peabody while campaigning. He was especially interested in more money for schools for white children. He protested distribution of state money which put more into Delta schools for blacks than hill country schools for whites. He was quoted, "The Negro already receives too much education. It ruins him as a farm hand and leads him to commit acts which for him mean death. This specter which endangers the civilization of Mississippi must be removed."

About the same time, speaking before a Delta crowd at Batesville, he said whites paid the larger part of schools taxes but the spending was larger for Delta Negro schools. Two years later he went further by advocating recruiting immigrants and changing land laws so that the big farms of the Delta would be replaced by small farms occupied by men from the North and West.

Still later these proposals were directed toward taking away the voting power of a small circle of Delta plantation men and putting the ballot strength in the hills. It is often overlooked that Vardaman, as a candidate in 1903, was endorsed by Le Roy Percy.

Vardaman advocated repeal of the Fifteenth Amendment, and parts of the Fourteenth. It was a logical development of a Vardaman attitude that had appeared more than twenty years earlier. In 1883, while still editing the *Winona Advance,* there was an uproar in Nashville, about a Negro constable shooting a white restaurant man. The Vardaman paper said that any town that tolerated a Negro official had "no right to complain."

For all of Vardaman's tremendous strength as a stump speaker, two outside influences contributed to his becoming governor. One was the introduction of the primary election, in which Mississippi led the nation. He lost the nominations under the convention method, but he won the first time the primaries were used.

The other outside influence was President Theodore Roosevelt. He sat down to eat with Booker T. Washington in the White House. He reappointed a Negro woman who had long been postmaster at Indianola. When the public pressures closed in on her she resigned, so Roosevelt closed the post office. Objections were numerous in Southern states, and thunderous in Mississippi, with Vardaman conspicuously shrill. Voting for Vardaman became a protest against Roosevelt.

As governor, his big push, against determined and powerful opposition, was to end the system of leasing convicts, which was enriching a few men while inflicting suffering on many. He came into office proposing that the governor's mansion be sold, and leaving governors to find their own shelter.

He got more state money for the common schools, but considered college expenses a problem for families of students. His opposition to Negro education went so far as vetoing an appropriation for Holly Springs State Normal, where some Negro teachers were trained. It was $2,000. He got a uniform textbook law that helped poor families.

Vardaman attacked the death penalty at every opportunity. In contradiction, he believed that lynching was necessary for Negroes who attacked white women, and he believed white women were in hourly danger. He specified quick death by hanging, and protested burning and prolonged killings. Yet he baffled his followers when, as governor, he raced across the state to stop a lynching, then did it again. In all, he saved nine lives from mobs. One of those rescued was later tried and freed, the first time it happened in Mississippi. He also obtained a strong vagrancy law, which forced some Negroes to take low-paying jobs.

He was an isolationist and opposed to imperialism, after almost a year in Cuba during the Spanish war. He said, "The American nigger is a gentleman and scholar compared to (the Cuban). Indeed I am disposed to apologize to the nigger for making the comparison."

Vardaman was without peer in swaying large crowds and building unquestioning loyalty. When he appeared, crowds that had been gathering for hours broke into cheers that drowned out the band. After two hours of oratory the applause was even louder and longer. He was dramatic, appearing once on a lumber wagon drawn by eighty white oxen. He was spectacular even in religion, marching down the aisle to an evangelist's mourners' bench after he had been governor.

His appearance was unforgettable. He was big, strong, assured, and immaculate from his well-brushed black hair to the tips of white boots. He was so dominant in action that listeners overlooked the fact that his sweeping gestures were all left-handed. His right arm had been torn by a corn sheller and was almost useless except for signing his name.

Yet when he won a Senate term neither his campaigning promises nor his attitude toward Negroes was as big a factor as the tactic of convincing a large part of the voters that he had been unjustly denied the seat.

Senator Anselm Joseph McLaurin had died at the end of 1909. It would have been reasonable for Vardaman to have been appointed for he had polled a large vote in losing to McLaurin. But the governor made a temporary appointment and left a successor to the legislature.

As the governor had left room for trouble by declining to make the appointment, the legislature again left space for an uproar by failing to simply elect a nominee. Instead the Democratic members of the legislature used a caucus. After each day's legislative session they went into a night session as a caucus. The meetings were public but the voting was secret. It was a retreat from the newly won advantages of primary voting to the old days of convention connivance.

Vardaman started way ahead with seventy-one votes on the first ballot. He stayed ahead and got up to seventy-eight. But eight-six were needed. The anti-Vardaman tactic was to keep nine other candidates with small votes in the race. The struggle went on almost two months, from 7 January through 22 February 1910. There were fifty-eight ballots, while Jackson overflowed with men interested on one side or the other, in the biggest news story of the era. Suddenly eight of the other names were withdrawn. The Vardaman vote went to up to eighty-two, but Le Roy Percy got eighty-seven.

While Percy was in the Senate, Vardaman campaigners criss-crossed the state with tales of a caucus corrupted by cash, liquor, women, and promises of jobs. The Percy forces did a thorough job of disproving the charges but the air was so filled with allegations that a majority of the people came to think there probably was corruption—and that the corruptors were being protected by the governor, the legislature and the courts. Vardaman went to Washington and Percy was sent home on a landslide of votes in 1911.

In Washington Vardaman was a radical reformer, contrary to his modern image as a stone-age conservative. He was an associate of Robert La Follette, George Norris, and other heroes of the liberal tradition. He considered labor unions the best protection against the power of big money. He wanted public ownership of the railroads, as well as electricity, natural gas, water, and street cars. He opposed business subsidies. He was an ardent prohibitionst. He opposed Sunday blue laws. He took a strong stand against antisemitism. He supported the cause of Mississippi's Choctaws. He supported the income tax, worked for a national law on child labor, and thought there should be federal old age pensions.

He got little notice as a liberal, partly because the eyes of outsiders were blinded by his blatant racism. His words were crude, in a time when others had similar ideas clothed in smoother language. It was common, in both North and South, to believe the Negro was a lower order of nature. Vardaman translated this into a campaign to bar the Negro from the voting booth and make it illegal for a Negro to hold office. But hardly anyone noticed that Mississippi had taken away the ballot by the constitution of 1890, before the Vardaman era. Nor was there much attention paid to the fact that none of the other big men in Mississippi politics took out after Vardaman on a contrary racial platform.

Vardaman was welcome in Chautauqua tents and big city auditoriums hundreds of miles from the cotton country. He only had one lecture, "The Impending Crisis." It was his most reliable source of income.

The Vardaman record in the Senate was more out of line with the times on national issues than his Negro attitude was irregular in his state. He wandered from party policy several times, especially on preparation for war, and he was one of the few who voted against the declaration of war. World War I was intensely popular in the magnolia country and in 1918 Vardaman was turned out in favor of Pat Harrison.

Vardaman's amazing magnetism remained in 1922, more than a

quarter century after his first run for the governor's office. In the senatorial primary that year he got more votes than anyone else, although Hubert Stephens won the run-off.

His splendid physique began to wilt in the 1918 campaign. In 1922 it had crumbled so badly that sometimes he merely sat on the platform while others read his words. His fiscal condition also was ailing. He had never had much of a law practice. His magazines were sometimes one-man publications. His campaign expense money largely came in from collections as he spoke, and there were times when he left the campaigning to friends while he went west to lecture and send back his fees.

Vardaman stories by the hundred are still told in Mississippi and yet the man came into the clear view of modern eyes only in 1970, when William F. Holmes, reared in Yazoo City, wrote *The White Chief.*

There were contradictions in Vardaman's personality and paradox in his career. Sometimes it seems that all stripes of Mississippi politicians share memories of Ole Miss law school, but Vardaman looked back to neither Oxford nor any other college town. Most office holders were born in the state, but Vardaman was born in Texas (26 July 1861). Neither did he die in Mississippi. His health utterly broken, and his only income a Spanish War pension, his last home was with a daughter in Birmingham, where he died (25 June 1930).

Vardaman accumulated nothing in the public service, nor did he build an organization of office holders. His basic hope had been to use government to better the lives of white farmers with a few acres, and workers with low wages. He was the champion of the little man at a time when the redneck needed help.

Peckerwood Prince

Theodore Gilmore Bilbo was Mississippi's governor from 1916 to 1920 and again from 1928 to 1932. He went to the U.S. Senate in 1935, was returned six years later, and was reelected for a third term but was barred by the Senate in 1947 from taking the oath again. Throughout his political wars he was in the news often, usually as "Theodore G. Bilbo, but often "Bilbo" was sufficient, and sometimes he was spoken of as "The Man." A national magazine once called him "Prince of the Peckerwoods."

The name is rarely heard today. In his day, small white farmers were numerous and he led them in a two-front attack—on the possibilities of

Theodore G. Bilbo (A.P. photo).

voting power for Negroes and on the accumulated power of the "elite establishment." Passing years have diminished the number of small farms because of farming with tractors, factory jobs, and welfare available in cities.

But Bilbo is a part of Mississippi history and his chapter was written within memories of the older generation. Bilbo came on the stage of state politics with a roar. He was an associate of James K. Vardaman, and his political heir.

The legislature of 1910 converted itself into a caucus which met at nights after the legislative session, to make a nomination for a Senate vacancy. Vardaman seemed to be way out ahead because of the size of his 1907 vote, although he had lost. The anti-Vardaman forces submitted nine other candidates before the caucus. Among them was Le Roy Percy, a Greenville lawyer and planter. The other candidates held on through a stalemate that lasted forty-four days. Suddenly all eight anti-Vardaman candidates withdrew in favor of Percy, who was nominated.

Soon after the election Bilbo announced that he, a state senator, had been bribed. He said he took the money in bills, put them in his safe, and voted for Vardaman anyway. He turned the bills over to the grand jury. But some of the money Bilbo turned in as evidence of bribery was printed after the event. The state Senate held a public hearing that amounted to a trial. When it was over a resolution was presented saying that "Senator T. G. Bilbo is unworthy to be a State Senator, and he is hereby expelled from membership in this body." A two-thirds majority was required and Bilbo came within one vote of being expelled. Instead, the Senate adopted a resolution saying that the "Senate of Mississippi pronounces said Bilbo as unfit to sit with honest, upright men in a respectable legislative body, and he is hereby asked to resign."

Rather than forcing him to resign, these words were almost advertising for Bilbo. The Vardaman campaign for election in 1912 began promptly. It was a long, vicious, and sordid campaign and it was won by Vardaman with a big margin. It is this campaigning that is recounted in a chapter of *Lanterns On the Levee,* without using the name "Bilbo." The book by Senator Percy's son, William Alexander Percy, is a masterpiece of writing. It was popular across the nation, with five printings required in the first five months after publication in 1941, and brisk sales for decades. It has been the introduction to Bilbo for thousands of distant readers.

In Mississippi he is better remembered as the governor. When he took office in 1916, Bilbo launched several reforms. William D. McCain, former president of the University of Southern Mississippi, writing in *A History of Mississippi* (edited by Richard Aubrey McLemore), says Bilbo "sets forth one of the most progressive and humanitarian programs which the state has ever known."

He pushed through the legislature much of his 1916 program. The State Tax Commission was a real reform which resulted in more equal taxation. The State Highway Commission was created and undertook to connect useful roads. The fee system of paying county officers, notably the sheriff-tax collectors, was abolished in favor of salaries. Much more state money was put into schools. Law enforcement was bolstered, especially against liquor law violators. He got a charity hospital in South Mississippi, a tuberculosis sanitarium, and a training school for delinquents.

In his second period in the governor's chair, beginning in 1928, Bilbo and the legislators often disagreed. But he must have pleased the people more often than the lawmakers did. In the 1931 elections, 121 members of the House were removed and only 19 reelected.

Especially remembered among the episodes of this period was the Bilbo "reform" of the state colleges and universities. He obtained new heads at Ole Miss, Mississippi A. & M., the Mississippi State College for Women, and the State Teachers College. He tried but missed at Delta State. Each of the Bilbo men then fired some faculty and staff.

The credits necessary for students in these Mississippi schools to go on to higher degrees outside the state or be accepted as faculty members elsewhere were taken away in 1931 by the Southern Association of Colleges and Secondary Schools. He was given a cold shoulder. His successors were left with the long process of rebuilding respectability.

The Great Depression struck especially hard in Mississippi, a state largely dependent on income from farms. Farmers had already been in depression for ten years before the nationwide financial troubles. One of the results was that state debt of less than $6 million in 1920 leaped to almost $29 million in 1930 and rushed on up to more than $50 million in 1932. There also were about $13 million in state warrants and certificates circulating when Bilbo departed the governor's office. In the state's treasury there was just $1,326.17. Teachers were being paid in certificates which were good for only ninety cents on the dollar, or eight-five and sometimes eighty.

Worst of all, state institutions had to produce cash to buy anything. The Mental Hospital at Whitfield ran out of food and the next governor had to write a personal check to feed the patients. Still, the voice of the people, speaking in ballots, sent Bilbo to the U.S. Senate in 1934. They chose him by a vote of 101,000 to 94,000 over Hubert Stephens, who had gone to the House in 1911 and to the Senate in 1922.

Before he got to the Senate, Bilbo had a period when he needed a job. Pat Harrison, who had been in Washington since 1911 as representative and senator, gave Bilbo a hand. Harrison arranged for Bilbo to get a job, making clippings for the Department of Agriculture. Bilbo became "Pastemaster General" his detractors said.

As a senator Bilbo voted with the New Deal, except on racial policies. He fell out with the veteran Mississippi senator and Harrison-Bilbo feuding went on for years, developing into bitter tension. There came a time when Harrison was a candidate for party whip. Senate Democrats were evenly divided when Bilbo announced he would vote for his Mississippi colleague if Harrison asked him to. Harrison said, "I wouldn't speak to that (expletive) if it meant the presidency of the United States." Harrison lost by one vote.

By that time Mississippi was habitually split along the Bilbo line.

Each person seemed to be either for Bilbo, beyond a mention of possible faults, or against Bilbo, beyond discussion of beneficial accomplishments. But neither friend nor foe was likely to talk about this crusader for under-privileged whites having a college background under his piney woods political character. He had gone away to school at Peabody, Vanderbilt, and the University of Michigan. He had studied to be both a teacher and a lawyer. He was, in fact, a public school teacher five years before he became a lawyer and a political officer holder in 1908. He lived on politics the rest of his life. And politics brought him down in the end.

Fear of Negro voting power had been a theme song of his campaigning for many years. The whites were the minority. In his second Senate term Bilbo became a figure on the national stage by filibustering the Fair Employment Practices Committee, and advocating deporting blacks to Africa. He became even more conspicuous in 1946 by telling white voters the time to keep blacks away from the ballot box was the night before elections. He said, ''I call for every red-blooded white man to use any means to keep the nigger away from the polls. If you don't understand what that means you are just plain dumb.''

On the first day of 1947 the Department of Justice announced an investigation of charges that Bilbo had intimidated Negroes to keep them from voting in 1946. Next day the War Investigating Committee said it had evidence Bilbo had used his office as senator ''for his personal gain in his dealing with war contractors.'' The committee accused Bilbo of receiving benefits of from $57,000 to $88,000.

In the 1946 voting, the political winds of the nation had shifted. The Democrats lost control of the Senate. Republicans took over committee chairmanships. The Republican Steering Committee recommended that Bilbo be barred at the door to keep him from taking the oath for his new term. Some senators protested on Bilbo's behalf with a filibuster that prevented all senators from being sworn. The log jam broke on 5 January when Bilbo departed Washington. He went to a New Orleans hospital and it was announced that his illness was cancer. He thought he could go back to Washington and fight it out. But he died in New Orleans on 21 August 1947. The ''Stormy Petrel of Mississippi Politics'' was almost seventy. He is buried near his Poplarville home.

Gamblers Kill Raiders

One night in 1904 raiders—in the name of the law—arrested more than one hundred fifty persons in a gambling house that had long been running openly at the northeast corner of Union and DeSoto (now Fourth). The players were Negroes. The operators were whites, who in the excitement took guns away from the deputy sheriffs, and killed two of them.

More than 6,000 persons jammed a protest meeting at the Lyceum Theatre at Second and Jefferson, and overflowed into Court Square. With lynch feeling in the air, the public response was channeled into a collection of thousands of dollars for a fund to reinforce the prosecutor.

Five men with an interest in the game were put on trial for murder, with the biggest names among lawyers lined up at long counsel tables. The extraordinary feature of the trial was a United States senator and a member of the House facing each other in Criminal Court. Congress was in recess and Senator Edward Carmack appeared for the state, with Representative Malcolm Patterson, the Memphis member of Congress, as one of the defense lawyers.

The gambling house on DeSoto was one of a syndicate operated by Mike Haggerty, whose lieutenant was George Honan, and whose friend was George "Bud" Degg. This game was run by Harry Hartley, whose helper was Harry Keene.

It was the game in which "Peco" was the cry of the winner who had five grains of corn in a line by a process far too complicated for understanding by outsiders, but thoroughly appreciated by Negroes of that time, both men and women. It was on the ground floor, in plain view whenever either the front or side door was opened. On the wall was a homey motto saying "The Lord loveth a cheerful player."

Raiders came from neither the police station nor the sheriff's office. They were organized by Squire Frank W. Davis in his justice of the peace office. At that time some magistrates rented space in downtown buildings. They and their deputies were dependent for their living on fees collected from losers in small debt cases or violators of minor criminal laws. Some deputies made a specialty of gaming raids, in which they tied all the players on a long rope and led them through the streets to the J. P. court to pay the fine, make bond, or be taken on to jail. If the raid on the peco game had been completed, there would have been about a thousand dollars in fees.

Nevertheless, on the fatal Monday night of 11 July officers were enforcing the law, with pistols and a warrant. The "DeSoto Street Riot" began when a deputy jumped up on a gaming table and read the warrant to Hartley and Keene. They had blocked the doors. The operators submitted to the warrant and a deputy began tying up the peco players.

Hartley was allowed to go to a telephone to call a bondsman. His call instead brought Haggerty, Honan, and Degg. There were angry words from a deputy who thought Haggerty had caused him to lose his badge. Shots were fired. The light went out. Everyone departed suddenly through windows and doors. The police riot squad found only a dark and deserted building. Houston Mitchell, a Negro deputy, had been killed.

Haggerty and Honan, the gambling house operators, walked up Union Avenue with Deputy J. J. Lawless, a raider, and gave him back his pistol. It was sometime later before they learned another deputy, Tom McDermott, had been shot. He lived a few hours, just long enough for a deathbed statement that Honan had shot him. Honan admitted it, saying he fired in defending himself.

Honan was immediately the center of attention. He looked like the Hollywood idea of a villain, with a big brown mustache, "steel blue eyes" and slicked-down black hair. All five were arrested during the night on murder warrants: Honan, Haggerty, Degg, Hartley, and Keene. They had been indicted and arraigned even before the public expressed itself Thursday night in the mass meeting that overflowed the theater.

They went on trial 21 July, just ten days after the killings. Judge John T. Moss presided in the old courthouse, at Main and Poplar. The state's strategy was to prosecute Honan, letting the fate of the others depend on that verdict.

In the early stages of the trial Carmack held the center of the stage. He was a former editor of *The Commercial Appeal,* and had won election to the House and then the Senate in support of silver coinage.

When the defense took over Patterson held the attention. He was a suave and polished lawyer who had been county prosecutor and had followed his father, Josiah, to Congress. Patterson did a thorough job of stripping majesty from the law of the raiders. He showed the peco game had been running openly without any kind of a raid until 9 July, the Saturday night before the "riot." That night Squire Davis issued five raid warrants, one of them for the DeSoto Street game.

The week before Squire Davis had gone with the raiders. Instead of the players being led to the squire's court on a rope, the squire accepted bonds from the fifty-four persons arrested right there. Gambling equipment seized by the raiders was given back to Haggerty, who signed a receipt. The game was going again as the squire went out the door. Honan had said to the squire, according to Honan's testimony at the murder trial, "Pull your men off. I am interested."

The riot raiders on Saturday included Deputy Sheriff C. W. Shoults. He had just lost a race for constable, with the backing of Squire Davis, to a candidate they thought was backed by Haggerty. On Monday the sheriff called Shoults on the carpet and reprimanded him for the mischief-making kind of raid. Another riot raider was Lawless, a twenty-two-year-old deputy. The sheriff took away his badge and commission Monday.

Monday night Squire Davis was visited at his office by Mike Shanley. He operated games in another syndicate, headed by Jim Kinnane, in competition with the Haggerty games. Shanley thought he was being treated unfairly. "The lid" had been put on and had closed the Shanley games but some others were still running. The Shanley theory was that the lid that closed one should close all.

Squire Davis agreed. He issued warrants for three houses that had been raided Saturday. Two were empty. The third was for the peco game. That warrant was issued on a complaint by John Smith, a Negro porter in the squire's office, who could neither read nor write. If he touched the pen while someone was helping write his name the complaint was legal, but testimony raised a question as to whether he touched it.

On Monday night Lawless was a raider. The sheriff had taken away his badge a few hours earlier, but Squire Davis made him a deputy again. Shoults, fresh from the sheriff's carpet for raiding the same game, was a raider. McDermott was only twenty-one and a new deputy who had just married the squire's daughter.

Mitchell, the Negro deputy, was deputized by the squire just before the raid. He had previously been deputized from time to time, long enough to serve papers from the squire's court on black defendants. He had gotten his pistol out of the hock shop that afternoon, and had also armed himself with a blackjack, and fortified his nerve with liquor.

Patterson closed his defense of Honan by saying to the jury, "As between the deputy sheriff who goes around under the mask of the law, preying upon the helpless poor, and the gambler, the choice is a matter of taste. For my part, I had rather be a gambler and take my chances with the law than to wear the mask of the law and plunder the poor."

Honan's fate was put into the hands of twelve "good men and true" on the afternoon of 26 August. On 1 September they were dismissed, the jury hung by three men who took the Honan side.

The outcome shocked the town—at first. But curiosity replaced shock when numerous jury stories began to circulate. One of the jurymen had two sons languishing in jail on murder charges while he was pondering whether Honan had committed murder. Another member of the jury was a friend of Shanley, the unhappy gambler who had obtained the raid.

Another celebrated his release from jury confinement by getting roaring drunk and going right back into confinement that night in jail. This added to interest in the story of a jury member who had a doctor's prescription requiring him to drink three times a day. Arrangements for delivering his medicine to the jury quarters opened the way for a steady flow of bottles to lubricate deliberations.

For entertainment the jurors could read about themselves and the evidence they had heard, according to one report of daily newspapers littering their rooms. About that time the public became weary of yards of stories about Honan and the center of attention shifted to Haggerty. On 3 September, just two days after the hung jury, a habeas corpus petition for release of Haggerty was filed before Judge J. P. Young in Circuit Court.

Judge Young ruled that Haggerty must stay in jail since "proof was conclusive that he was an accessory." But his lawyers went before Judge Jacob Galloway, another Circuit Court judge, with the same plea 9 September. Four days later Judge Galloway turned Haggerty loose under $24,500 bond.

An appeal was rushed to Nashville and on 15 October the Supreme Court overruled Judge Galloway and upheld Judge Young. But the Haggerty lawyers were back before Judge Galloway on 19 October with a new habeas corpus plea. They said they had found two Negro women peco players who said Haggerty and his associates had nothing to do with the shooting. Judge Galloway opened the jail doors for all five.

Next day Judge Moss, who had presided at the murder trial, ordered the immediate arrest of Haggerty. When the sheriff was sent after him, Haggerty was gone.

On 2 November a defense lawyer took two doctors and Deputy Sheriff Ernest Miller to Shannon, Mississippi, to open the Mitchell grave. Contrary to uncontested evidence at the trial that the black deputy had been shot four times, it was found that only one bullet had hit him. On the train back to Memphis the deputy ran into—actually bumped into—Haggerty in a corridor.

The gambler was wearing a fine cutaway and freshly pressed trousers, and carrying a silk-lined overcoat. The deputy and the gambler knew each other and settled down on the cushions for a talk. Part way into town the officer remembered to tell Haggerty he was under arrest. That was a bit awkward, for Haggerty was going back to surrender the next morning, but he hoped to spend the night with his wife and children. Because of the accidental meeting he had to be taken from the depot to the jail house.

A week later the tired old habeas corpus act was staged again before Judge Galloway and Haggerty returned to his normal life, which included operation of gambling houses for several years after. In early December a futile attempt was made to get another jury for a second trial. It came time for Patterson to report for a session of Congress and he withdrew from the case.

In January another defense lawyer, Ralph Davis (unrelated to the squire) demanded a second trial. Week after week the defense requested another trial, but the Honan-Haggerty case remained on the shelf.

The delays were brought to a jolting end. All five men indicted for the killings surrendered and were jailed. The defense then went before Judge Galloway with one more habeas corpus petition. This one said they were being denied their constitutional right to a speedy trial. All were released. The case was closed. It was less than a year after the double deaths.

Separate and Unequal

The memories of many Memphians include the years when blacks were forbidden to use public parks. Whether city taxes were to be used to build a special park for blacks only was debated issue in public affairs in the era of 1911–1913.

The wave of U.S. Supreme Court rulings against segregation was extended to parks in a lawsuit from Memphis decided as recently as 1963. But young people now would have a hard time shifting mental gears to a time of all-white public parks, when citizens with brown skins were frequent users of Church Park and its auditorium, a private investment by the original Bob Church.

For those too young to remember, an introduction to the old atmosphere may be found in an article in a special edition of *The Commercial Appeal*, 28 November 1915. An article headlined "Recent Progress of Negro Race Has Been Notable" begins:

Church Park Auditorium, 1906 (from *The Robert R. Churches of Memphis* by Roberta Church).

> The status of the negro in Memphis, and not only in Memphis but throughout the entire territory which is tributary to Memphis, is one which is the cause of abiding satisfaction to all friends of the colored race. There are exceptions, numerous and notable enough, but generally speaking there has been a wonderful improvemert in the condition of this people, mentally and materially, during the past decade.
>
> This improvement is witnessed in the number and character of the farms owned and operated by negroes; in the growing agregate of their bank deposits; in their invasion of the ranks of skilled labor; in the number and importance of the schools and colleges maintained by them and for their benefit; in their disposition, slowly gathering momentum, to think and act for themselves, to believe in themselves and in each other.

The writer gave a large part of the credit to Booker T. Washington and his followers. Some of the local credit was given to Le Moyne Institute, which then had a faculty of 22 and 600 students.

Other credit was assigned to Howe Institute, with 500 students, which had academic courses but emphasized an alternative industrial course of manual training and domestic science. It said, "This school makes a specialty, for one thing, of furnishing trained houseboys for the people of Memphis—sending into this service as many as 100 each year." The University of West Tennessee Medical School was said to have 100 students. Public schools were using about 100 black teachers for about 6,000 children.

Adjoining this summary of black progress is an advertisement for the Fraternal Savings Bank & Trust Company, 358 Beale, offering three percent for savings and mentioning Christmas savings clubs. One line said, "Payments one cent, two cents and five cents per week."

This was published in the year blacks had attained—in a manner of speaking—the dignity of a separate park. Ed Crump had been in the mayor's chair only a few weeks in early 1910 when he called attention to the lack of recreational facilities for blacks, and suggested the Park Commission should build a park for them. This was one political issue on which *The Commercial Appeal* and Crump took the same side.

In 1911 there was a response, of a kind, from Robert Galloway, chairman of the park board. The three-man commission was largely independent of other local government. It had its own tax rate and some income from fees and its spending of operating funds was without supervision. The chairman was also an independent personality. He was wealthy and had put a large amount of time and energy into the new park system since becoming one of the original commissioners in 1900. He also had made large contributions, most notably the full expense of obtaining and shipping the temple stones from Memphis on the Nile to Memphis on the Mississippi.

The Galloway response to Crump was a suggestion that Presidents Island be converted into a park for blacks. The island was a true island then, surrounded on all sides by water, and nothing was said about a bridge or ferry. But the annual spring floods were mentioned. Galloway said the overflow would enrich the land and increase the growth of trees and bushes and he said the black "ought to be in his glory among all that tropical growth."

Several months later, with the chairman cruising on his yacht in the Caribbean, a park commissioner proposed buying fifty acres somewhere east of the city for a park. Crump supported this plan. When Galloway got back to town he wrote to the mayor and said he was ready to appear before the City Commission in opposition. But the City Commission took the Galloway side temporarily and storm clouds blew up in Park Commission sessions, with Commissioner Abe Goodman taking the Crump side against the chairman.

In February of 1913 the conflict flared on another front, which had nothing to do with blacks. Galloway wanted the city to buy Jackson Mound, a privately owned entertainment center on the bluff edge. The City Commission refused and Galloway reacted with a letter challenging Crump to a debate, with Galloway offering to pay for the hall and the band and then "eat him up."

A few weeks later the City Commission followed the Crump plan by buying fifty-three acres for $600 and establishing Douglass Park, a short block north of Chelsea west of Holmes. (It was outside the city line until 1929.)

In 1913 the Park Commission pushed the creaking gates open a little wider by allowing blacks to visit the free zoo during limited morning hours. In the spring of 1914 the gates opened an inch or so more when blacks were allowed to use Overton Park on Tuesdays. It was a brief experiment. On 17 June a vigorous protest was made at the Park Commission meeting by a delegation from the Evergreen Club. This was an early civic club with a clubhouse at Evergreen and Overton Park, surrounded by the homes of some leading citizens. June Rudisill, an outstanding businessman, was one of several men who spoke.

It was alleged that black Memphis was pouring into Overton Park in hordes while the suburban acreage of Douglass Park was still being converted for park purposes. Blacks showed up in the early morning and stayed until long after midnight. They overloaded streetcars on Tuesdays to the distress of patrons who had to get to and from work every day. They were accused of being disorderly, loud, and having disgraceful restroom conduct. They were using the wading pool and those who had automobiles were beginning to drive through the park any time they pleased, it was claimed.

These heated words poured in a flood on the shoulders of Colonel Galloway, who, in this case, took the black side. He said he had spent a large part of his Tuesdays in the park to see for himself what was happening. He disputed the Evergreen words repeatedly. The shouting culminated in a direct confrontation in which Rudisill claimed to have seen blacks in the wading pool and to show them to Galloway, while Galloway replied that he had watched the pool, had never seen a black in it, and would show Rudisill. But in spite of Galloway's support it was announced on 23 June 1913 that the following day would be the last black Tuesday for Overton Park.

About the same time the City Commission bought Jackson Mound and renamed it DeSoto Park. But Galloway felt his years of public service in founding the park system were being spurned and he resigned.

This background of blacks being kept out of city parks, while whites argued about favors for blacks, underlies the high importance of Church's Park and Auditorium. Memphis had neither Overton Park nor even a Park Commission when the senior Robert R. Church bought 300 feet of frontage on the south side of Beale, near Fourth, in 1899.

There he created a park with six acres of flowers and walks, the biggest floral display being a rounded bed with a banana tree in the center, circled by rows of red cannas, and bordered with white periwinkles. Peacocks roamed. There was a picnic ground, a playground and a bandstand. Most of all there was the auditorium with about 2,000 seats. It was said to be the largest theater in the United States owned by a black. Under the big stage was a banquet hall and there was a bar and a soda fountain. Park and building represented a $100,000 investment.

When it was new it was operated as a theater, advertising vaudeville nightly, with a new bill weekly. Admission was fifteen cents. Sometimes there was dancing, stopped exactly at midnight Saturday to observe the Sabbath, and Handy's Band was heard at intervals. President Theodore Roosevelt spoke there. So did Booker T. Washington. Some names that became big in music or the theater were seen. Conventions were held there and commencement exercises, and rallies that launched some of the early moves toward civil rights.

The city bought the park and, in 1941, took off the Church name, substituting "Beale Avenue Park." Years of protests from blacks were successful in restoring the Church name in 1956. Then came purchase by the Memphis Housing Authority—and then the big bulldozers. It was announced the park would be reshaped and sold back to the Park Commission, for building a replacement community center.

A large bronze placque was paid for by the city's Sesquicentennial Commission, an imposing work of art with high relief busts of both Robert Church and Robert Church, Jr. and a capsuled account of their careers. For lack of a building to mount it on, it sat in storage for several years before being added to the Mississippi Valley Collection in the library at Memphis State.

There was an abrupt end to remaining independence in management of the parks in 1948 when City Hall took over and required the Park Commission to submit a budget for the year's spending. The policy on blacks in the parks changed much more slowly. In 1952 the petition approach was used by thirty-one black organizations. Blacks were still barred entirely from the fairgrounds amusement park, the art gallery, and the Pink Palace, although they were admitted to the zoo on Thursdays.

Then there came a time when the art gallery was open to blacks only one day a week, late in the 1950s. It was a change overlooked by a large part of the public with the result of a most remarkable incident. Two estimable ladies at Greenville, Mississippi, set out for an all-day trip to see a special exhibit at the gallery. Their driver left them at the door and went on to the parking lot. The art lovers were turned back at the door. They had never heard of "Negro Day." But they rose to the occasion with magnificent aplomb. They walked to the car, made themselves comfortable, and sent the driver in to enjoy the art.

The National Association for the Advancement of Colored People called in the power of federal courts in a suit filed in 1960. Jesse Turner was a president of the Memphis chapter and A. W. Willis was attorney.

Late in 1960 there was a quite removal of the one-day signs on the art gallery and zoo. On 15 June 1961 Judge Marion S. Boyd ruled for a ten-year desegregation plan. The NAACP appealed. The Park Commission opened the fairgrounds and five of the seven golf courses and made a ten-year schedule for other changes. But the Supreme Court ruled on 27 May 1963, ordering immediate and complete ending of racial barriers. And that was the end of it, although the city kept all swimming pools closed that summer and the next.

Courts of Injustice

Until 1936 the courts of Shelby County included some privately owned establishments where fees collected from losers were the income of the magistrates and his deputies. It was a system that bore down hard on the poor and the stranger. Raided crap games after pay day, or a little friendly rolling of the dice in the alley any night, were big producers of fees. So were those who had almost paid out the installments on a set of bedroom furniture or only owned another payment on the Easter suit. Letting the rent wait to pay something on an old doctor bill could bring a deputy to the door with an eviction writ and fees.

Thousands of persons with painful memories of that "justice" are still here, and yet the reform that closed the fee courts has been all but entirely forgotten. Perhaps it is hard for those who have never seen it to believe what went on. Or perhaps memory slippage has been helped by poor recordkeeping in the magistrate's courts.

The change was so drastic and so abrupt it should have been remembered. It came on the afternoon of 22 July 1936. A few magistrates who kept their noses clean and a few who were comparatively clean were summoned to the courthouse. There they found themselves face to face with E. H. Crump, unofficial manager of city and county business, and his chief lieutenants, Mayor Watkins Overton, County Commission Chairman E. W. Hale, Attorney General Tyler McLain, and Frank

Rice, back tax collector who looked after election details and Nashville contacts. With them was Guy Joyner, who was about to become sheriff.

The chosen magistrates were told how they were about to reform. More than that, it was written out for them. There was a pledge list of nineteen items in which they promised to end abuse of the law on garnishment of wages, wholesale arrest of gamblers, use of their courts for loan shark collectors, arrangements with professional bondsmen, and so on in very specific detail.

There was a pledge for each of them to sign as a public document. With it was a set of qualification papers, prepared by the Crump organization, for elections about to be held. It was a time when candidates for public office without the organization support might as well stay home. Those who signed the pledge were in. Other magistrates, and the deputies and constables attached to them, were high and dry on the beach.

There had been fourteen justice of the peace courts in 1929. In 1933 there had been thirteen. Beginning 1 September 1936 there would be only five. Those chosen were: Will Bacon, whose office was in the basement at 156 Madison; C. L. Clancy, upstairs at the northeast corner of Madison and Front; George B. Coleman, upstairs at 68 Madison; E. E. Jeter at 91 North Second; and Alma Law at 55 South Third. There were to be two other squires, without courts; John Dudney, who was paid a salary as county court chairman, and Joe Boyle, whose salary was as courthouse custodian.

The theory was that there would be enough legitimate fees to support them when the competition was stopped. The legal method was a reduction of Shelby County's civil districts to two. There had been eight until the legislative session in 1934.

The theory of justice of the peace courts was based on frontier conditions of few roads and winter rains that made them impassable. It was necessary to have a magistrate nearer than the county seat—a day away if the roads were open—to rule on minor cases. The loser could appeal and get a hearing in a higher court at the courthouse. But many a small dispute or crime could be disposed of without the journey to town.

On the same theory, each incorporated town had a magistrate, a feature of the law which gave the small towns and rural areas control of the county court years after more than half of Shelby County's people lived in Memphis. When the magistrates met as the county court (the local legislative body), the wishes of the majority of the people—who lived in Memphis—were overwhelmed by magistrates representing the rural minority. This was so even though most of the county's taxes were collected in Memphis.

It was a local habit to think of the county government as managing local government outside of Memphis, without realizing that the county was collecting taxes on Memphis homes and stores and diverting much of the money to schools and roads outside of Memphis. Creation of another civil district with another squire was a popular thing to do. There came a time, about 1905, when Memphis had fifty-two magistrates.

Memphis men, the few who knew about it, were more amused than outraged when the squires gathered at Gaston's Hotel the night before a county court meeting to make the trades that would show up next morning as county court actions. A squire who wanted a new school had to support another squire's bridge. And if one squire got a bridge another squire demanded the same. An old courthouse story tells of a squire who got his bridge, only to find that it stood in solitude without a road at either end.

This management sometimes produced good results, as in the building of the courthouse. Roads and schools were considered better than in adjoining counties. Some worthy men became squires and were a steadying influence.

Nevertheless it was the county court actions that got first attention when E. H. Crump took over city government as mayor in 1910. His city method was the commission form of government, so he established a County Commission of three members in 1912. It stripped from the county court a large part of its traditional strength. There came a time when decisions were made by the county commission and only approved by the county court. Sometimes the squires went to the office of Will Hale, commission chairman, and were handed slips of paper telling each one what he was to do and how he was to say it in the court meeting opening a few minutes later. There was rigid control of what they did about taxes, especially. A low tax rate, and hope of lowering the tax rate, were of prime importance.

As individuals, operating magistrate's courts, the squires had loose restraints. There were too many of them. They had to rent downtown space and pay for it out of their fees. Their only income from the county was fifteen dollars a day for attending county court sessions, of which there were twelve a year, three days at the opening of each quarter.

It took a lot of fees to pay the expenses and have living expenses left over. If a squire had a deputy who brought in overdue accounts for a clothing store the fees might be steady. For instance, the court costs on a debt collection case often were $10.75. A deputy who handled evictions for a landlord with dozens of rental places brought in good business.

When a dice game was raided the bill for each player usually was $9.30, which was $4 for the arresting officer, $3.30 for the magistrate, and the $2 fine for the state. Taken before the magistrate at night, from the game to court, they could plead guilty, pay, and leave. Or they could post bond, by paying another fee, for returning to court later. Or they could be carried from court to jail. Unless they raised the money for the fine and costs the final scene was at the Penal Farm where these fees and others accumulated along the way were worked out at one dollar a day.

As might be expected, when the raiders and their prisoners got to the justice of the peace office, there was a rush for telephones in the hope that rescue money could be raised from wives, brothers, foremen or bosses.

The crop of fees was so good that it was standard equipment for the raiders to carry a rope, to which the prisoners were tied for a long walk through the city streets to the so-called court of justice. At least one gang of raiders added the refinement of a long chain, with handcuffs, and a truck for a quicker trip to court.

It was these raids that gave the magistrate's courts an especially ripe odor, particularly when the victims began to talk about "decoys," black men hired by a magistrate's deputy to get a game started for the sole purpose of raiding it. There was one magistrate who spent most of his time in police station corridors waiting for the arrest of persons who could afford to pay for release on bond. The bonds already signed by property owners were in the squire's pocket, complete except for the name of the accused.

It must be remembered that we had some squires who never opened a court, serving only on days the County Court was in session. It also is true that some courts earned a living on collecting accounts, without using the gambling game raid device.

Still the whole method of justice, in which the squire had a fee if he ruled one way and none if his ruling went the other way, came into disrepute. In common speech "justice of the peace" was reduced to "J. P." and that was translated into "judgment for the plaintiff."

At intervals newspaper reporters were assigned to spend Saturday nights in magistrate's court where hanky panky was suspected and long stories were written about the unjust ''justice.'' The pressure of public opinion built up when hard times came down during the depression years.

The essential fault was that magistrates were ruling on cases in which they had a financial interest in the outcome. But justice of the peace courts were deeply imbedded in Tennessee law and were older than the state. In rural counties and in the rural dominated legislature, reform seemed beyond reach.

The Crump organization in 1936 simply used its raw strength to force reform for Shelby County. It was a landmark in betterment of the part of the court system most often seen by men and women whose income was small and irregular. But it has had very little attention since, either in writing or in conversation, so little that it seems almost everyone has forgotten had bad it used to be.

One of the reasons for neglect is that a short time later the Crump efforts were turned toward a statewide law. The obvious cure was judges with steady salaries, regardless of how they ruled, and salaried deputies, regardless of how many cases they handled.

Unable to break resistance of rural squires, Crump settled for a private Shelby County Act establishing the Court of General Sessions. Similar courts in Nashville and Knoxville had demonstrated benefits.

General Sessions judges took up the small claims and petty crime cases on 1 September 1942. That is a date more likely to be remembered because of the beginning of uniform court records. Originally there were four judges. The only magistrate who became a judge was Will Bacon, and it was publicly announced that the others would be expected to follow his lead. He was a former sheriff, a former Memphis Juvenile Court judge, a lawyer, an Army colonel, and a one-time Arkansas newspaperman and his standing in the community was high, in part because of the cleanness of his magistrate's court before the 1936 shakeup. Sam Campbell, former assistant prosecutor, was another of the first judges. Robert A. Tillman, former public defender, became a General Sessions judge. Robert I. Moore was one of the original judges.

In 1945 the fourth division of the court, where Judge Tillman presided, was abolished and three judges carried the load. The fourth division was restored in 1955. The rising population seems to include the normal number of persons who spend faster than they earn, or think a bigger loan is the cure for being unable to pay off smaller borrowings. And for those who are old enough to remember this is one more reason for refusing to join in moaning for what some persons call ''the good old days.''

3
Blood, et cetera

Dangerous Days

The Civil War part of the story of Lamar Fontaine includes twenty-seven
pitched battles, fifty-seven heavy skirmishes and more than a hundred
individual skirmishes. He counted sixty-seven wounds. He told of being
captured five times, with each incident accompanied by a daring escape.
But the Civil War came only after he had sailed the Arctic, visited the
Great Wall of China, taken part in Perry's expedition to open Japan,
seen the Taj Mahal, made a caravan journey across the Sahara and
toured South America, as well as won a medal from the Russians as a
marksman in the Crimean War.

He was especially proud of his ability as a poet. He earned his living
as a civil engineer, surveying for the first railroad through the
Mississippi Delta, and maintaining an office for many years at Lyon,
near Clarksdale.

Without waiting to grow up, he had enough unusual experiences as a
boy to make a book. He was born in a tent on 10 October 1829 when
Texas was wild. In that unlikely location he was taught Latin, Greek and
Hebrew for about seven years beginning when he was three. His instruc-
tor was a German baron, graduate of Heidelberg and exiled Polish
general who was also his nurse when he was small, his teacher of
boxing, fencing, riding and especially of markmanship, while entertain-

Lamar Fontaine (from *My Life and My Lectures* by Lamar Fontaine).

ing him with stories from world history. He wrote later that at ten he had almost as much learning as some college students, including mathematics.

But when his tutor died and he was sent to a school with other children, he was soon whipped by the teacher and ran away. On his way to Mexico he was captured by Comanches who held him slightly more than four years. He astounded the Indians by his ability to kill deer and turkey with a rifle while riding horseback, and he killed a grizzly with a single shot. His clothes wore out and he went naked, summer and winter, until his whole skin was as tough as his hands.

When he was barely fourteen the Comanche chief gave him permission to go home—if he walked. There were 750 miles as the crow flies between the Indian camp and Austin, Texas, and eighty of those miles were desert. He got through without seeing another human being, and he wrote years later that Austin held the last white men before the Pacific Coast.

His story of life among the Indians was hard to believe, and his tale of that long trip home by himself was just too much. He was young and he was small. When he had grown some more he got up to fifty-eight pounds at age sixteen. Only his mother believed him. Others thought he was a scout preparing the way for an Indian raiding party.

His father got him out of the unfriendly town and back in school by driving a team, with spare horses, more than a month all the way to North Carolina. Another student falsely accused him of something for which a teacher whipped him severely. Fontaine took care of the teacher in a stickball game, corrected the student who had caused his trouble, and departed. When his father got back to Austin, the boy had beaten him back by two days.

So the father took Fontaine to see his relative, Matthew Fontaine Maury, pioneer in oceanography, who was a Navy lietutenant. He was aboard a ship at Pensacola, Florida, and young Fontaine found himself tricked into going to sea, while his father remained ashore. He had six years of instruction from an expert in navigation and in the higher branches of mathematics.

Fontaine enjoyed the sea and the travel. He became a Buddhist priest. He became a Russian soldier. He was a civil engineer in the jungles of Honduras when he heard Lincoln had been elected. After First Manassas he had the experience of stopping a burial party about to lower him into a grave just dug beside him, learning that his father had a casket on the way from Richmond, and reading a flattering obituary about himself.

Fontaine told the story of a friendship with another soldier so close that, beyond eating and sleeping together, they each carried pocket books of poetry and read to each other, Fontaine from Byron and his friend from Burns.

One of his most extraordinary anecdotes tells about a kind of local peace between Confederates and Yankees on opposite sides of the narrow Potomac. A Yankee picket called across to ask about exchanging newspapers. A man from each side waded to midstream, traded papers, stood in the water to talk over recent fighting and wound up with the Yank taking the Rebel to the other side for dinner. Before dinner a written agreement to stop pickets firing at each other was signed in duplicate. The Yankee tobacco was so bad, a Blue Coat was taken across the river into the Confederate camp to get some good chewing plugs and pipe twists. Then the Northerners swam in their half of the river, while the Southerners laid their rifles on the bank to read papers from the North. That night when it turned cool, the Rebel pickets built a fire in the open, relying on the cease-fire agreement. A Yankee picket used the fire light to take perfect aim at the head of Fontaine's friend.

Fontaine wrote about that killing as the beginning of his resolve to never trust a Yank.

He got a "Dear John" that made him so bitter he wrote the girl a long set of verses, including a line about sullied orange blossoms in her bridal wreath. He then exposed himself on a battlefield and called attention to himself by holding up a battle flag. Bullets shortened the staff and pierced the flag but rejected his death wish.

He was a scout for Stonewall Jackson, and stories of his marksmanship include the time he was on a hill above the Rapidan River, opposite a federal artillery battery on the other bank, more than five hundred yards away. With Stonewall Jackson watching, he pointed out a man in blue, felled him with one shot, picked out another and felled him, until twenty men were down. Then Robert E. Lee came up, and Fontaine knocked down forty more. That was sixty men without a miss in less than an hour before his ammunition ran out.

One of his assignments for General Joseph Johnston was to map fortifications built by the Yankees in Memphis. He made himself up as a Union refugee from Austin with a tight wig of white hair and a daily rinse of his entire skin with iodide of iron which produced wrinkles. At the bridge across Nonconnah Creek he bought a cart and an old mule, hired an aged Negro, and came to Memphis to sell a load of wood. His Negro helper made daily trips with wood while Fontaine measured the battlements.

He considered that his wartime exploits came to a climax of danger—and of accomplishment—when General Johnston sent him through the thousands of troops beseiging Vicksburg with dispatches and 18,000 musket percussion caps. He got through cliff-hanging perils. Then he got out through more perils, with dispatches and with messages to Confederate relatives. All the time he had three unhealed wounds and his right arm was partially paralyzed. His wounds were numerous and severe but the only one that left a permanent handicap was a bullet in the right ankle late in the war. He limped for the rest of his life.

The full name of this man of adventure around the world was Jacques Mirabeau Bonaparte Lamar Fontaine. He was a member of the family of Patrick Henry, of the Maurys of Maury County, Tennessee, and of Patrick Henry Fontaine, surveyor general of all land south of Tennessee with headquarters at Pontotoc, Mississippi, as well as other persons of prominence.

When he entered the Confederate service he was thirty-three and had grown to a quarter-inch more than six feet, but he was still thin at 160 pounds, a slender frame for such physical feats and medical recoveries as he described.

The war had been over more than a year when he, at thirty-seven, married Lemuella S. Brickell. They had four sons and four daughters. He made an irregular living as a ginner, school teacher, and draughts-man, until moving to Mississippi, where he was county surveyor at Yazoo City and then a railroad surveyor. The line he surveyed became the Yazoo & Mississippi Valley, now the Illinois Central Gulf. He said "My feet have trod upon every square mile from Horn Lake on the north to the mouth of the Yazoo River above Vicksburg, on the south."

He might have done well as a writer, for his narrative style moves fast and his descriptions are bright with detail. His belief in his own abilities was boundless. As a military expert he felt qualified to exalt Stonewall Jackson to the ultimate heights. He wrote, "When the military student comes to survey the genius and generalship of Stonewall Jackson he will have to lift his eyes to a towering height, far above the plane of ordinary humanity, and it will be a snow-shrouded and cloud-dimmed peak that will greet him. Centuries will roll away before his equal will again tread the fields of martial glory." He wrote of his own poetry: "It is a monument of word painting that will endure as long as the civilized white man exists on Earth."

Such extravagant words and such an elaborate set of adventures as an Indian captive, a sailor, a soldier, a jungle surveyor, and a traveler from Greenland to the Sahara stretch the credibility of readers. And yet the outline at some length was published in the enlarged edition of *Old Guard in Gray* in 1899, more than thirty years after the events de-scribed. This was followed by extensive detail in a book *My Life and My Lectures* by Lamar Fontaine, C. E., Ph.D., in 1908. A full summary of his career was published in *Who's Who in America,* and is still included in *Who Was Who,* although there is nothing in the item to indicate what schools conferred upon him the engineering and philosophy degrees. A grandson, however, remembers a framed Ph.D. from the University of Florida in the Fontaine home.

When he died on 1 October 1921, *The Commercial Appeal* used his picture and the story at the top of two columns on page 1. He had attained the age of ninety-two. He had lived more than fifty years beyond his adventures. He had told his extraordinary stories at least three times in print. But still the only hint of a question was the word "claimed" in one line of his newspaper obituary. It said, "He claimed to have taken part in the following battles among many others: Bull Run,

Stonewall Jackson's campaigns, Second Manassas, Sharpsburg, Chickamauga, Missionary Ridge and Spottsylvania Courthouse.''

It is to be expected that one or more modern Mississippi historians would either call attention to Lamar Fontaine's spectacular life or expose holes in his stories. But we have examined the entire file of the *Journal of Mississippi History*, which begins in 1939, without finding a title that either lauds Fontaine or discredits him. Fontaine gets brief notices in the two-volume *History of Mississippi* edited by Richard Aubrey McLemore, especially as a poet.

It is unlikely that his book will become a part of the recent flow of photographic reprints. For the story includes several incidents that would repel present-day readers. The six lectures that conclude the book take up such subjects as racial superiority, and a theory that civilization originated in the mountains of South America. One of his lecture subjects is ''Where Did Cain Get His Wife?'' Lamar Fontaine had an extraordinary life and what he wrote holds high interest but some of his ideas have been only curiosities for many years.

Seven-Week Battle

Everyone who knows anything about the Civil War knows about Shiloh, the two days of massive killings on the bank of the Tennessee River about a hundred miles east of Memphis. In the rainy, muddy April of 1862, more men went to battle than ever before fought on North American turf. Only the struggle at Gettysburg is a rival for the attention Shiloh has had from men, boys, soldiers, students, scholars, and casual readers of books and magazines.

A great many persons learn in their early contact with the Shiloh story that the reason so much strength on both sides was put into the contest was that two railroads crossed at Corinth, Mississippi. They were the Memphis & Charleston, the only rail line across the South, and the Mobile & Ohio, the longest north-south line in the South.

The South, determined to hold its supply lines, massed every unit within reach at Corinth. The North, fresh from conquests near the Tennessee-Kentucky line, aimed a juggernaut at the Corinth junction. So the South moved out in front of the town to meet the threat before the attackers were ready.

Yankees were pushed back through the fields and trees on 6 April but, with a fresh army, regained the ground on 7 April. Confederates splashed along puddled roads in rain and fell back to Corinth.

The next scene in popular history shows squads of soldiers in blue guarding the railroad tracks they have won. But that is a shortening of the narrative. The South had been turned back at Shiloh on 7 April, but it was more than seven weeks before the North got into Corinth, on 30 May. It was only twenty miles. Almost as obscure in common knowledge is the fact that the South returned to Corinth with such strength as to break through the North's defenses into the heart of town six months after Shiloh, on 3 and 4 October.

Modern residents of Corinth have undertaken to make better known the defense of the town through the weeks after Shiloh and especially the October renewal of the April contest for possession of the rails.

Corinth was created by the railroad crossing. Railroad builders moving eastward out of Memphis and north from Mobile met there in 1854. Just east of the junction a scraggly settlement appeared and was called Cross City, until the residents looked to classical Greece for the more attractive name of Corinth.

The rails were less than ten years old when the Confederates gathered an army at Corinth and sent it to the Virginia battlefields. Another army was assembled at Corinth and sent into the Tennessee campaigns. For the third time the soldiers in gray were collected at Corinth, and it was this army that moved out to Shiloh to hold the armies in blue away from the rails.

There were about 40,000 men in the army that moved toward the river. Another 40,000 attackers were camped at the river just twenty-two miles from Corinth. But the attackers had about 25,000 fresh troops for the second day of fighting. When the Shiloh guns were stilled, the losses were remarkably even: 1,754 Union men killed, to 1,723 Confederates. The Union wounded numbered 8,408, the Confederates 8,012. It was a battle so fierce that there were more casualties than in the Revolution, the War of 1812, and the War with Mexico combined.

Yet the winner was in doubt. The Union armies, all three of them, stayed on the battlefield without following the Confederates to Corinth, much less claiming the rail prizes they had come after. General Henry W. Halleck built his troop strength to 100,000, the largest army ever assembled in North America, before he began to move down the roads to Corinth. Each day they moved a short distance, then dug entrenchments for protection during the night.

Halleck was exercising extreme caution because he had heard that the Confederates had 146,000 men waiting for him, and that more were on the way to bring the defenders up to 200,000. More than a month after

Shiloh, the Federals were still beyond the range of Confederate guns at Corinth.

Actually, General Pierre Gustave Toutant Beauregard had fewer than 52,000 men on duty, only half as many as were moving slowly toward them. The official rolls were much longer, but battle wounds and contagious illness had converted Corinth into a citywide hospital. Churches, schools, and homes were all taken over. More troops died in Corinth during the Federal advance than had died on the battlefield.

The Rebel army dug trenches and massive earthwork defenses. Great success was attained in getting alarming stories of Corinth strength to the Federal high command by way of escaped prisoners. A triumph of deceit was accomplished as the Union army moved close to town. A locomotive was brought to a stop, band music floated over the hills, and mighty roars of welcome came from massed throats. The train pulled away quietly and a short time later roared into town again, with more band music and another crowd of cheering welcomers. Then the same engine, the brass band, and the same roar of welcome did it again.

In the Union trenches it sounded as though the Rebel trenches were being packed with thousands of freshly arrived troops. In the official war records there is a dispatch from a Union general saying, ''The enemy is reinforcing heavily by train, in my front and on my left. The cars are running constantly, and the cheering is immense every time they unload in front of me.''

While the Union attention was being held by the arrival of the fake troops, the actual movement was a withdrawal southward to Tupelo. Beauregard had gotten his whole command out of town. When Halleck finally attacked Corinth 30 May, the Confederates were gone. The Federals let them go and spread their huge strength in garrisons along the M&C tracks to protect the rails that had cost them so much.

The Confederates had conserved their strength, notably General Earl Van Dorn's army in North Mississippi. There was some consideration of winning back Memphis or Bolivar, but the tired survivors of the attempt to retake Corinth were able to hold the Federals off and move back to Ripley.

It was a costly part of the war. In addition to the much better known battle at Shiloh, and the almost overlooked weeks of assault from Shiloh to Corinth, three days fighting at Corinth used up 4,233 Confederates killed, wounded, captured and missing. For the Federals the total was 2,520.

For the sake of the Corinth railroad junction, the South had withdrawn troops from New Orleans, the South's largest city and the commanding position in river trade, and the city had fallen into Federal hands. For the protection of Corinth, an army that was headed for St. Louis was drawn back to Corinth, and Confederate control of Arkansas was lost. Such concentration of resources and such lengthy casualty lists were justified, following events showed. But they were in vain. The rails at Corinth had been lost, and strength of the South west of the mountains was on the decline.

Memorials to the dead, and preservation of trenches, forts, and battle sites have been strangely neglected at Corinth. Shiloh is only a few miles away, and it has been well-developed for tourists and historians, with some benefits to Corinth. But that ignores the time and effort between the fight at Shiloh and the Federal possession of Corinth's rails. Skirmishes elsewhere, with little influence on the tides of war, have handsome monuments, while both the advance on Corinth and the big battle in October have been ignored.

The modern industrial city has, principally, a national cemetery and a little park where the Federals built one of their string of defenses, Fort Robinett. It contains six graves, two markers and a cannon without wheels. One of the monuments helps preserve the name of the special Confederate hero of the battle for Corinth, Colonel William P. Rogers of the Second Texas Infantry. Against seemingly impossible odds, the Texans captured the fort before eleven bullets cut down Colonel Rogers. His daring leadership was so impressive that the opposing commander, General Rosecrans, ordered him buried exactly where he fell, with full honors.

Corinth is still a railroad junction, although the names of the lines have been changed to Southern Railway and Illinois Central Gulf. Now the city is undertaking to win distinction as an urban national battlefield park, with places where history was made easily available to visitors in the city's streets. The distinction is there. It is the recognition that is sought.

A Little Dandy

General Thomas Carmichael Hindman was a little dandy. He was only five feet two at the most, yet he commanded attention with patent leather boots, elaborately ruffled shirts, rose-colored kid gloves and a cane. His is an honored name in Tippah County (Ripley), Mississippi, because he grew up there. His boyhood home, which had two floors and an entrance

Thomas Carmichael Hindman (from *Generals in Gray* by
Ezra J. Warner).

ornamented by four pillars, was preserved and pointed out to visitors
until it burned in 1938. His name is even more honored in Phillips
County (Helena), Arkansas, where he was a lawyer, a member of the
lower house of Congress, and the top Confederate commander for the
whole area west of the Mississippi River. A cemetery monument calls
attention to his youthful career.

There is nothing to commemorate his old age—because he had none,
even though he lived through the war. While a West Point education was
common among generals on both sides, Hindman had none, but he did
have military experience. Nor did he attend a law school, reading in the
office of a legal firm instead.

His father, Tom Hindman Sr., was the first boy born in Knoxville,
Tennessee. The future general was born there too on 28 January 1828.
He attended school at Jacksonville, Alabama, where the family moved
in 1832 and at Ripley, the family home after 1841. He then journeyed to
Lawrenceville Classical Institute, in New Jersey near Princeton, and
was graduated with honors at eighteen.

The senior Hindman was a veteran of the Battle of New Orleans, and when war with Mexico came he went out in the uniform of a colonel and went to war in a Mississippi regiment, taking with him two sons.

One son was Robert Holt Hindman, whose life ended at twenty-seven, a few years after he came back from Mexico. The Tippah County Historical and Genealogical Society recently published an account of General Hindman, which says his brother's grave is marked by the words, "Killed at Ripley, Miss., by W. C. Falkner, May 8, 1849." This was one of the earlier episodes in the Falkner life that was ended by another killing on the streets of Ripley. The younger brother, just out of school, raised a company of neighbors and went to war as a lieutenant. He won captain's bars by gallantry in action.

Back from Mexico, Tom Hindman went into the Ripley law office of Orpando Davis for three years of study. He became a Ripley lawyer in 1851 and the same year was elected to the Mississippi legislature. He concluded that states had the right to secede as early as 1851. In 1857 he became conspicuous in the Democratic Party. He became a friend of Jefferson Davis. He was only twenty-three when he debated Senator Henry Foote, and at twenty-six accepted a debate challenge from James Lusk Alcorn, later governor and senator.

But Hindman turned from the Mississippi legal practice and politics to Helena. He had hardly opened his law office when another young lawyer saw the little fellow being mauled by a much bigger man. The other attorney, Patrick R. Cleburne, rushed into the street to even things up. Hindman's injuries were minor but Cleburne was seriously wounded. So Hindman carried Cleburne across the river to the Hindman home at Ripley, and stayed with him during weeks of recovery. They were friends for life and both became Confederate generals.

He also stood out among the men of Helena in 1856 when yellow fever struck. There was the usual fast exodus. There were only three doctors, and the fever got one of them. The other two issued a call for volunteer, unpaid nurses. In what had been a town of 1,500 only three stayed to nurse and help the ill: Tom Hindman, Pat Cleburne, and one Rice, a youthful Methodist preacher.

Hindman's Democratic party activities in Mississippi were renewed in Arkansas and he soon became prominent. In the voting of 1858 Hindman went to the House of Representatives on a huge majority. In 1860 he was reelected but when it came time to take the oath the following March the winds of Fort Sumter were blowing hard and he declined. Instead he went into the army of the South.

He was in command of "Hindman's Legion." After 28 September 1861 he had the rank of brigadier general. He was wounded while commanding a regiment at Shiloh and was recognized for gallantry in action there with promotion to major general on 18 April 1862. Hindman was given command of Arkansas, Missouri, Northern Louisiana and the Indian Territory but there was hardly any army to command. He had to raise his own army, which was difficult because men and boys who wanted to go to war had already gone. They were fighting on the other side of the river.

Hindman had, however, a conscription law and he used it, without much attention to the fine points of what could be done legally. The involuntary soldiers needed rifles, so Hindman set up factories to make some. The rifles needed ammunition so the general organized chemical works to make powder. He operated lead mines to get lead for bullets, and tanneries to make boots. He even organized women into sewing circles to make uniforms.

His accomplishment is one of the most remarkable feats of the war story, for he raised and equipped an army of 16,000. That brought on some complications. The upper command at Richmond had less interest in defending Arkansas than in holding Vicksburg and wanted the Hindman strength assigned for that purpose.

Hindman had, in addition to the difficulties with higher officers, an unhappy people in the countryside he was defending. He tried to slow the Federal advance from the northwest corner of the state, where the Battle of Pea Ridge was fought 6–8 March 1862. So he put bushwhackers to burning bridges, destroying food, putting the torch to cotton bales and contaminating wells, by killing a cow and throwing the carcass into the water.

That tactic took away things that could be used by the invading army but it was as rough on the people being defended as on the blue army. There was a real question as to whether it would be better to be conquered or to be defended by such methods. The people cursed Hindman as much as they did Major General Samuel Curtis, who moved his men across the state. Curtis made Helena, Hindman's home, his strong point. In fact, he moved into the comforts of Hindman's house.

Arkansas's residents complained so bitterly and so often that an order came out from Richmond on 12 August 1862, demoting him to a field command. The top post went to Major General Theophilus Hunter Holmes. Hindman was so offended that he resigned, rather than take orders from Holmes. But he soon returned to uniform. The situation west of the river was more than Holmes could handle and he was replaced for the final years of the war by Lieutenant General Edmund Kirby Smith.

Hindman made several plans for resuming the Confederate move across the Missouri line and threatening St. Louis. There were heavy additions to federal troops in Missouri, for one thing, and the high command at Richmond wanted Hindman's strength used for defense of Vicksburg. Eventually more invaders came south past the Pea Ridge battlefield and Hindman took his army into another confrontation in the northwest section of the state 7 December 1862. There was a day of fighting in the cold at Prairie Grove. It was a standoff, but during the night Hindman withdrew. His little handmade army dwindled.

Even so, his name might have been more familiar in history books, except for the unusual circumstances of a battle far from his command. The Confederates had built Fort Hindman at the old capital, Arkansas Post, near the mouths of both the Arkansas and the White rivers. They installed twelve big guns and assigned six field artillery pieces to the troops.

Fort Hindman was a strongpoint, where Confederate boats could be protected between dashing raids down the Arkansas and out into the Mississippi to capture Federal boats on their way from Memphis to Vicksburg with ammunition for the assault on Vicksburg. It was a thorn in the Union side.

So the federal forces organized an amphibious assault. They sent thirteen rams and gunboats, led by three ironclads. They followed up with 30,000 soldiers on 50 transports. The outcome was clear when defending troops numbered 5,000. But the expedition that started on 8 January 1863 was able to take over the fort only on 11 January. It was a considerable battle and the number of men was very large in comparison with other battles in Arkansas. Yet it was only a preliminary to the big event at Vicksburg and only historians know about Fort Hindman.

General Hindman went on to another career on the other side of the river. He was a division commander under General Braxton Bragg, and his performance was good at Chickamauga, the seige of Chattanooga, and the defense of Atlanta. In the Atlanta campaign he was wounded a second time on 27 June 1864 so severely that his war service was ended.

With the war over, he wrote his mother he had fought too hard for the Confederate States of America to "remain under the flag of her conquerors." He moved his wife and three children to Mexico City. The Mexican government was impressed by his military record and offered him a good place in the army. He turned down the offer and took up writing. His two books on military subjects produced an income for living expenses. He also was attorney for "The American Colony of Yucatan." The colony was planned as a refuge for Confederates fearful of postwar treatment. Legal preparations were complete when Mexican politics took an abrupt turn.

The French had undertaken a Mexican adventure while the United States was busy with the challenge of the Confederacy. When the North neared victory the French pulled the props out from under Emperor Maximilian, his government collapsed, and he was shot. The southerners went home.

So Hindman went back to Helena and leaped into Arkansas politics with a strident voice against the carpetbaggers who had taken charge in Little Rock. It was a time of loud voices and violent deeds. The row of carpetbagger mansions along a Little Rock ridge was commonly called "Robbers Row." The Ku Klux Klan and other whites fought a miniature war with the militia, almost all black.

The governor had to order guns and ammunition from St. Louis for the militia. The boat delivering the arms got as far as Memphis, but downstream at night some masked men came aboard and unloaded in the middle of the river. Two radicals on their way to a political meeting at Clarendon were shot from ambush.

Even in such an uproar Hindman made himself heard with burning words in a debate with the governor. He was so vitriolic that the governor had him arrested for treason. He had been back from Mexico less than a year. Then came 27 September 1868. Feelings in Helena were excited that day by the posse's lynching of a black. That night General Hindman sat by the fireside to read a newspaper. Someone stepped up on the porch, fired through the window, and killed him. His fortieth was his final birthday. He lived long enough to say, "I do not know who killed me, but, whoever it was, I forgive him."

"Incredible Yanqui"

Lee Christmas was a railroad engineer from Memphis who, when he lost his job, went south of the border—way south. He got a job in Honduras, running a banana train from Puerto Cortez inland for sixty miles. One day a revolution blew off around him and his train was captured. The rebels put a gun on him and told him to take them to where they could see the government line of battle. So he joined the revolt, which made the

Lee Christmas (from *The Commercial Appeal* files).

barefoot revolutionists so happy they made Christmas a captain. That made him so happy he offered to run the train right through the government barricades, which he did, whereupon the insurrectionists promoted him to the rank of general.

That was in 1897. For the next twenty years he made news in Honduras and sometimes in Nicaragua, El Salvador, and Guatemala, setting up some presidents and pulling some down. He was credited with engineering almost a dozen revolutions. Herman B. Deutsch, New Orleans newspaperman and author, did a book about him, *The Incredible Yanqui*, in 1931. In the Richard Harding Davis book, *Soldiers of Fortune*, he is said to be the model for the character "Clay," but similarities with the real life of Christmas are few.

As the '80s turned into the '90s, Lee Christmas had been an engineer on the Yazoo and Mississippi Valley Railroad, now part of the Illinois Central Gulf. He ran trains up and down the Delta of Mississippi, and he lived on Kentucky Street. He was well liked by his associates in Memphis. On 29 November 1891 he crashed his train head-on into another. According to one account, he had gone to sleep at the throttle. But that must have been unofficial, for during his extended recovery from severe scalding, he planned on climbing back into the cab.

Unfortunately for his plans, someone in the Chicago railroad offices decided it was important for engineers to be able to tell the difference between red and green semaphore signals. After his crash but before he returned, railroad doctors began testing engine crews for color-blindness. Christmas was color-blind.

A friend told him banana companies were short of engineers. He said the trains ran only in daylight and hired without testing for color-blindness or anything else. So Christmas shipped out of New Orleans for Honduras.

His first taste of politics by rifle suited him so that he made a career of it and also made numerous enemies. Those who objected to him and some of his unsavory methods were once so numerous, he decided he must have bodyguards. He hired two Americans and put one in a hotel room on each side of his sleeping quarters. One writer said he fought thirty-six major battles, without attempting to number the skirmishes and brief encounters. Neither did anyone attempt to count his wounds beyond seven, but one was obvious. His left arm was limp and useless because of machine gun fire.

Stories about him were numerous, colorful, and often true. Aside from the opportunities open to a filibusterer in the land of fragile governments and fickle loyalties, he had a marital career of four marriages, and he had a profane vocabulary that went far beyond fabled accomplishments of drunken sailors.

He was backing President Bontilla of Honduras when the government was overthrown and Christmas was chased through town by the whole army and a howling mob. He managed to get to the back door of the armory, slip inside, and bolt the door. He was the only man inside but there were 1,500 rifles and a large amount of ammunition. He fired through a porthole, ran to another and fired, then another, making like a squad of determined marksmen. The pursuers kept up the seige for hours and he kept picking them off for just as many hours.

Christmas thought he knocked off eighty. Later writers say he was too modest, that he got a hundred, maybe more. However many lives he shortened that day, there came a time when a truce seemed advisable. So he came out and when the attackers saw he had been holding them off by himself, a cheer went up, and he was made a general on their side.

Another time—this time he was commanding some troops—he ordered a night attack on enemies sleeping in the jungle. The question came immediately of how his men could tell foe from friend after action started in the total blackness. Christmas had the answer. He ordered his men to strip off every bit of clothing. He told them: "When you feel flesh, you'll know it's a friend. When you feel a man with clothes on, you'll know he's an enemy, so let him have it."

He once was made police chief of a capital city but joined the revolt against the regime which had put him in office. A new government in Honduras paid him off by making him governor of the department of Cortez. He was given valuable mining and railroad concessions. At one time he operated a large hotel.

One of his most spectacular actions, related by several chroniclers, came when he was helping General Estrada revolt against President Zelaye in Nicaragua. General Christmas asked President Cabrera of Guatemala to send 500 soldiers across the border but the president of Guatemala hemmed and hawed about taking part in another nation's revolt. He stalled so long that General Christmas ran out of patience and wrote a telegram. It said:

> Manuel Estrada Cabrera, son of a cur, President of Guatemala,
>
> You dirty dog I put you in as President of this republic and you have refused to let me have money or men for the Nicaraguan campaign you cowardly pup if you would fight I would beat your brains out if you would duel I would chop you to bits I spit on you Hell with you I have quit.
>
> Lee Christmas.

Eventually Christmas did quit. His fighting days were over in 1911, after only one brush with the United States government. Washington acted when he ran guns out of New Orleans to a revolt in a friendly nation. But when World War I came, he thought his battle experience was needed. He applied for a commission and an assignment in France. President Wilson turned him down with a formal letter. The general was furious. He offered to "lick" the board that turned him down, one at a time or all together—with his one good arm.

During his adventures in Central America he had kept his citizenship in the United States and he considered Memphis his home. He had left two daughters and a son here. His address was listed once as 902 Barton. Opportunities to make millions, some of them legitimately, came his way and a great deal of money passed through his hands, but in his final days he was penniless. He died on 28 January 1924, with anemia listed as the cause of death and his age given as sixty-one. He was living in Memphis when the final illness struck, but he went to New Orleans and died there unknown to readers of *The Commercial Appeal* for two days.

The Bolton Killings

Wade Bolton is remembered as the center of the bloodiest feud in Shelby County history. This might be unfair, since his name has been preserved because he left a large part of a big estate to found a school, which has been in the news at intervals ever since. He was never indicted for killing anyone. On the contrary, he was a victim, and after he was dead the death roll lengthened to eight names.

The administration of his estate is the oldest active case in Shelby County courts and almost another century of life is assured for the bushels of records in Chancery Court. When the will was filed the estate was estimated at $500,000 plus the 1,200-acre farm. The school has been built and other bequests delivered but the estate is bigger now than it has ever been. His will directed that his grave be marked with a monument that looked like he really looked. So the sculptor gave him a vest button awry and untied shoe laces. The legend says only, ''Founder of Bolton College.''

When he died on 23 July 1869 there was an extraordinarily instant knowledge of his will in many parts of town, including the fact that the school was to be built. Yet the main talk that Friday morning was of another clause. He had left $10,000 to the widow of Thomas Jonathan ''Stonewall'' Jackson, because he read that she had sold household furnishings to pay his debts.

Interest was strong because Bolton had been shot on Main Street by a former partner in business, Thomas Dickens, before daylight witnesses. Wade had been prominent several years as a partner of his brother, Isaac Bolton. Before the partnership was formed, Isaac had been the biggest slave dealer in Memphis. The company was a huge dealer in cotton, with branches in Vicksburg, Mississippi, Richmond, Virginia, and Richmond, Kentucky, as well as the slave business. Partners in Bolton and Dickens were Isaac and Wade Bolton, Thomas Dickens and Washington Bolton, who was unrelated to the two Boltons but the brother of Mrs. Dickens.

Wade Hampton Bolton was a member of one of the very first families to settle in Shelby County, coming from North Carolina, probably in the pre-Memphis days. It was a leading family in the Big Creek community, where there was early opposition to the John Overton politics in Memphis.

His birth date, 8 December 1812, shows he was almost eight years old before there was a Shelby County government. Wade seems to have

Memorial to Wade Bolton (from *Elmwood: History of the Cemetery*).

gone into business separately from his brother. At least he put only the name "W. H. Bolton" on an advertisement in *The Memphis Appeal*, 2 December 1846. It said:

> I have again returned to this market with 20 likely negroes. I have located at Main and Adams Streets. I have for sale plenty of boys, men and women and some very fancy girls. I intend to have a constant supply through the season and will not be undersold by an agent in this market. My motto is 'the swift penny: the slow shilling, I will never get.' I will also pay highest cash for young negroes.

Later he advertised that he had moved from the Main Street corner down Adams to "Bolton's Negro Mart." In 1849 the name of Bolton and Dickens was used.

In 1857 a Kentucky associate brought to the firm a twenty-three-year-old Negro, who was sold by Bolton and Dickens to Thomas B. Crenshaw, a Methodist preacher. The man said he was free, got to court, and proved it, and the dealer had to refund the purchase money. While drinking, Isaac Bolton accused the Kentuckian of tricking the firm, fired four pistol shots, and fatally wounded him (Death number one).

A long series of court hearings followed and eventually a jury in Covington turned Bolton loose. Newsmen at the time said there was corruption and a later account said every member of the jury was bribed. Defense expenses were more than $100,000.

Wade Bolton wanted it paid from company money. Dickens refused. He thought Isaac Bolton should pay. The argument broke up the company and left Dickens unsatisfied. Courts allowed payment from company funds, eventually. During the war, in 1862, Washington Bolton died, and in 1864 Isaac died, in debt. That left Wade Bolton and Dickens bitterly arguing about the Isaac Bolton trial expenses and settlement of the company finances. Wade Bolton wrote by hand a long will of fifteen clauses, with repeated words abusing Dickens, which he signed 10 August 1868.

In January, 1869, someone tried to murder Dickens in his farm home near Raleigh. He accused Bolton, without evidence. A few weeks later, while Dickens was having supper with friends at his home, two men walked in and began shooting. A man in the house, Green Wilson, was killed (Death number two). So was Nancy, a Negro servant for many years (Death number three). A young man, Robert Humphries, was wounded. Another bullet hit Dickens in the right eye and another struck his arm.

One person in the Dickens home said he had seen the two gunmen in company of Bolton associates. Dickens then accused Wade Bolton of hiring the two to kill him and all witnesses to the lawsuits, and to get from his house some documents involved in the suits. On 17 June the pair was recognized on a Memphis street. They resisted arrest and both were shot. One said he was named Morgan and was from near Russellville, Alabama, and then died (Death number four). He said the other, who got away, was James Inman, also from Russellville.

Dickens's son, Samuel, notified Russellville authorities and a few days later learned that Inman, badly wounded, was in a cave near his mother's home. Samuel prepared to go to Russellville after the accused gunman.

Apparently waiting for the train, Samuel walked along Main Street with his father. They came upon Wade Bolton, with his back to the fence around Court Square near the Main Street gate to the park. Bolton was talking to a friend when Dickens, without a word, pulled out a pistol and fired a bullet hitting Boltons's left shoulder. Bolton ran down the street and found a deputy sheriff, exclaming, "I am murdered. Old Tom Dickens did it. Arrest him." Dickens was arrested and put under $2,500 bond. Bolton was sure the wound was fatal and refused to let a doctor even probe for the bullet. So he died on 23 July 1869 at the home of a friend, F. M. Cash (Death number five).

Without waiting for Bolton's death, Samuel Dickens had gone to Alabama with Humphries, the young man wounded when Tom Dickens was fired on. He enlisted a posse of seventeen and two guides into an area of caves in the face of a steep bluff. They wounded another Inman and killed James Inman (Death number six). The body was brought back to Memphis by young Dickens on 26 July 1869. Then Thomas Dickens was tried for the killing of Wade Bolton. After twenty-six days of trial his name was cleared. Both Boltons were dead, and it was assumed that the feud was over.

It was only a lull. The killing returned on 30 July 1871. Dickens spent the night with his friend, John C. Bolton, on Big Creek, about six miles from his Raleigh home. In the morning he was riding home on horseback when he was shot from the roadside (Death number seven). Evidence of the killer having waited behind bushes was found. The buckshot-mangled body was in the Loosahatchie Bottom road. His horse had galloped home with an empty saddle. One week later, at the same place on the road through the bottoms, the younger Dickens was shot and killed (Death number eight).

Meantime the Bolton lawsuits had gone on, with some new ones because of the Wade Bolton will. It was an extraordinary document. Even though his grave with the famous monument is in Elmwood, his will ordered his burial in Pleasant Ridge Church burying ground. He named E. M. Apperson executor, without bond, and Beecher & Belcher as attorney.

An unusual clause says:

> Fidelity is the noblest trait of human beings and should be rewarded, therefore I hereby give and bequeath to my loyal slaves, now called freedmen, that has stayed with me during the war, and has remained with me on my plantation ever since, in my employ or working my land, and has never left it to work or labor on any other farm, to all these that continue faithful in this way up to my death, I instruct my executor to pay the heads of families of all such, three hundred dollars, and to single ones one hundred dollars each that has no families; to Mary Ann I give five hundred dollars.

To "My Beloved wife, Lavinia Ann Bolton" he left 300 acres for life, some personal property, $10,000 and a $10,000 insurance policy. But she dissented and sued the estate. The only children of Wade and Lavinia Bolton were three girls, each buried in Raleigh Cemetery before she was a year old.

Several clauses of the will gave $5,000 to individuals, including some nephews and nieces on condition they assist in turning back the Dickens claim. One clause begins, "I give and bequeath my niece, Josephine Bolton, now the wife of the notorious Doctor Samuel Dickens (the Judas of the family), five dollars, one sixth of what Judas Iscariot got for betraying the Lord."

Near the end Bolton wrote, "Should I die before this fraudulant suit of old Tom Dickens, and his tool and ally, Sarah W. Bolton, has instituted against me and Isaac L. Bolton's estate is decided, I want my executor to defend the same to the bitter end and, as I know, and the world should know, I don't owe him one cent, or they would not sleep on their rights for eleven years, and myself and Isaac L. Bolton both being solvent, and punctual to pay our debts on demand."

Having attended to these instructions, Wade Bolton turned to his big plan. He wrote, "I hereby give and bequeath, after the death of my wife, the three hundred acres (in which she had a life estate) to the trustees of the free schools of Shelby County, Tennessee, and their successors in office, forever, for the purpose of erecting a college of learning on the same, and hereby give and donate ten thousand dollars for the purpose of erecting a college of learning on the same, to be called Bolton College."

Many disputed parts of the will and the suits against the estate were settled by state supreme court rulings in 1880. The college was set up in 1887. In 1911 a good two-story school building was erected, with barns and other outbuildings, for 200 students. It is near Brunswick.

Bolton College became an agricultural high school and was turned over to the county school board. In the days of small farms Bolton College instruction was designed to improve rural living. There was a new set of buildings in 1924 and in 1979 a new vocational building was dedicated. In modern times of wide farms and large machines it has taught the standard subjects, in the county's smallest high school, with about 365 pupils, 75 percent of them black. The county has use of the buildings and the 18.69 acre campus, without paying anything. There is net income from renting the remainder of the old plantation to neighboring farmers. There also is income from investment of surplus income, which has been accumulating for years. Supervision is in the hands of Chancery Court, which reviews accounts annually. The 1977 report, filed by R. Grattan Brown, Jr., attorney, shows land income of rental $55,000 a year and accumulated investments of $589,000, most of it in municipal bonds.

Sin City Doomsday

Sin got pretty bad in Memphis in 1906. It got so bad that a black minister told of the devil leaving hell on a vacation in which he "stopped over at Memphis, sat down on Beale Street and rewrote the Ten Commandments, leaving the NOT out of each commandment," according to Fred Hutchins, writing in *What Happened in Memphis*.

The downhill skids had been greased just two years earlier when operators of a gambling game that had long run wide open at Union and DeSoto (now Fourth) took guns away from raiders and killed two deputy sheriffs. Another load of grease had gone on the skids in 1905, when a reform ticket was elected. The head men were true reformers but their campaigners included a big gambler. Months later he had 200 premarked ballots, a surplus beyond what had been necessary for the "right" to win on election day.

At this time there was a saloon that ran all day and all night. It truly never closed, for it had nothing like a door, a swinging panel, or an entrance barricade to close. There also was a large building of several floors, known in the trade as the largest brothel in the nation. Cocaine could be bought in drug stores, like aspirin. It came in little flat round containers of wood, known as "lids," at fifty cents. *Bagnio* girls had lots of pains, including frequent tuberculosis, and used drugs to get them through the night. Small boys, venturing down the passageway beside the big emporium in the early morning, sometimes found the ground covered like snow with discarded lids, tossed out the windows. Both of these establishments were in a little night-life cluster far from the sin bins of Beale Street and the famous joy spots downtown.

In this sinful city the preachers, of course, warned of the wrath of God. Then there appeared a wrinkled old black woman who despaired of the power of ordinary preaching, predictions, and prayer to drive the devil out of town. She took her stand at Main and Madison, on 5 March 1906, to say God was so angry that, unless Memphis straightened up, He was going to sink the town in a hole so deep that the tallest buildings would go out of sight.

People had only a short time to mend their ways or get out of the way of the approaching wrath. She announced that doomsday would be 27 March, although she said there would be a final warning in the form of two days of darkness preceding the disaster.

The story of the seeress who took her predictions to the busiest street corner in the city, and told of a giant hole about to open in the earth, spread rapidly through kitchens across town and into the dining rooms. Most of the town, white and black, seemed to be talking about it. There was an enlargement of the story, probably added by jeering young white men, in which, before the earth began to crumble, a yellow dog would leap from the top floor of a high building to escape the falling bricks.

Newspapers took up the doomsday warnings. As the dreaded date neared, a red ring around the moon forecast trouble. The ignorant began to foresake Memphis. Fred Hutchins, whose book has a detailed account of doomsday in Memphis, says railroads offered excursion rates to Little Rock, Jackson, and Nashville for those who wanted to avoid the chance of being "buried alive" in the city of sin. Bishop Thomas F. Gailor mentions the scare in his partial autobiography, *Some Memories*.

Doom was scheduled for a Tuesday. The Sunday before, many a Memphis household found itself without a cook, a maid, or a yardboy. It is also reported that many a white man, and numerous women, found it a time to visit relatives back on the farm. Then came Monday, destruction day minus one. It was a day without a sun. Dark clouds hung low. Smoke from factory stacks came out of the top and immediately sagged to the ground. It rained and then poured until the clouds were sending it down by the bucket. There was lightning and especially there was thunder, so close that buildings seemed to quiver under celestial blows.

About 4 P.M., with the darkness, the rain, and the crashing thunder in full control, so many frightened whites and blacks were trying to get away from the downtown danger that traffic almost clogged at Main and

Madison. Tony Devoto was the sole representative of police law and order when an emergency descended. A black woman, with her face full of excitement, was eagerly moving southward, dragging along her husband. Just as they passed the policeman the loudest thunder bolt of all smashed down. The old woman threw up her hands, fell limp to the sidewalk and screamed, apparently a direct hit from above.

"Lawd, lawd, Mollie wanted me to take her to Little Rock yesterday, but I put it off too long. It's too late," her husband moaned. Cold rain in the face revived her a little and she tried to sit up, but there was so much water in her eyes and the rain was so thick the downtown buildings seemed to be gone, and she collapsed again. Some of her fright was calmed when the policeman stopped a passing buggy and sent them on their way to the depot and Little Rock.

That was on the day before doomsday. When it arrived someone tossed a dead yellow dog out of a high window to the sidewalk, just in front of a crowd of blacks. But Memphis pulled through—and so did the devil.

4

For Profit

It Really Picks

A cotton picking machine that impressed newspapermen and magazine writers was demonstrated on 31 August 1936 at the Delta Experiment Station in Stoneville, Mississippi. Before a month had passed the public from coast to coast knew that a momentous event had occurred. A swirl of newspaper stories had been followed by accounts in *Time, Literary Digest, Newsweek,* and *Business Week* magazines. The demonstration was the triumph of John and Mack Rust, after years of effort and disappointment, the same disappointment that had come to a host of inventors and investors for many years.

There followed years of modifications of the picker and efforts to bring the cost down to a practical level for growers. The Rust line was developed by Ben Pearson, Incorporated, at Pine Bluff, Arkansas; by the Allis-Chalmers Company which built a new plant at Gadsden, Alabama, the J. I. Case Company; and Massey-Harris-Ferguson, Incorporated.

On another line of patents the International Harvester Company took a strong hand in the making of pickers. The harvester company announced late in 1942 that it was ready to go into production, the first commercial volume manufacturing of machines. War shortages slowed the development but there was another milestone in 1944 when

John D. Rust

International pickers were used on the Hopson brothers place at Clarksdale, Mississippi, to produce the first cotton crop grown and harvested without hand labor. It was 1948 when Harvester completed a plant at Memphis, which has been a big element in the cotton picker business and in the growth of Memphis.

A mechanical cotton picker that worked, and one that could be sold at a price growers could pay was a monumental change in cotton farming and a revolutionary alteration for the rural population of the South. For many years thoughtful men had looked forward with foreboding to the time when an inventor would solve the picker problem and thousands of persons who knew nothing about earning a living except in cotton fields would be unemployed. John Rust made extensive preparations for easing the shock socially while working bugs out of the machine.

By good fortune the mechanical solutions were found at a time when rural labor had rushed to war jobs and postwar boom employment in the cities. What could have been displacement of cotton hands by the machine was, in large part, an emergency purchase of pickers by growers unable to find enough help to get the cotton out of the rains.

This transition was fast. The picking machines built in 1946 and left over from all previous years numbered only 107, by National Cotton Council figures. During 1952 the number of pickers manufactured for sale in the United States was up to 4,590.

It had been a long time coming. The same generations of clever men who made machines that harvested wheat, baled hay, and put gang plows behind tractors turned their talents to cotton. But cotton remained a crop usually grown with one mule working one row at a time, weeds chopped out with a hoe, and picked by men, women, and children who dragged bags up one row and down the next.

There had been several periods when it was difficult to find enough hands. During such a year, 1820, a Louisiana cotton man sent to Brazil for monkeys. He tried to train them to pick cotton.

The first patent for a cotton picking machine was issued in 1850 to Samuel D. Rembert and Jedediah Prescott of Memphis. Cotton picking by air, blasted or sucked through rubber tubes, appeared in 1859 and continued to be a favorite idea. It attracted the intense interest of International Harvester in 1922. In 1924 a model appeared which could be pulled by one mule while a gasoline motor produced the suction in four tubes, each handled by a man who put the end of the tube to an open boll.

The use of electrical attraction was patented in 1868. L. C. Stuckenberg of Memphis had a great deal of attention in 1922 with a machine that used a vacuum, with brushes turned by electricity at the end of each tube. He had been improving the device fourteen years. It was hailed by *Scientific American* in an article entitled "The Successful Cotton Picker."

W. C. Durant, better remembered for his accomplishments in automobiles, thought he had the answer with rotary blades at the end of suction tubes. He built 500 machines in St. Louis, but the market in the United States turned him down and he let the Russians have his machine.

There was a time when strippers or sledders dragged over the cotton stalks by growers in the Texas panhandle seemed to be the answer. Deere and Company was attracted and a commercial stripper was demonstrated in 1927. In 1932 Deere was producing 500 machines a year.

Hiram Berry of Greenville, Mississippi, patented a machine in 1923, demonstrated it in 1926, and did so well that the Deere company bought him out in 1943. The Berry device used spindles to pull the open cotton from the boll. But Deere gave up on the Berry type in 1946.

A very long story of an effort with a successful outcome began in Chicago in 1885 when Angus Campbell took up the quest for a cotton picking machine. He had only vacations from his regular job to go south to try the improvements he had been making all year in his spare time.

By 1910 he was able to make a demonstration of five machines at once at Waxahatchie, Texas. But it was 1924 before International Harvester dropped the vacuum tube machines and bought out the Campbell patents.

Harvester had taken an interest in cotton picking machinery since 1902. The company put more than $5 million into experiments. The Campbell line of patents ran back to 1895 but it was 1948 before modifications brought Harvester to the point of opening the Memphis plant for big-time production of pickers using revolving spindles to twist the cotton off the stalk.

By that time there had been more than fifteen hundred patents issued for cotton pickers. Cotton growers, disappointed in the several announced "successes," leaned to the belief that there never would be a cheaper device for picking cotton than the human hand.

For anyone inclined to tinker with wrenches and cogwheels there is fascination in the picker portion of the book *The New Revolution in the Cotton Economy*, by James H. Street. For a few years just before the picker was successful there was a variation in which machinery took over the growing but the harvesting was done by thousands of hands taken out of the cities each morning on old buses and trucks. Another variation of that period was the use of braceros from Mexico.

As the use of twirling spindles to pick cotton neared practical usefulness and inventors struggled with the problem of getting the cotton off the spindles, there developed increasing worry about what all-machine cotton growing would mean. What could the cities do about millions of persons whose only experience was in cotton grown and picked by hand? The Street Book tells of E. H. Crump, the center of Memphis and Tennessee politics, urging a law to prevent use of cotton picking machines in this state.

What the Rust demonstration at Stoneville in 1936 did was a double whammy. It convinced growers that inventors had really triumphed at last. It came with a plan for easing human problems of change.

The Rust story, as written by John Rust, is an often consulted document in the 1953 edition of *The West Tennessee Historical Society Papers*. It tells of two Texas boys who picked cotton as children. John was a harvest hand in the wheat fields when he studied automotive engineering and mechanical drawing by mail. Mack had a degree in mechanical engineering.

John went to bed one night in Kansas City in 1927, puzzling over the cotton picker problem, when he remembered that on dewy mornings cotton stuck to his fingers. "I jumped out of bed," he wrote, "found some absorbent cotton and a nail for testing. I licked the nail and twirled it in the cotton and found that it would work." That was the turning point. He took out a patent in 1928. Working out of Leesville, Louisiana, in 1931 the Rust brothers made a machine that picked a bale a day. Working out of Lake Providence, Louisiana, in 1933, they had a machine that picked five bales a day.

In 1934 he came to a convention of engineers at the Hotel Peabody with movies that excited promises of plenty of financing. So he moved to Memphis and lived here for the next fifteen years. The Rust Cotton Picker Company had an office and shop at 2369 Florida. In 1936 John Rust built a machine that picked thirteen bales a day.

He had the enthusiastic support of W. E. Ayres, assistant director of the Delta Experiment Station and John T. Fargason, Jr., of Memphis became a supporter and arranged a demonstration on his Clarksdale, Mississippi, plantation. It showed a crop that averaged $16.12 a bale in hand-picking cost, while machine picking cost was a mere $5, and the reduction in price because of trash in the machine picking was only 40 cents a bale.

The move to Memphis brought another kind of change. *The Commercial Appeal* had announced the move and the prospects with a display four columns wide on 18 April 1934. Other towns where the Rust brothers had made early models used similar space but the news stopped in each locality. The difference was that wire service writers made nationwide news of the Memphis stories. These resulted in a comprehensive article in *The American Mercury* of February 1935, followed by a condensation for the millions of readers of *The Reader's Digest*. It included a discussion of the problems of surplus cotton field labor. This was the background which brought newspaper and magazine writers to Stoneville for the big event of 1936. The nation as well as the cotton growers learned that the cotton picker had broken the hold of hand labor.

There were still troubles ahead, such as a war that shut off steel. In 1941 John Rust had to take a job at Canton, Ohio, and Mack Rust at

Pittsburgh, and their wives took jobs at the Army Supply Depot here. Unable to pay franchise taxes, the company lost its state charter. Equipment in the shop was sold to pay old debts in 1942. That was the year Mack, who had worked with John since 1928, gave up and moved to Arizona. He later moved to California, where he died on 11 January 1966.

But John still had his brain and his drawing board. He started over again with sturdier parts and improved designs. He was in Washington in 1944 to patent new features when Allis-Chalmers asked for a manufacturing license. That connection put the Rust machine on the track for the postwar boom. It enabled John to go back along the way he had come paying back everyone who had ventured investments in his devices, more than $250,000 altogether. Stockholders in the Memphis company got two dollars for one dollar. An oil field worker who borrowed money to get the original machine started in 1927 got back four dollars for one dollar.

The Rust patents were given to the Rust Foundation, which found the best attack on social problems brought by the picker was preparation of teachers to lift the former field hands into the new era of jobs. Among the first to get Rust Foundation funds were the University of Arkansas and Memphis State University.

John left Memphis for Pine Bluff, Arkansas, in 1949. By 1952, he was able to consider the mountain of mechanical problems climbed at last, and profits assigned to the nonprofit trust. When that year ended, almost 12,000 pickers of all brands had been produced, about a third of them in that one year.

It was near the end of his life. He died in Pine Bluff, 20 January 1954, at sixty-one. A generation was growing up that had never known about thousands of years when cotton demanded bent backs and crawling knees in the frosty mud.

Bridging Generations of Business Growth

One rainy night in October of 1901 Goldsmith's moved to its present location with the help of a bridge over South Main Street traffic. The new building was at the southwest corner of Main and Gayoso with a second floor window knocked out to let in the bridge on which rolling bins of merchandise arrived.

The other end of the bridge was a building at the southeast corner, where the Goldsmith business had grown to overflow size. When rain

J. Goldsmith

came, tarpaulins had to be found and installed while electric lights on each side of the bridge twinkled out "Bridge of Success" and the carts moved at a lively pace.

On the east side, the store closed early at 4:00 P.M. On the west side, the store was ready to open on time at 9:00 A.M. Organization had been so complete that the whole stock had been moved and displayed at 11:00 P.M. the night before.

The southwest corner had been occupied for many years by Menken's, the leading store of another age. That building and its neighbors had been destroyed in one of Memphis's most disastrous fires in 1899.

Napoleon Hill, banker and cotton factor, cleared away the charred ruins and put up a building on speculation. It was big, intended for five stores, although it neither reached as far down Main as Hotel Gayoso, nor was it as deep as Front Street. Hill rented one store, on the corner, to Goldsmith's. Then the Goldsmith management lifted its sight to a broader future and rented a second store. Before Hill had completed the roof, Goldsmith's had leased all five stores. Goldsmith's bought the building in 1919.

The store also made additions that carried it up to an alley along the hotel and expanded in the back to Front. In 1948 Goldsmith's bought the hotel itself for more than $1 million. The store continued to operate the hotel for several years but gradually converted hotel space to store uses. The entire hotel is used by the store now, and so are buildings on the other side of Front.

The energetic center of this dramatic growth was Jacob Goldsmith, a man of small stature who usually reduced his name to "J." But the business was twenty-seven years old before his name appeared at all. He had a brother two years older, who reduced Isaac to "I." The name of the store that moved across Main Street was "I. Goldsmith & Bros." Ike died in 1884 but Jacob kept the name until 1904.

Roots of the big Memphis store go back to a log cabin provisions store on the Military Road near Forrest City, Arkansas. Before the Civil War there was a store at Taylor's Creek, operated by a German immigrant, Louis Ottenheimer, whose family lived behind a partition in the rear.

Ottenheimer did well enough in the country to move to Memphis. In partnership with Moses Schwartz, he opened a dry goods store at 348 Main. That was on the east side, about midway down the block between Union and Gayoso.

He continued to do well and in 1867 was able to visit his hometown, Hainstadt, in the German province of Baden. His sister had two sons. Jacob, born 3 February 1850, had just completed the government supervised school. The older boy, Ike, was working without much prospect.

Ottenheimer brought the boys to his home at 123 Pontotoc. They were to clerk in his store and be paid only board and room while they learned English and storekeeping. Then they were paid ten dollars a month, each, plus board and room. They could save a large part of the cash and they did, until they had accumulated $500.

They used it to go into business for themselves in 1870. The first store was at 81 Beale on the south side of the street in the middle of the block west of the city Market House and Hadden Street (now Third). They had fifteen feet of frontage on an unpaved street where ox carts sometimes got stuck in the mud. The store was sixty feet deep, and that was more than needed to display such a small stock. Jacob slept in the rear.

Gross business the first day amounted to twenty-five dollars. The sales force consisted of the two young owners. The first customers must have come back and brought their friends because space was soon expanded to one side and the rear, and the address was lengthened to 81-83 Beale. It was 75 feet by 125.

Opening a new business in Memphis—population about 30,000—in 1870 was doubtful. In 1873 Memphis was struck and badly hurt by the worst yellow fever epidemic ever known here. The fever came back much worse in 1878 in the famous disaster that almost depopulated the town. There was a return of the fever in 1879 that brought on municipal bankruptcy and caused the city of Memphis to cease to exist, while the state government took over with a taxing district.

The fever became so bad in 1878 that Goldsmith took his family to Brownsville, Tennessee, but the fever followed. He came back and rented a cottage in the country on Pigeon Roost Road. He then reopened the store and kept it open a few hours each morning. The 1879 fever caused him to move to St. Louis for three months and close the store. When frost stopped the epidemic he came back and his business revived quickly.

By 1881 the Goldsmith business was big enough to move to Main Street. At Number 348 the firm of Ottenheimer & Schwartz was replaced by I. Goldsmith & Bro. But Goldsmith kept the Beale Street space and operated at both locations, at first. Three years later Goldsmith's needed more Main Street space and added the adjoining building No. 350. The same year, 1884, Ike died. Jacob bought Ike's share from his widow but kept the name until J. Goldsmith & Sons Co., was formed in 1904. Jacob Goldsmith had personal talents in addition to guidance from his older brother, help from his sons, and contributions from his associates. He was astute in his judgement of character. He was friendly without having to work at it. He was cheerful, knew it was an asset, and required his help to be cheerful. There were other plusses in his character and, beyond that, he was lucky.

One of the luck stories still circulating in the store tells of a shopper asking the price of a blouse in a window. A clerk told her to go to the blouse department and ask. The owner, having overheard, asked her to wait while he went out on the sidewalk to see. As he got to the display window he paused to pick up a five dollar bill.

Goldsmith enjoyed his grandchildren and the grandchildren of others. About 1907 he began going to the Poplar Street Depot to welcome Santa Claus and show him the way to Goldsmith's. He soon had young helpers and their progress down Main Street became a Christmas parade. Decorated floats were added while it was a Goldsmith event. Later other merchants joined in a cooperative promotion.

Christmas at Goldsmith's one year got so out of hand that police took over the doors to keep shoppers out until those inside had thinned enough to make space for newcomers. Another time there was danger in a Goldsmith's Christmas. Children were invited to talk to Santa by telephone. At the appointed hour executives joined the switchboard girls, and youngsters from Muscle Shoals, Alabama, to the Missouri Bootheel reached for telephones, as well as thousands of Memphis children responded. The flood of calls blocked out the whole "8" exchange and that was the exchange used for the police and fire departments.

Attractions of Goldsmith methods must have been obvious early, for the space at 348 Main, even with Number 350 added, was soon out-grown. In 1894 the store moved into a building built for Goldsmith's at the southeast corner of Main and Gayoso. Less than 10 years later came the move across the street to a much bigger building.

Goldsmith's was a wholesaler, as well as a retailer, for several years. It was the first store in the South to arrange merchandise by departments, bringing in the era of the "department store" in 1902. It led the way into the age of full-page newspaper advertising in 1903, with "The Yellow Ticket Sale." It was at the head of the parade into another form of advertising in 1922 when the Reichman-Crosby Company operated radio station WKN. Part of the live music broadcast was made by "Goldsmith's Supreme Jazz Band." Reichman-Crosby sold its radio equipment to *The Commercial Appeal* which put WMC on the air in 1923. Goldsmith's introduced the "Charga-Plate" method of credit in Memphis in 1937. The first Memphis department store to have electric stairs was Goldsmith's, in 1950. There had been one in a variety store, however, years before.

Goldsmith's moved in strongly on the parking problem in 1953 by building a ramp garage across Front Street. A tunnel entrance to the store is the shortest possible walk and is out of the weather. Until the Gayoso Hotel was closed, at the end of 1962, the tunnel was popular with hotel patrons, too.

Jacob Goldsmith lived until 24 November 1933. At eight-three he was still president of the company and still able to read the the news-paper without glasses. He left three sons, four daughters, fifteen grand-children, and six great-grandchildren. The sons were Fred, Elias, and Leo.

In memoriam the children gave $200,000 to build the Goldsmith Civic Garden Center in Audubon Park, which opened in 1964. Fred, the oldest son, became the second president of the company. He was the father of Jack and Fred, Jr., as well as Dorothy, wife of Dr. Joseph A. Gronauer.

During World War II, when most of the Goldsmith men were in

uniform, responsibilities fell on Elias, the second son, and Dr. Gronauer. Elias J. Goldsmith was the father of Elias and Robert, who remained at the store longer than the others.

Jack, the son of Fred, was the third president of the company in 1959 when Goldsmith's became part of Federated Department Stores, Inc., the nation's largest and most profitable organization of department stores. It includes Filene's in Boston, Bloomingdale's in New York, Burdine's in Miami, and Shillito's in Cincinnati. The Goldsmith family was paid $13.5 million in Federated stock.

The business on South Main, still headquarters, has since become much larger with branches in East Memphis (1961), Whitehaven (1966), and Raleigh (1971). Federated has prospered, turning in new highs in earnings. And Goldsmith's had been a major factor. In 1972 Ralph Lazarus, chief executive of Federated, said Goldsmith's was the "fastest growing and most profitable division" of the business.

Sober Wholesaling

When he was sixty-six, William R. Moore set up a partnership to carry on the big wholesale dry goods business he had established. A document was drawn up which began with a page and a half of type in which each member of the firm obligated himself to take away part of the ownership of any other partner who drank often or who "treated" friends or customers to drinks. Before anything else was agreed upon, this long paragraph had such language as:

> No man deliberately sets out in life's career to become a drunkard; but occasional drinks lead, unconsciously, to habitual drinking, and habitual drinking leads inevitably to both financial insolvency, and to the drunkard's grave. Daily observation, therefore, of these self-evident and eloquent truths, leads us to specially provide in this article of co-partnership against the fatal future possibilities to which all men are liable; and in order to provide effectively against them, it is hereby expressly agreed that no member of this firm or co-partnership shall be permitted to indulge in habitual use of intoxicants; nor shall the habit known as "treating" of individual friends or business be permitted.

There is much more on this theme, including the business results of a "muddled brain," the low value of customers obtained through the bar of a "drinking saloon," and the evil example for employees.

Then comes the clincher in which any member of the firm who gets out of line is to forfeit one third of his holdings to the others for the first offense, another third for the second offense, and the remainder for a third offense. A majority of the other partners had final power to say when there had been an offense and each of them agreed in advance to submit. Then each partner agreed to stay out of any other "outside avocation or trade."

Capital was set up at $188,000, with contributions of $50,000 by Moore, $40,000 by Robert M. McLean, $10,000 by Orrin M. Peck, $6,000 by Walter B. McLean, $4,000 by William J. Armstrong and $2,000 by Frank L. Lang. Another clause set up salaries at $450 per month for Moore, $350 for Robert McLean, $292 for Peck, $292 for Osgood Armstrong, $150 for Walter McLean, $150 for William Armstrong and $150 for Lang. But they could draw more if they paid six percent, which was what each was being paid for his capital invesment. Another clause of the partnership contract agreed to pay Moore $147 a month for the building he owned, then numbered 389-397 Second.

This was a three-year contract signed on 1 January 1897. It was renewed for three years on 1 January 1900. Meantime Moore had bought the property then numbered 396 Main and the new rent clause called for the business to pay Moore $4,400 a year on Second Street, and $2,400 on Main. The Wm. R. Moore & Company partnership document is among Moore's personal papers recently added by *The Commercial Appeal* to the Memphis Room of the Public Library.

William Robert Moore was a strong man who stood firm against the custom of his time as to drinking and treating at the bars. He was even more conspicuous in opposition to secession, the Southern side of the Civil War, and glorification of the "Lost Cause."

He had been a Whig, like many merchants and some large plantation operators. When the cannon roared at Fort Sumter almost all of the former Whigs in the South changed their minds overnight about secession, rushed into the armies of the South, and for many years were the "Bourbons" who took control of the Democratic Party below the Ohio River.

In contrast, Moore went into the Republican Party, as many Whigs in the North did. He was a young businessman with an infant business in Memphis but he supported Lincoln. He was publicly abused, villified, and held in contempt. The attack was so severe the Presbyterian congregation of which he was a member threw him out. He stayed out the rest of his life. He stayed in business, but he quickly converted Confederate money into real estate on Main and Second, and he built on it. When the war was over he had land and a building, while those who had Confederate bills had only resentment. His business expanded and his reputation was good in spite of his politics.

Moore was the only Republican elected to Congress in the Memphis district during the long decades after the 1872 election of Barbour Lewis, a former Yankee officer. In the election of 1880 Moore defeated Casey Young, a former Confederate officer, who had been in Congress three terms. Young returned to Washington for two more terms after the Moore interruption. Moore was renominated in 1882 but one term was enough and he declined. At the 1888 Republican convention he had to take the floor to cut off an attempt by Mississippi and Tennessee delegates to nominate him for vice president. In 1890 he declined a nomination for governor.

For William R. Moore to defy his community on whisky and on the Democratic Party was only part of a total independence that brought him through a hardscrabble boyhood. He was born on 28 March 1830 in the hills near Huntsville, Alabama. Six months later his father was dead. His mother moved to Beech Grove, Tennessee, and when he was six, to Fosterville, in Rutherford County. At twelve he went to work as a farm hand and worked barefoot in the fields for twenty-four dollars a year and board and room. When the year was over he had saved twelve dollars. He went to school a little until he was fifteen but for the most part his learning was self-taught.

The boy got a much better job selling dry goods in a Nashville retail store, and then became a wholesale salesman in Nashville. He moved to New York as a wholesale salesman. It was a time when retailers in the South talked of boycotting New York wholesalers because of abolition politics. Moore did such a good job of holding the Southern storekeepers that he was made a junior partner. When he was less than thirty Moore went into business for himself. He came to Memphis, then the fastest growing city in the nation, in 1859. Moore brought with him his nephew Robert M. McLean, and from the New York firm where they had worked together, O. M. Peck.

They set up a wholesale house in a narrow building on the west side of Main, against the alley below Madison. After they closed the store for the day the three young men went to the basement and packed the goods they had sold. Then they climbed up to living quarters over the store.

None was married. Moore was forty-eight before he married Charlotte Blood. They lived at first in her father's home, which was on the north side of Union, near Third. It was a childless marriage. Robert McLean later married and his daughter Bessie, married E. H. Crump.

These young men had established a sound business that did more than survive disorders of war and reconstruction, the yellow fever of 1873,

1878, and 1879, and the depressions of 1873, 1893, 1907, and 1921. It prospered and expanded. The main building at Third and Monroe continues to be one of the largest used by a single firm in downtown Memphis and warehouses occupy much more space elsewhere.

When the sober partnership ran out in 1903 the company was incorporated. Younger men within the organization moved up, notably W. R. King. He began as Moore's stenographer, became president of the firm, and president of the Bank of Commerce as well. In 1954 stockholders sold to a dealer. Years later it developed that the buyer was a combination of businessmen headed by Charles G. Fury.

In his later years Moore became a writer of both prose and rhymes. He also gave increasing attention to finding the best way to help boys past hardships like he went through in getting started. He wrote his will over and over again. One of the discarded wills signed in 1902 is among the papers newly presented to the Memphis Room at the Library. It shows plans for a trust fund that would provide a life income for his widow but otherwise be devoted to building and paying operating costs of the "William R. Moore College of Technology." He signed himself "Wm." and he used "Wm." in the firm name but his will spells out "William" for the school.

The will said he wanted to benefit "the community in which I have so long resided, and where I have accumulated the means that I may leave at my death." He also said he wanted to pay tribute to "the aggregate of good citizenship in our midst," and he hoped to show his "abiding interest in the welfare and success of this portion of our common country." The purpose of the school was set out as "education and training of youths in the mechanic arts and sciences, including electricity, and the operation and maintenance of a manual and scientific training school."

When Moore died on 12 June 1909, his will was attacked in court. Distant relatives objected. Mrs. Moore, left $10,000 a year in the final revision of the will, chose to take instead her dower right to one-third. She died in 1919 but her will was lost and the estate was back in court. The outcome was that everything she owned went to the school.

Trustees of the school had organized but the substantial Moore estate was insufficient to carry out his instructions to use "methods and principles observed in the best institutions" of its kind in the United States. They were to use one quarter of the bequest for buildings, grounds, and equipment, and invest the remainder to produce income for operating costs.

So the trustees put the money to work and waited for it to increase. Their major income was from a little frontage on South Main leading to a large warehouse on Second. This was leased in 1919 by the school trustees to Lowe's theater organization for ninety-nine years. It was converted into Loew's State, a leading downtown movie house.

Investments produced income that was put into other investments until the trust fund reached $2 million. Then they bought the old Montgomery home at Poplar and Bellevue and built the school. It opened on 2 January 1939. Several persons, admiring the school and agreeing with the Moore philosophy of education, had added to the endowment.

It is entirely self-supporting, without tuition, although students pay for materials they use. The school year is eleven months long and equipment gets double use two nights a week, for night classes. There are about 220 students all the time. Several are older men and there have been a few women. Each day begins with a Bible reading and inspirational talk. Otherwise it is all classroom and shop work, mostly shop. They learn about electronics, automobile mechanics, machine shops, architectural drawing, welding, refrigeration, and woodworking.

It is a school that rarely appears in the news. It neither has appeals for funds, recruitment teams seeking students or football players, efforts to add to the jobs waiting for graduates, campus disturbances, nor even administrative changes. There have been only three directors, J. Lister Skinner, G. Edwin Shofner, and Gaylon Hall.

All over Memphis and its surrounding counties are young men hoping their applications for admission will be chosen from the stack on hand, and businessmen hoping to hire a graduate, some times too impatient to wait for the diploma. This must have been about what William R. Moore had in mind as the best way to contribute to the community in which he prospered.

The House of Bruce

In 1921 the E. L. Bruce Company opened a plant so huge it could produce a million dollars worth of oak flooring in one year. It was the first time the industry had such a large plant anywhere, and it was the beginning of many years of promotion of Memphis as the hardwood capital of the world. It also was the preliminary to full-page advertising in national magazines directing Bruce mail to Memphis.

Bruce operations grew until the company had plants in Bruce, Laurel,

C. Arthur Bruce

and Columbus, Mississippi; Nashville and Jackson, Tennessee; Cairo, Illinois; Center, Texas; Ishpeming, Michigan; Vrendenburgh, Alabama; a second plant in Memphis; and the old plant in Little Rock, Arkansas. At Bruce the sawmill in the woods grew into a town and transportation of the wood became the Mississippi & Skuna Valley Railroad. Bruce also was the world's largest maker of furniture parts. It made flooring for freight trucks and railroad cars. It made hardwood panels. It made waxes, finishes, and floor care products. It had a door plant.

Soon after Bruce became the leading flooring company the public became alarmed by termites. Bruce became the authority on the insects with the establishment of the Bruce Research Laboratory in 1927, which developed new chemicals and new methods tried out in Memphis for two years, and then offered across the country in 1930 as "Terminix." Franchise distribution was used.

For a time Bruce was deep in prefabricated housing for Oak Ridge, before it was known that the atom bomb was being made there, and for the Tennessse Valley Authority. When the company was well along in years, and known largely for oak floors, it bought the company that made about half of the nation's maple floors for gymnasiums, schools, and bowling alleys. That was the Robins Flooring Co., of Ishpeming, Michigan, bought in 1962.

The major Bruce accomplishment probably was the development of ways to use a large part of the low-grade oak which is abundant in the South. At the same time Bruce enlarged the market by reducing the price of a flooring previously used only in fine homes. Oak flooring became standard.

The founder of this giant company was Edward Lawson Bruce. His father, Charles Bruce, had a sawmill on the bank of the Kansas River at Lawrence, Kansas, and ambition for his son to be a lawyer. But E. L. Bruce was far more interested in selling lumber than in college studies. He opened a lumberyard in Kansas City in 1884 and lost it to a flood in 1903. He rebuilt it and lost the new lumberyard to another flood in 1905. He built the Kansas City Hardwood Flooring Company and lost it to a fire in 1912.

He moved his flooring business to Little Rock in 1914. All four of his sons joined him in the business: Robert G., Frank E., E. L., Jr., and C. Arthur. The title of sales manager went to Arthur, who had tried other occupations and had practiced law before going into lumber.

But selling was the founder's specialty and there came a time when he left his boys to run the plant while he got out and sold the flooring. Eventually it came time to retire and he moved to Los Angeles. While in "retirement" E. L. Bruce built the company's largest sales outlet in Los Angeles. He died at eighty-nine on 17 August 1944.

The Bruce plant in Memphis occupied forty-three acres on Thomas. When it was built it was outside the city limits, although the city was just on the other side of Thomas and arrangements were made for the Memphis Fire Department to leave the city for Bruce fires. When the plant was running at full speed there were about a thousand jobs there. One of the sights of the city was the Bruce gate in the morning where hundreds of men clustered in the hope of a prize in the daily hiring. That was before unions.

In 1958 Bruce bought the Welsh plant at 1218 Hollywood, where wall paneling was made. Net sales for the twelve months ending 30 June 1963, reached $52.5 million, and net profits were $1.2 million. However the figures showed that while sales were rising expenses sometimes were rising faster.

In March of 1958 the company skipped its quarterly dividend, which led to one of the most bizarre incidents in modern business. Edward M.

Gilbert was a man of thirty-four who was reaching for the jet set with a villa near Monte Carlo, a fortune of $20 million largely based on the family-owned Empire National Corporation, and an Eastern lumber firm. It seemed to Gilbert that the missed dividend would be considered by others a sign of Bruce weakness and an indication of the time to buy Bruce Stock. The stock leaped from $16.87 a share in March to $77 in June. In July Gilbert claimed control of Bruce. The Bruce family disputed it in court and in the market by buying more stock.

By June of 1961 Eddie Gilbert and his father, Harry, said they had eighty-one percent of the Bruce stock. They merged their Empire Company with the Bruce company. Young Gilbert became president of Bruce. E. L. Bruce, Jr. gave up and became chairman of the board. Arthur Bruce, having lost his official position, fought on against Gilbert control. The enlarged company did a bigger and more profitable business until 12 June 1962. Suddenly it was learned that young Gilbert had dipped into Bruce bank accounts for $1,953,000. He resigned his presidency and flew away to Brazil.

He had undertaken to buy control of the Celotex Co. for merger into the Bruce-Empire complex. He bought Celotex stock on margin. When the market collapsed he borrowed from friends, and when the market slid on down, he propped up his trading accounts with Bruce cash. Gilbert came back after about four months. A New York grand jury indicted him on fifteen counts. Eventually he went to prison for two years from which he emerged in 1969. The U.S. Tax Court in April of 1976 ruled that he owed $1,467,000 in 1962 income taxes. Strangely, he had offered to pay at the time of his original trouble and was then able to pay in full.

Arthur Bruce went back into the Bruce management when Gilbert fled. The restored Bruce control brought in fresh management. The new president and member of the board was W. H. Gonyea, of Eugene, Oregon, a large lumber operator. Another new board member was Edgar Eisenhower, a Tacoma, Washington, banker who was the general's brother. Before the end of 1962, direct loss of the June trouble had been reduced to $1,498,000 with a large surety bond still to be collected. Company assets were almost $33.5 million.

Bruce business was hit hard in 1968. Oak floors had been standard for homes for many years. But that year the FHA began to guarantee home loans in which the mortgage included wall-to-wall carpeting. There have been recent years of little building of any kind of homes or apartments.

There was also a loss to the company and to Memphis in the death of C. Arthur Bruce on 22 December 1966. The "C" stood for Charles, but he was known as "C. Arthur." He was a graduate of the University of Chicago and of Harvard Law School who joined the Bruce company when he was about thirty-one. He came to Memphis in 1919, when building of the plant began, before headquarters were moved in 1921. He became vice-president in 1945 and board chairman in 1954.

In common with many of the timber men from Indiana and Michigan who began to come to Memphis after 1895, Arthur Bruce kept his Republican politics. He was the Republican candidate for governor in 1932 and in 1940, long before the popularity of the party in the suburbs. He was a member of the county election commission for several years. He repeatedly accepted civic responsibilities, as president of the Chamber of Commerce, of the Community Chest, and of the Chickasaw Council of Boy Scouts. He also was finance chairman of the Boys Club. One of his chief interests for many years was LeMoyne College, of which he was chairman of the board. He was a national vice-president of the American Unitarian Association.

The company, of course, continued with his brother, E. L. Bruce, Jr., as chairman of the board. But the big Bruce plant on Thomas had been closed since late in 1965. In 1968 it was announced that Bruce had been bought by Cook & Company, Incorporated, which had been largely in grain and cotton. Bruce became a wholly owned subsidiary. Former holders of Bruce stock became the owners of 1,093,871 shares of Cook.

J. E. Rainey, a Cook man, took over as president of Bruce in 1974. Headquarters was moved to the CTH Building in the Ridgeway development on Poplar at I–240. On the night of 11 January 1977 fire destroyed the big building of the Bruce plant. The machinery had been silent for years. The property had been sold about a year earlier to the next door neighbor, Kraft. Workmen demolishing the machinery were blamed for the fire. Still, it was an unwelcome end.

A few days later on 13 January, E. L. Bruce Jr., died at eighty-five. He had been the last Bruce to head the company. Another few days brought the announcement on 16 January that three Bruce hardwood flooring mills at Nashville and Jackson, Tennessee, and Center, Texas, had been sold for $14 million to the Triangle Pacific Corporation of Dallas.

Heroine of Rice

Rice riches came into Arkansas farming in 1903 at the hands of a grieving widow and her sons. She was Mrs. Emma Thompson Morris, who lived near Lonoke in the Grand Prairie country. Her accomplishment was a good crop on ten acres of rice.

John Morris moved his family from Nebraska in 1894 to the Prairie Longue portion of the flat country. He did well with a dairy herd on pasture of native grasses, while raising some corn, oats, and stock peas.

The hope of rice in Arkansas came from Emma Morris's half-sister's husband, W. H. Fuller of Carlisle. In 1897 he put down an irrigation well and planted rice but lost the crop to poor pumping. The next season he rented a farm near Jennings, Louisiana, and undertook to learn at first hand how the Louisiana rice growers did it. Fuller's efforts in Arkansas continued to fail, perhaps because he counted too much on rain. At least he never got enough pumped water. But Fuller convinced his brother-in-law, Morris, that there was reason to hope for rice in Arkansas. In 1901 Morris and some friends installed a well and planted fifty acres. It was lost when pumping was unsatisfactory.

In 1902 Morris tried again on five acres. He dug a small well and pumped with a steam boiler. That effort produced a crop of sixty-four bushels per acre. It was so encouraging that Morris laid out a fifteen-acre plan for 1903. He went down to Louisiana before planting to see what he could learn from the rice growers. A heart attack killed him in Louisiana.

That was when rice money for Arkansas hung in the balance. Mrs. Morris became a heroine in the prairie area when she undertook to go ahead with his plan. She and her boys got a good crop on ten of the acres. The result was good enough for Mrs. Morris to expand to fifty acres of rice in 1904, with a ten-inch well.

Another change had come in 1903. A new member of Congress that year was Joseph T. Robinson, a Lonoke farm boy. He helped get $2,500 from the Department of Agriculture for a University of Arkansas rice experiment station at Lonoke. At first the experts did little teaching. The experiment station staff members were more like students, learning from the Morris-Fuller family about mistakes to avoid. But they spread the word.

Expansion of rice acres in Arkansas was dramatic after 1903, although it had been slow in starting. The root was, strangely, a new railroad in Louisiana. The Louisiana Western Railroad from Lafayette,

Mrs. John M. Morris (courtesy of Merlin Morris).

Louisiana, to Orange, Texas, was completed in 1881. The rails, which soon became part of the Southern Pacific line, ran through prairie which had long been neglected by settlers. Since it was treeless it was assumed to be poor land. Some of it could be bought for twelve cents an acre. Some 160-acre homesteads were available for fourteen dollar down payments. The railroad needed farmers and speculators had an opportunity. They took aim at farmers who were having a hard time in the Kansas-Iowa-Illinois region. Some of them were ready to leave the winter storms, the high interest on mortgages, and the summer clouds of grasshoppers.

These were men accustomed to planting wheat with drills, in contrast to the South's preference for cotton and hoes. They were independent capitalists, in a small way, instead of tenants. They were constantly experimenting with machinery. At first they grew some native rice to eat. Then they tried better seed and wheat growing methods. The wheat and corn with which they were familiar were failures. The rice did well and one of the Midwestern farmers worked out a way to alter a twine binder for wheat so that he could harvest rice. That was in 1884. So in 1888 the Deering company brought out a rice binder. Steam tractors and steam threshing machines were brought in. Drought forced development of reliable irrigation in 1894. The rice boom came on so fast that Louisiana growers sent two million pounds to New Orleans mills in 1886 and 200 million in 1892.

This was the rice experience into which Morris and Fuller dipped for guidance in Arkansas. When Arkansas rice began to show profits there was another campaign to get Midwest farmers to move. At one time the Stuttgart Land and Development Company offered free excursion trains to prospects each first and third Tuesday. The St. Louis Southwestern Railway promoted the Arkansas prairie as the Southern Pacific had pushed Texas and Louisiana land.

In 1906, only three years after the ten-acre success at Lonoke, Arkansas had its own rice mill. Stuttgart businessmen built it. There were five Arkansas rice mills in 1910.

Rice growing became so popular in Arkansas that by 1915 there was a rice mill in Memphis. Joseph Newburger was president of the Memphis Rice Mill, and J. D. Marks was manager. In 1920 when "The Mid-South and Its Builders" was published there was recognition for Arkansas rice farmers from C. P. J. Mooney, editor of *The Commerical Appeal*.

As might be expected, the growing of rice spread out of the Arkansas prairie to the East Arkansas flatlands, and across the river to the delta country of Mississippi, bringing a golden glow of profits to a vast part of the Memphis trade territory. The rice fields came to an abrupt halt at the hills just below Memphis. The only rice in Shelby County in 1974 was a five-acre field farmed by Joe Linhoss, near Eads.

In Arkansas dollar-a-bushel rice before World War I brought on a rise in land prices that paid out many times over for the speculators. The rice went on up to three dollars a bushel in 1920. A depression the next year knocked the price down to thirty-two cents, which caused formation of the Arkansas Rice Growers Cooperative Association. Through the co-op, the rice growers own their own dryers, mills, and sales organization, selling their brand, "Riceland."

Rice farming with machines and with an unusually successful branch of agricultural science allows Arkansas rice to be grown at a profit, then moved to gulf ports and shipped all the way to the Oriental markets— and still sell in competition with the rice from traditional paddies of the Far East.

When Arkansas had only the fate-filled ten acres of rice on Mrs. Morris's farm in 1903, Louisiana had more than 376,000 acres in rice and Texas had 234,000. These two states had more than ninety-nine percent of the rice acres of the United States then. Arkansas rice passed Louisiana long ago. It has recently passed Texas. In 1973 Arkansas became the number one rice state of the nation, only seventy years after the tiny success on the widow's farm at Lonoke.

A Memphis Automobile

Memphis once had a company for making automobiles—The Southern Six. The Southern Automobile Manufacturing Company, Incorporated, was advertised as "A Million Dollar Organization Composed of Southern People." Offices were in the Hotel Chisca and a plant was announced at Mallory and Latham. Officials were W. A. King, president; L. P. Miller, vice-president and general counsel: W. A. Schibley, secretary-treasurer; and W. N. Frazese, general sales manager.

This information comes from the 1920 city directory, but the company is missing from the 1919 and 1921 directories. At least two automobiles were assembled, probably three. H. Parks Tigrett, Jr., of Newbern, Tennessee, in a letter written in 1971, recalled one of them fondly. His father got it through his brother-in-law, Schibley, the company treasurer.

Tigrett remembers the Southern Six as a "thing of beauty," and "way ahead of its time." He wrote, "Unfortunately this classic automobile was no match for our dirt and mud roads and it was a sad day for all of us when my father traded it for a tractor. The last we heard of our Southern Six it was owned by James H. "Buck" Osment of Dyersburg." Mr. Tigrett was told three Southerns were built.

David L. Hutkin of 432 North Highland also wrote in 1971 of seeing the Southern on display at the curb in front of the Chisca. He said design and styling were "far ahead of its time." He had a vague memory of a second Southern.

A clear account of the demonstrator comes from Frank Cubbins of 25 South Barksdale. When he lived at 429 Vance he had the job of putting finishing touches on the car, although he never saw an assembly plant. He was hired after the automobile had been moved to the second floor of the Chisca Garage, a building still standing in 1971 on the west side of Main, between Pontotoc and Vance. It was moved to the Chisca on a float.

For about two weeks Cubbins had a job at intervals. He installed the running boards and he ran errands. But most of all he polished the car,

Death of the Southern Six (by Bill Herrington for *The Commercial Appeal*).

kept it covered with a dust cloth overnight, and then polished it some more the next day.

The chassis and body, except the radiator, were bought from a Lexington automobile plant. The radiator was of unusually graceful shape, somewhat like the Cadillac design. The word "Southern" was slanted across it with a "6" above and another "6" below. In a time when most automobile bodies were angular the Southern was slim, the first of the "sports" bodies remembered by Cubbins. The motor was a very long "red seal model" from the Continental plant. The color was fire-engine red. "A pretty car," he recalls. It looked so good that Cubbins expected the company to do well in the sale of stock.

But the demonstration was dramatically cut short before enough stock had been sold to get the company into high gear. Police found a bootlegger or a gambler at Main and Linden and chased him. He ran to the Chisca Garage and up to the second floor. The law and the outlaw shot it out in a gun battle that ended when death of the outlaw silenced the guns. Police in those days used .44 calibre ammunition with a huge slug that tore gaping openings in anything it failed to knock down. The Southern Six, beautifully polished and innocently awaiting fame for itself and fortune for its builders, died as the outlaw died—full of bullet holes.

Buggies and Autos

There once was a young man whose buggy making plant did so well that he retired at thirty-four. But he went back into buggies and made a great deal more money, shifted into automobiles, and eventually made a car

"IT SPEAKS FOR ITSELF"

RUSSELL E. GARDNER

THE CONFIDENCE OF THE AMERICAN PUBLIC IN THE GARDNER ORGANIZATION WAS STRIKINGLY DEMONSTRATED IN THE RECEIPT OF 5,372 INQUIRIES FROM AUTOMOBILE DISTRIBUTORS AND DEALERS PRIOR TO PRODUCTION.

MANY WANTED TO SIGN UP "SIGHT UNSEEN" ON WHATEVER TYPE OF CAR WE DECIDED TO BUILD.

THESE DISTRIBUTORS AND DEALERS KNEW FROM A PAST RECORD OF OVER 33 YEARS' SUCCESSFUL MANUFACTURE THAT WHATEVER CAR RUSSELL E. GARDNER BUILT WOULD BE GOOD—A 100% VALUE—A CAR EASY TO SELL, AND EASY TO KEEP SOLD.

THE RECORD OF THE MANY THOUSANDS OF GARDNER LIGHT FOURS IN ACTUAL USE DURING THE PAST YEAR HAS JUSTIFIED THIS CONFIDENCE.

THE GARDNER MOTOR CO., INC.
ST. LOUIS, U. S. A.

that carried his name to a nationwide market. Then he retired again to homes in Memphis and Miami Beach. The name was Russell Gardner. It is a name known well to those whose memories include the 1920s.

As a child in the northwestern corner of the state he lived in the small town of Gardner, named for his family. At ten he went to work in his father's mill at Union City, where wagon wheel spokes were made. In 1869, when he was nineteen, he struck out on his own and became a clerk in a spoke and wheel plant at Gallion, Ohio. Two years later he was secretary of the company and a stockholder. He objected so strongly to some company methods that he got out and sold his stock, even though all he got for the certificates was a carload of wagon wheel hubs. He traded the hubs for some whole wheels.

On this background he came to Memphis about 1872 and opened a buggy making business. Reviewing his life years later, *The Commercial Appeal* said his plant was on the west side of Main in the first block below Poplar. He soon moved to Columbus, Ohio, and then to St. Louis.

The time in Memphis was so brief that neither the plant nor Gardner show up in city directories from 1871 to 1876. A short stay here fits into the situation. Memphis had several established carriage plants then. Yellow fever hit so hard in 1873 that some other businessmen moved to St. Louis. The city government went bankrupt a few years later.

Municipal debt probably was more of a disaster to Gardner than to ordinary men. He was conspicuous among buggy men because when they were advertising credit terms he announced, ''We sell for cash and cheaper.'' He required full payment in advance from buyers and he paid his bills promptly in cash, operating his plant absolutely without debts either coming in or going out.

He found a fast road to bigger sales by doing without salesmen or dealers. He made his sales with an attractive catalog. Buyers sent their money by mail and got their buggies shipped directly from the plant. Of course there was nothing to discourage a country merchant from buying a buggy, and paying for it in expectation of resale. Gardner was one of the first manufacturers to try direct mail orders.

Profits came fast. The price was very long hours for an owner without executives. Gardner himself kept the books, wrote the letters, mailed the catalogs, and shipped the buggies. Four years was plenty of that pace. He had $150,000 clear, which was a small fortune in those days.

So he sold out and went home to Gardner. But leisure was too quiet. He became a banker at Gardner and soon had other banks at Dresden,

Martin, and Greenville. In two years he was tired of the monotony of calculating interest on farm loans. He turned back to St. Louis and buggies. He established the Banner Buggy Company in 1893. Somewhere along the line he had learned to delegate responsibility to helpers. Banner buggy sales became much too big for a one-man front office.

The Banner was a best seller among buggies. It was said to be made in the nation's largest buggy plant. The price was good. It was a sturdy vehicle in an age of mud roads. It was especially popular in West Tennessee and West Kentucky because of quick delivery on St. Louis boats running to dozens of landings along the Tennessee River all the way up to Muscle Shoals.

It was a Gardner principle to restrict his efforts to one thing at a time. His letterheads once said, "Buggies, Buggies, Buggies—Nothing but Buggies." That shut out early automobiles. It was the Gardner opinion that they would only be playthings for the rich.

Some of his mechanics experimented anyway. They mounted an engine on a surrey and rigged up a steering wheel. They called the boss to show him they had a horseless surrey that would run. It put-putted down the street toward the river, went over the top of the levee and picked up speed on the slope. The experimenters, in their anxiety to get the carriage to move, had done nothing whatever about stopping it if it did move. They had a brakeless wonder. The driver leaped out just before the splash. "Let it lay, boys," Gardner said as he turned his back on the disaster.

Just the same, Gardner was keeping track of automobile developments. A major one was that the self-starter allowed women to drive by releasing them from the tribulations of cranking. Another was the appearance of the Chevrolet.

Louis Chevrolet, the race driver who beat Barney Oldfield, built the first car bearing his name in 1911. He had the help of William C. Durant, who had lost control of General Motors the year before. Chevrolet lost faith in his car and sold his interest to Durant in 1915, but Durant was building the Chevrolet company with the goal of getting back General Motors.

It also was in 1915 that Gardner came into the automobile picture. The Gardner buggy plant was licensed to assemble Chevrolets in St. Louis. In 1916 the Chevrolet company went after the low-price market with a touring car called the "Four Ninety," which emphasized the $490 price. In 1918 Chevrolet became part of General Motors. Gardner did well. He sold out to General Motors in 1919 for a price reported at $2.5 million. It may have been higher.

He went right back into automobiles, an independent in competition with General Motors. Aiming at a market that paid more than Chevrolet and Ford prices, he brought out the "Gardner Light Four." The Gardner was boosted by the prestige of full-page advertising in the *Saturday Evening Post*. The *Post* ad in the issue of 30 October 1920 said public confidence in Gardner products was so high that 5,372 distributors and dealers had inquired about handling his car before there were any to show them. "Thousands" of Gardners were on the road by the time the ad appeared. Another *Post* advertisement, 27 November 1920, mapped the dealers from coast to coast. In Memphis the Gardner dealer was the Chickasaw Motor Car Company. This ad also pictured Russell E. Gardner, Jr., vice-president for sales.

Gardner automobiles lived through the Roaring Twenties, when it became acceptable for a man to drive a mortgaged car, and when the name of Chrysler appeared. Then came the Great Depression. In 1930 Gardner simply liquidated the Gardner Motor Company and retired again. This time he came back to Memphis. His last home was at 1876 Central where he died at seventy-two on 17 September 1938.

He was considered a wealthy man both here and in Miami. He was also "well connected" in the old phrase, his brother, Fred Gardner, having become governor of Missouri, and his sister's husband, Malcolm Patterson, governor of Tennessee. Several relatives live in Memphis, notably Mrs. Mary Gardner Patterson Phillips, a niece, and Mrs. Lee Gardner, Sr. and her granddaughter, Jan Gardner. Lee Gardner was Russell's cousin and was associated with the motor company. Gardner was also considered gruff. His charity was muted by his custom of giving directly to individuals and requiring that nothing be said about it.

His obituary told of his being superintendent of the Congregational Sunday School in St. Louis. An old clipping says W. C. Handy dedicated "St. Louis Blues" to Gardner. A family tradition says he was the first president of the St. Louis Athletic Club. In the days when only sportsmen bought automobiles, Gardner's sport was backing balloon-racing crews.

At various times he owned several boats. Long before modern roads made it easy to get to Horseshoe Lake he bought a big spread of land near Bruins, Arkansas, for hunting and fishing. Gardner also had an interest in baseball. He bought the Memphis Club of the Southern League in 1914, and immediately sold a controlling interest to his son-in-law, Thomas R. Watkins. The club was run for many years by Watkins, during the time afternoon newspapers put out a baseball edition whenever the final "out" was called and the Memphis Street Railway assembled extra cars to get the crowd home.

Games were played in a Madison Avenue park across the street from Baptist Hospital. In 1922 a fine new diamond with unusually good grandstands was completed by Watkins, who used part of his wife's father's first name in naming it Russwood Park. Russwood Park was built for baseball but it was the big sports arena of the era before Crump Stadium. That was where the Tennessee Doctors displayed their football genius and where big college and prep school games were played in the days when baseball stopped before football began. Wrestlers and fighters also appeared there.

Until destroyed in the Easter night fire of 1960, Russwood Park was a name and location known to everyone. But by the time flames wiped it out almost everyone had forgotten that the "Russ" stood for Russell Gardner who made his first fortune—and his second—in buggies.

Big Insurance

Joseph E. Walker went to Alcorn Agricultural & Mechanical College without either high school credits or money, a seventeen-year-old Negro from the Port Gibson, Mississippi, country. In his struggles for an education he earned money as a teacher in country schools, and eventually took an examination which resulted in his becoming the only black holder of a first grade certificate as a teacher in Jefferson County.

He was graduated in 1903, won an M.D. at Meharry in 1906, and became a doctor in Indianola. He was still penniless but he had credit and kept up a good front. There he met Wayne Cox, husband of Minnie Cox, postmistress at the center of a Theodore Roosevelt uproar. He was the wealthiest Negro in that part of the state and the Cox home was a magnet for other influential blacks.

In 1912 Cox made Walker president of the Delta Penny Savings Bank. In 1917 directors of the Mississippi Life Insurance Company made Dr. Walker president. Assets were $48,000, which rose to $467,000 in 1922. Meanwhile, the company had moved to Memphis in 1920.

There was strong opposition to this move from the established leadership of Beale Street, and from within the company. One of the results was that Dr. Walker founded the Universal Life Insurance Company in 1923, with backing from the wealthy A. W. Willis family. This com-

Joseph E. Walker, MD

pany built a three-story headquarters building at Linden and Wellington, and has grown into a substantial position in Memphis finance. It had $434.3 million of insurance in force in 1978, when the annual premium was $18.6 million. The company does business through thirty-eight offices in ten states, with an $8 million payroll each year.

There once were some white investors and a few whites on the staff, but it is all black now. This insurance company is by far the largest black-owned business in Memphis, and the first to install its own computer. It is the fourth largest black-owned insurance company in the nation. The South's first large subdivision, Riverview, for black homeowners was financed by Universal Life, which has provided financing for several others.

Dr. Walker stepped out front personally as the first black candidate for office in modern Memphis, when he was a candidate for the school board in 1951. His life has been given special attention in *Mississippi Black History Makers,* published in 1977. He also is the subject of a book, *The Driftwood of Bayou Pierre* by T. J. Johnson. He was born on

31 March 1880. Dr. Walker was also the founder (1946) and first president of the Tri-State Bank, at Main and Beale. He died in 1958 and has been succeeded by his son, Maceo.

Invented Here

The invention of the automobile lift is one of the distinctions of Memphis. Until this device appeared mechanics working under a car were in a dirty and awkward position, even if they had a platform on casters and were only changing oil. There were some concrete pits with steps at one end but space was cramped and the pit was likely to accumulate trash and spilled oil and grease. It was a big change to be able to drive an automobile on to a pair of metal tracks and raise it into the air by simply pushing a lever.

Fifty years ago there were repeated newspaper accounts of Peter J. Lunati inventing the lift. He had learned about automobiles and trucks as a soldier assigned to the transportation corps in France during World War I. He opened a little garage and filling station at 1656 Lamar, near the Famous Cafe and a Mr. Bowers' Store.

He undertook to build a better "jack" to make it easier to work upward from beneath a car. His basic ideas was that filling stations had compressors in order to offer air for tires. The air compressors were already there and he undertook to use their pressure on cylinders that would lift the car. There were many difficulties before he had a workable design but it was able to lift only 200 pounds. However, he had a patent by 1925. That was almost the end of the road. For a year he was unable either to sell the patent or to interest men with money in backing him.

Fortunately Lunati's lawyer was Malcolm S. McGehee, partner of Henry Livingston, with offices on the eighth floor of the Exchange Building. McGehee had accepted a quarter interest in the patent as his legal fee.

Among other clients of McGehee was P. F. O'Brien, who had both business experience and capital. McGehee showed O'Brien the patent with the result that O'Brien took an exclusive license for use of the patent, put up the money, and organized the Automobile Rotary Lift Company. The first office was on the eighth floor of the Exchange Building.

The office later was moved to the twelfth floor of the Union Planters Bank Building; B. B. Jones, an associate of O'Brien, became president, and F. M. Henderson, secretary. A plant was built at 1055 Kentucky.

Raymond J. O'Brien later became president and Jones moved to Berry-ville, Virginia.

O'Brien's company had a slow start. It lost $50,000 the first year and doubled the loss the second. It began to make some money the third year, 1928. After 11 years annual sales were still reaching toward $400,000 and the payroll was less than a hundred.

The new manufacturing plant added to the size of local business and made the name of Memphis more widely known. After dropping "Automobile"from its name, in 1936 Rotary Lift moved into elevators and began the expansion which took it into the Dover Corporation in 1958. One of the Dover plants is just across the state line in DeSoto County. The company still makes automobile lifts, but they are a small item in sales and none of the patents is in the name of Lunati.

Lunati was on O'Brien's payroll during parts of 1925 and 1926, as an engineer. A small fraction of the company stock was paid Lunati for the license to use his patent. There were good royalties for several years but Lunati had only a flimsy "mail order patent" which eventually was thrown out in court.

Another man had founded the company that used Lunati's patent. Other men had obtained more important patents in perfecting his idea. But none of this was important to Pete Lunati, a man without ambitions to become a business tycoon. What he wanted was to be a preacher.

Nearness of death on the battlefield of France had made a deep religious impression. He began preaching at YMCA buildings and recreation centers for soldiers. He was jobless when he took off the uniform but he was determined to preach. He prayed for success in making an automobile lift and he promised God the profits and his time if his prayer was granted. "My invention was successful only because God willed it," he said.

The first year of royalties, 1928, opened the way. He put $23,500 into building a church at Manassas and Looney, then furnished it, and became the minister without salary. He promptly provided his family with a good home at 1778 Jackson, including an organ in the living room. He had lived for years at 905 Faxon.

Having provided the church building and a solid income for his family, he was soon putting full time into religious work. He preached every Sunday morning and again Sunday night, and he conducted Thursday prayer meetings. There was talk of an additional Tuesday night service. Mrs. Lunati played the organ at all services, and led a Monday night Bible class.

He called the church the Christian Assembly. It welcomed everyone from all Christian denominations, for Lunati objected to denominational divisions. He also objected to being addressed as "Reverend." After almost seven years he moved on from the Christian Assembly. He was at one time a teacher of the Strand Bible Class, a large interdenominational group meeting in a downtown theater. He became pastor of Ward Memorial Church. He took up evangelistic tours.

When he became ill his son and namesake left Bob Jones College to carry on the evangelism. Peter Lunati, Jr., had become a Baptist minister. In addition to preaching he played the cornet. His three sisters played the vibraphone, accordion, and piano and they all sang as they toured in hundreds of tent meetings, including such cities as Detroit and Washington. They once came back to Memphis and pitched their tent several blocks from the church their father had built. It had passed into the hands of the Salvation Army. Peter Junior later became a pastor at Muscle Shoals, Alabama.

In his later years Peter Lunati had an even bigger dream. In 1935 he bought hundreds of acres of gullies near Holly Springs, Mississippi. He took up scientific farming, with electric power and irrigation on part of the land. He planned to establish a religious training school where students could earn their way on the farm. He talked of a tabernacle. But his life ended on 19 October 1946 before he could live that dream.

Rebels on Rails

In 1935 the Memphis region acquired the proud distinction of becoming home to the South's first streamlined train. It was the second in the nation.

The nation was traveling by rail then—and counting a Pullman trip with drawing room privacy and vast expanses of white napery in the diners as one of the world's highest luxuries, which it was. Just then the newspapers and magazines were full of the newest advance in railroad science, the Burlington Zephyr between Kansas City, Missouri, and Lincoln, Nebraska. It was a train of aluminum, removing a large part of the weight and the rumbling noise of the best previous trains. The locomotives were diesels, quieter, cleaner, and more powerful.

Less than a year after the first Zephyr took up daily service, the Gulf, Mobile & Northern brought this innovation of streamlined trains to the South. People along the tracks from Mobile, through Jackson, Tennessee, to St. Louis rode the supercars at every opportunity.

GM&N Rebel of 1940

This GM&N train was the Rebel. It wore distinctive colors of bright red and silver. Pullman car names included Old Man River, Forrest Park, King Cotton, French Quarter, and Black Gold. These GM&N speedsters led the nation by being the first to add pretty college graduates as stewardesses to the uniformed train crew.

The trains later became known as the Little Rebels because the fleet was increased in 1940 by addition of Big Rebels. For many years a Rebel departed Mobile at 3:15 P.M. and arrived at St. Louis at 8:15 A.M. Another left St. Louis at 6:00 P.M. and got to Mobile at 10:55 A.M. They had met in the middle of the night at Jackson, Tennessee. These were fine trains, fondly remembered in Ripley, Mississippi, Cairo, Illinois, and many another town. But after World War II passenger traffic dried up. Good highways had been built. Persons of ordinary means found it easier to get credit for automobile purchases. And airlines became more reliable. The Little Rebels were retired in February of 1954. The Big Rebels kept on until losses mounted to $4,500 a day. They made their last run on 13 October 1958.

This remarkable railroad was the accomplishment of a most remarkable preacher's boy who became a Jackson, Tennessee, banker and then went into railroading from the top. Isaac Burton Tigrett was his name, but everyone, high and low, called him "Ike." He was so friendly that an old conductor once told him about breaking a rule, explained why, won approval, then asked the head man to say nothing about the incident to any railroad official.

He was born at Friendship, Tennessee, the son of Samuel Tigrett, a Baptist minister. He took his college work at Union University in Jackson. In 1904 he entered banking as cashier of the Bank of Halls, later becoming cashier of the Union & Trust Company of Jackson. He was a thirty-two-year-old bank cashier when a friend asked him to look after the money as treasurer of the Birmingham & Northwestern. Regardless of its ambitious name, this was a line with forty-nine miles of rusty track between Dyersburg and Jackson, with two locomotives, both second-hand. It was suggested that the railroad's name might just as well have been Hell & Seattle. A year later, in 1912, Tigrett was president. The promoter had withdrawn, leaving Tigrett to answer some unhappy stockholders.

Nearly 400 miles away in Mobile, the Gulf, Mobile & Northern put Tigrett on its board of directors in 1917. This line came out of government management after World War I in a badly wounded condition. The board was evenly divided as to which of two experienced railroad men could best solve problems of recuperation. So as a temporary compromise until they could agree on the new president, they put Tigrett in the head chair. It was a temporary job that lasted as long as he lived.

First, the GM&N absorbed the little Birmingham & Northwestern. Second, it took over the Memphis & Meridian, with another name longer than its tracks, which stretched thirty-three miles from Meridian, Mississippi, to Union, Mississippi. Third was a still shorter pair of rails, the Jackson and Eastern, which went on from Union to Lena, Mississippi, fifteen miles. Under Tigrett management the Jackson, Mississippi goal was reached in 1926.

A major enlargement came in 1929 when the New Orleans and Great Northern was leased. This added a Jackson-New Orleans track and put the GM&N in the port of New Orleans, as well as Mobile.

Tigrett management held the expanded lines together through the depression years to the satisfaction of bond holders and other bankers. On this solid foundation in 1940 the GM&N was able to take over by merger the Mobile & Ohio, which was bankrupt. It greatly strengthened GM&N because the M&O tracks had a route connecting Jackson, Mississippi, and Mobile. The two railroads had duplicate lines only a few miles apart. There was even greater strength added to the GM&N by adding M&O tracks into the Midwest at St. Louis. The change was so great that the GM&N changed its name to Gulf, Mobile & Ohio.

The GM&O was a major railroad. It was the first in the United States to become all-diesel, discarding every steam locomotive. It was also notable for operating the Gulf Transport Company, which had bus and truck fleets to complete transportation of both passengers and freight. Either at the beginning or the end of the service on rails, the same ownership offered the highway miles. In replacement of railway mail cars, Gulf Transport had the nation's first highway post office cars. The GM&O also was the first to demonstrate the value to railroad freight business of newspaper and magazine advertising. Tigrett's ideas of modernization went so far as an application for authority to build an air service between New Orleans and Chicago.

By this time the GM&O ancestry included the names of about fifty old railroads, with the biggest addition of all still ahead. Charles B. Stout, Memphis flour dealer and a GM&O director, called to the attention of a reluctant Tigrett the Chicago & Alton, which was old and infirm. Eventually Tigrett accepted the Stout view and a long unraveling of financial tangles began, with the result that in 1947 the GM&O bought the Alton, by assuming Alton debts.

This line served Chicago and the Great Lakes, Kansas City, and the Missouri River area, as well as strengthening the St. Louis service. The combined lines then bought $25 million in new equipment, including 121 diesels. Travelers could board the sleeper in Mobile and go all the way to Chicago. The new name was the Gulf, Mobile and Ohio, Alton Route.

To this was added a Memphis connection. Using Southern Railway tracks, a long train of freight cars left the GM&N tracks at Middleton, Tennessee, each day and rolled toward the big railroad center on the bluff. It was matched, of course, by another long train rolling out of Memphis to the GM&N junction.

The Gulf, Mobile and Ohio, Alton was a big and busy system of rails with almost 3,000 miles of track. It had been stitched together in a mere 35 years, starting with the 49-mile run from Dyersburg into Jackson.

The builder was felled, unexpectedly, by a heart attack 2 May 1954. He left a railroad able to compete for the Great Lakes-Gulf freight. This was also the area served by the Illinois Central, with deepwater ports at New Orleans and Gulfport. That line had come down from Chicago by way of Jackson, Tennessee, and gone down through Jackson, Mississippi, and the middle of that state. It obtained control of other railroads that let its cars run all the way from Chicago to New Orleans in 1873. Then the IC acquired the Huntington rails along the western parts of Kentucky, Tennessee, and Mississippi, which allowed moving of the main line from Jackson, Tennessee, to Memphis in 1896.

Thus formation of the Gulf, Mobile & Ohio system resulted in two routes to the Gulf down the eastern part of Mississippi competing with two other routes in the western part of the same state, operated by the IC. Four parallel lines of rails to the Gulf through Mississippi were abundant, to say it mildly, in a time when passengers had departed. The nation's taxes were building superhighways for trucks, and towboats for barges were being ordered faster than they could be built. So, on 3 October 1967, there was a merger agreement uniting the Gulf, Mobile & Ohio with the Illinois Central. The biggest railroad in Memphis is now the Illinois Central Gulf and the familiar IC has become ICG. The "G" remains as a reminder of the spectacular achievement of Ike Tigrett of Jackson, Tennessee.

Memphis Airline

When aviation was a young and thrilling business, and commercial planes were smaller, Memphis was headquarters for Chicago & Southern Airlines, Incorporated. The pilots and the stewardesses lived here, mechanics tore down the engines and put them together again in an airport hangar built for them, and international advertising announced the head office was at Municipal Airport, Memphis 2, Tennessee.

A timetable dated 9 September 1948 has a map of Chicago and Southern routes in which the original Chicago-Memphis-New Orleans service is almost overbalanced by the other side of an "X" serving Detroit-Indianapolis-Memphis-Little Rock-Houston. But both reach mundane cities compared with the map lines that offer flights from both New Orleans and Houston to Havana, Kingston, Aruba, Curacao, and Caracas. Another route runs from Memphis to Kansas City.

This timetable offers the vacationist "a magic-carpet air lane to romantic New Orleans, glamorous Havana, and Caribbean Islands fabulous in history and charm." It also calls attention to the "New Little Rock Cut-off," saving a full hour between Chicago and Hot Springs. Of course the heavy traffic was to cities on the "X" that crossed at Memphis, advertised by the airline as "gateways to the industrial heart of the United States." Chicago & Southern was also a handy link in the middle of the nation for connections to east-west airlines. It was, in addition, known for careful operations that increased safety. In this timetable are large letters announcing "C & S has had a perfect safety record for over 12 years." After eleven years the company had a clear record for almost 547 million passenger-miles.

Carleton Putnam in 1945

A few weeks before the September timetable, C & S had celebrated its fifteenth birthday on 25 June. It had become a company with 1,320 employees, who were paid $4,426,000 a year, of which $238,000 was the Memphis payroll. It had a net worth of $3 million at the end of 1947. At the start in 1933 the net worth figure had been $114,000, consisting of two five-passenger Bellanca planes. On their sides they bore the words, "Pacific Seaboard Airline." It usually sold three tickets a trip between Los Angeles and San Francisco and usually lost money. A mail contract was refused in Washington. But mail was the foundation of the airline success story.

The Pacific Seaboard line was the brainchild of Carleton Putnam, who had a new law degree from Columbia University when he went to the coast. Putnam had a pilot license and an old Bellanca, and bought another. He had the close association of L. D. "Hap" Anderson, an experienced commercial pilot. For many years Anderson was chief pilot as the new airline expanded. In May of 1934 Putnam bid 17½ cents a mile for the mail contract between Chicago and New Orleans. It was the lowest ever received by the Post Office.

Consequently, the Pacific Seaboard line was moved suddenly to Memphis and doubled in size—by purchase of two more Bellancas. The staff was also strengthened by the addition of R. L. "Doc" Anderson, brother of "Hap," and Bruce Braun. They got mail in the air on 3 June 1934, which met requirements of a $50,000 performance bond. Passengers were added on 13 July. The Chicago & Southern name appeared on 1 February 1935. Business was good and better planes were obtained. The Bellancas were replaced by trimotor Stinsons. The Stinson could carry seven passengers, in place of five, and it could fly at 120 miles per hour, in place of 110.

This business had expanded to one flight daily each way on the Chicago-Memphis-New Orleans route. On 1 April 1935 night flights were added, without a stewardess or a copilot. A Chicago-St. Louis service was added. In the summer of 1935, headquarters was moved from Memphis to St. Louis. It was explained that management was needed nearer the winter weather problems at the northern end of the flights.

Business was so good that bigger and faster planes were needed in 1936. The new Lockheed Electras had seats for 10, space for 500 pounds of mail and speed of 160 miles an hour. The increase in business was marked by such reports as were issued in October of 1936 when, compared with the same month a year before, Memphis passengers were up 110 percent, mail was up 50 percent and express climbed 102 percent in volume and 300 percent in revenue.

In 1939 Chicago & Southern had three flights daily each way on the Chicago-New Orleans run, and was an applicant for a new Memphis-Houston service. This compared with four flights a day by American through Memphis between Newark and Los Angeles. Eastern was flying a Memphis-Birmingham-Tampa run.

Memphis stood out on the airways map as a crossroads. Travelers said the Memphis terminal was better than they found in other cities, including the New York landing at Newark. The whole airport was along the north side of Winchester Road. It was enlarged eastward when the city bought more land and built a hangar to be leased to C & S. The airline was coming back from St. Louis.

The company was much bigger. On 1 May 1940 it had moved up to the fabulous DC-3 classic of reliability which has 21 passenger seats and 170 mile-an-hour speed. The return to Memphis was scheduled for 25 May 1941. While the move was being organized authority was obtained for the run to Houston beginning March 1. In 1945 the Detroit route was added.

Chicago & Southern became an international line in June of 1946, flying to Havana, Kingston, and Caracas and to islands along the way. For flying over the Caribbean the company added the DC-4, which had four engines and fifty seats. In 1948 a Memphis-Kansas City service was started. By 1950 C & S had revenue of almost $13 million a year, of which $856,000 was profit. Only 6 airlines in the United States were larger.

The Putnam efforts came to a kind of culmination in 1948, the year the company was fifteen years old, obtained the Kansas City route and expanded into international flights. That was the year Putnam turned the presidency over to Sidney Stewart, who had been executive vice president. He became board chairman. Putnam and his wife had a home in 1948 at 2220 Union. A short time later he moved to Washington.

In 1953 Chicago & Southern was combined with the smaller Delta line, and consolidated management moved to Atlanta, although the crew base and overhaul operations remained in Memphis for a time. Only four airlines in the United States were larger than the new company.

Putnam's retirement from a highly successful company when he was only fifty-two was a puzzle. But he is an unusual person. Even though he wrote about himself in a book published in 1945, *High Journey: A Decade in the Pilgrimage of an Airline Pioneer,* he was quiet, contemplative, and reserved. Some newspapermen came to the conclusion that it was a case of a man who had found sociology and writing more interesting than the day-to-day running of an airline, and more important to him than compiling a larger fortune. It also was a situation in which a man could afford to do what he wanted to do.

Born in New York, he was educated at St. Paul's New York Military Academy and St. John's Military Academy. He went to Princeton where he won a degree in science in 1924, honors in history and politics, and the distinction of being editor of the literary magazine, *Nassau.* There followed some foreign travel, work in a New York law office, a year in the law school at Harvard, some New York politics, and some research on Southwestern pioneers. He went back to study at the Columbia law school in 1930, from which he was graduated with a law degree in 1932.

But by then he had been attracted to air transportation. He flew his own plane to the West Coast to examine possibilities. He was in the office of the Lockheed Aircraft Corporation one day in May of 1933, when the first commercial transport was still in the Lockheed shop. Robert Gross, president of Lockheed, asked Putnam, ''Why don't you start an airline?'' So he did.

When his restless mind turned from the airline to sociology and history, the change was more gradual. Yet he was back in the news following publication of a long letter on the editorial page of *The Commercial Appeal* on 10 November 1958 and in some other papers about the same time. In fact there was a Putnam Letter Committee in Birmingham sponsoring widespread publication of the letter. In it, this famous businessman with a New York background attacked both the Supreme Court reasoning on schools segregated by race and the theory that Negro accomplishment was determined entirely by environment.

The public hears few of the airline details that once were daily news, but within the Delta organization are several men who began their climb in Chicago & Southern uniforms. Carleton Putnam is still on the board of directors of Delta. The chairman of the board is W. T. Beebe, who was a C & S official in Memphis.

5
Some of Our Best

Fame of an Artist

A Memphis girl who grew into fame as a painter in Paris became a big name in the news of 1904-05. She was Katherine Augusta Carl, whose friends called her "Kate." Hers was the first portrait ever done of Hsiao-ch'in, Dowager Empress of China. It was exhibited at the World's Fair in St. Louis, where it attracted a good deal of attention both as a portrait of an unusual person and because it was delivered by members of the royal family and constantly protected by two kneeling guards.

The artist became much more famous when English newspapermen mixed their ideas of the "Tiger Lady" of Oriental politics with Miss Carl's ideas on her return to the West. In the news accounts she lambasted her hosts when she actually had been favorably impressed. In corrections, she wrote of her experiences in the Summer Palace at Peking. The public interest was like attention given to President Nixon when his trip allowed reporters and cameramen to penetrate the modern Bamboo Curtain around Chinese mysteries. But the curtains Miss Carl opened showed a still more closely guarded royal court of exotic splendors.

Miss Carl's window into the ancient Manchu world began to open in the October 1905 issue of *Century Magazine*. Hers was the leading

大清國慈禧皇太后

The Empress Dowager by Kate Carl

article in this prestigious publication, loaded with advertisements for books, schools, pianos, and automobiles like the Pope electric from Indianapolis and the air-cooled Franklin from Syracuse. The opening article was given twenty pages, with five full pages of the artist's work. Other articles followed in the November and December issues, and then it came out in book form, titled *The Empress Dowager*.

Kate Carl told of a charming little woman, a thoughtful hostess with amazing youthfulness. Seeing the Empress before being presented, the artist supposed she was some member of the court in her forties. She was almost seventy, without a line in her face and without a touch of cosmetics. This unlined face is the high point of her portrait, almost unbelievable at her age but true to life.

While it was still unusual in the West, the Empress smoked, both a water pipe and cigarets in very long holders. Dignitaries were carried about the huge grounds in "palace chairs," six men lifting the poles of each chair. Eunuchs, "a dozen or more" of them, were assigned to wait on the visiting artist. When the empress went boating her barge was towed by big yellow ropes from two boats, in each of which twenty-four rowers stood. Sitting was forbidden in the presence of the empress under any circumstance, except that in the throne room cushions could be used on the floor.

Palace meals included such delicacies as shark fins, deer sinews, fish brains, shrimp eggs, and the famous geese and ducks. Rice came from a side table. Tea was never served with meals. There was heated wine casually available during the meal. The tea came afterward, without either milk or sugar.

Kate Carl was told she was the first resident in the Palace from the West since Marco Polo. She lived there eleven months and, although none had been done before, eventually painted four portraits.

This strange world of concubines, marble, elaborate wooden carvings, jade and jewels worth millions was unfolded by a woman born in New Orleans and reared in Memphis. Her father was Captain Francis Augustus Carl, a tourist from Germany when he met a tourist from Ireland, Miss Mary Bredon. He organized a company for the Confederacy and was killed in the war. The young widow came to Memphis to teach at the State Female College. She taught English and eventually became head of the school, sometimes being spoken of as the "lady president."

This school had been founded in 1858 at McLemore and a new street named College. It had quickly attracted daughters of wealthy families from several states. It was occupied by Yankee troops during the war and General Nathan Bedford Forrest fought a skirmish there during the raid into Memphis in 1864. The main building stood until 1957.

There had been several changes in ownership when Kate Carl was graduated in 1882. She had shown artistic talents. One of her mother's relatives was Sir Robert Hart, then on the British diplomatic staff at Paris. He took her into his household and she became a student of art in Paris. She attained membership in the *Société Nationale des Beaux Arts,* the International Society of Women Painters, the International Jury of Fine Arts, and the International Jury of Applied Arts. In 1883 and for ten years thereafter she exhibited her paintings at the *Salon des Artists Français.*

At one stage in her career she came back to Memphis and opened a studio in a building at Main and Madison. But she moved on to her own studio on Washington Square in New York. And then she returned to Paris for many years.

Meantime, Sir Robert had also taken an interest in her brother, Francis, who had been born in Osyka, Mississippi. The brother entered the customs service of China and rose to become a commissioner, as well as a mandarin of the second degree.

Kate Carl was visiting her brother in Shanghai when the wife of the ambassador from the United States at Peking prevailed upon the Empress to break the taboo against pictures of royalty. Resistance was overcome with word that Queen Victoria's picture would be at the St. Louis Fair. So Miss Carl went to the Summer Palace and at the hour chosen by scholars of the court with the aid of calendars and almanacs she was standing at her canvas before the Double Dragon Throne when all eighty-five clocks in the room chimed, struck gongs, and played tunes to announce the time for the artist to begin her charcoal outline.

Kate Carl returned to Memphis for the first time in twenty-seven years just before Christmas in 1930. For a week she was the guest of Mrs. Alston Boyd of 1560 Central for a round of luncheons and parties with her schoolmates. She again had a studio in New York when she died on 3 December 1938. She was in her eighties.

During the years there had been a dwindling of interest in the Dragon Throne. But when the Empress died she was buried in a casket filled with jewels worth millions, which were described at column length in *The New York Times* when grave robbers stole them. The picture at the St. Louis Fair had been given to the United States government. Visitors to the Smithsonian Institution can see it to this day. The yellow silk embroidered covering in which it traveled is more often seen than the portrait, for it is used as the background for display of historic documents in the Smithsonian.

At least once the portrait has been taken from Washington and displayed for throngs, at the Chicago World's Fair of 1933, still in its intricately carved camphor wood frame. The frame alone had a value of $40,000 in 1904.

The popular favorite among her works here probably is her painting of three children blowing soap bubbles. It hung in the home of Mrs. D. P. Hadden, whose husband was head of the Memphis municipal government. Later it was seen for many years in the Vance Avenue home of Mrs. Wharton Jones.

When Florence McIntyre reviewed Memphis art for the West Tennessee Historical Society in 1953 she found three other Carl paintings, in the homes of Mrs. Daisy Neely Mallory, Mrs. Neely Grant, and Mrs. Elizabeth Falls Maury. Most familiar to modern viewers is the Kate Carl portrait of Mrs. S. H. Brooks in a riding habit, sometimes displayed near the entrance to Brooks Memorial Art Gallery.

The generation of young ladies of Memphis who were taught art by Miss Carl, in Memphis and in Paris, is gone. But she left a deep impression. Her talents and personality were frequently brought to the attention of students of Mrs. Annie Stephenson Morgan, an outstanding teacher of art here. Miss Carl had taught Mrs. Morgan.

More directly, during her many years in France, Kate Carl helped young people from the United States, especially girls from Memphis. There were several of them, including Bessie and Martha Boyd, Frances and Minnie Lee Falls, Lillie Dunn and Bessie Vance. Miss Carl spent months traveling in Europe with Miss Vance, to the great advantage of modern Memphis. Miss Vance became the wife of S. H. Brooks and in his memory she gave the Brooks Gallery to this city. Kate Carl was one of the original trustees of Brooks Memorial and she continued on the board for many years. In addition she was one of three jurors named to rule on acceptability of works of art offered to the Brooks collection.

Kate Carl was a good artist. She benefited many other persons. She was influential in the founding of the cultural jewel of the Brooks Gallery. It is odd that such a person should be best remembered for what she wrote about Manchu China.

The Gallery Brooks

Brooks Memorial Art Gallery is, in one way, the result of a fortune made by Hamilton Brooks as a Front Street cotton factor. In another way the art gallery is the fruit of the love for fine art taught to Bessie Vance by a Memphis painter who attained recognition after moving to France. The words "Brooks Memorial" are often spoken both because of the art displayed there and the architectural jewel of a building that adorns Overton Park. Yet hardly anyone can tell who Brooks was.

His full name was Samuel Hamilton Brooks and he was known in the family as "Hamilton." He came into the fast-growing town on the bluff in 1858 at the age of twenty-four. His brother William, two years older, was already here in the firm of Brooks & McCall. He had been here about two years when war came. Although he had been reared at Marietta, Ohio, and his family background was in Massachusetts, Hamilton Brooks put on the gray uniform.

Back from war, Brooks went into a new firm, Brooks, Neely and Company. His partners were J. C. and H. M. Neely. In its early years the firm was at 276 Front (old numbering) but it was moved southward to 367 Front, where it stayed many years. This business is often described briefly as "wholesale grocers." But if there is enough space there are the added words, "cotton factors, commission merchants, liquor dealers." The meaning was that his firm, and others like it, furnished on credit everything needed by a cotton grower and his store serving the tenants and then sold the crop for him. The Brooks, Neely firm prospered. Hamilton Brooks moved "out east" to 348 Jefferson Extended (old numbering). He was accustomed to living well.

The Brooks family had come from England to Chelsea, Massachusetts, in 1636. John Brooks I had a line of sailing vessels in the Boston–Havre (France) trade. John Brooks II married the daughter of a Paris banker. Hamilton Brooks's father, Samuel, married Mary Malissa Dodge of Beverly, Ohio. Her family had come from England to Salem, Massachusetts, in 1626, even before the Brookses. Her grandfather, John Dodge I, was a partner in a mill that was the "first company formed in the Ohio country for any purpose whatever." He accumulated great wealth, for the times.

Hamilton Brooks was only four when his father died in Texas. His mother and her three sons returned to his grandfather's home in Ohio. It was an elegant home, but the New England background required hard work of every member of the family and put emphasis on religious training. It was from this home that Brooks came to Memphis and made

Hamilton Brooks (by Cecelia Beaux, in Brooks Memorial
Art Gallery).

his own fortune. His huge home at 674 Jefferson had tall magnolias in
the yard and an iron fence. The spiral staircase was three floors high.
The vast expanse of the parlor was matched by a fireplace, and above the
mantel, a mirror that reached toward the ceiling.

Brooks retired from the cotton factoring business in 1897, when he
was sixty-three. He continued to be vice-president of First National
Bank, and of the Bluff City Insurance Company.

His wife died the next year. She was the former Lida Ballance of
Cincinnati. There were four children, but three died while young. In
1902 he married again. The second Mrs. Brooks was Bessie Vance,
daughter of Calvin and Margaret Vance. She was about thirty-four.

Bessie Vance had advantages of the best in schools. She was one of
several Memphis girls sent to France for guidance in art by Katherine
Carl. Miss Vance's parents arranged for this artist to take Bessie on a
tour of months in the famous European galleries, especially in Italy. The
Kate Carl influence remained strong in the life of Mrs. Brooks, as long
as the artist lived.

Mr. Brooks died in 1912. Less than a year later Mrs. Brooks had arranged with the Park Commission to give the memorial art gallery to the city. She specified that Kate Carl was to be a trustee of the Brooks Memorial. A Kate Carl painting of Bessie Vance as a young woman sometimes is hung near the entrance, although another painting of her is more often displayed.

Mrs. Brooks planned to provide $100,000, but alterations raised the cost to $115,000. James Gamble Rogers of New York designed the white Georgia marble structure. It was formally presented to the people of Memphis, fully paid for, by Mrs. Brooks in 1916.

While the gift was by Mrs. Brooks, it was characteristic of him. He was one of the first to contribute when businessmen got together the fund with which the Court Square fountain was built. Mrs. Brooks wrote of him: "He was full of sympathy and charity for this fellow men, especially those in sickness and sorrow. . . . He was social, loving; though quiet and gentle, always responsive . . . under all conditions a gentleman, devoted to his city of adoption, public spirited, giving liberally to every good cause. . . . He disliked above all things display, and always impressed us with his sincerity, honesty and highest ideals of life."

Mrs. Brooks moved to Daytona Beach, Florida, in 1918. She lived to be seventy-five, dying on 5 December 1943. The nearest relatives were two nephews and a niece of Mr. Brooks. The niece, Mrs. D. T. Schoolfield, who was Edith Brooks, wrote a little more than three pages about Brooks and his family in 1921. It is all the record there is of his career and it has to be supplemented by research in old newspapers and city directories. But the short record in writing is greatly enhanced by the white marble memorial in the park.

Persuasive General

In 1879 there was an assembly in St. Louis of some of the former leaders of Memphis who had been scattered by the yellow fever disaster of the year before. The question was whether Memphis could be saved. Gloomy speakers held the floor. There were talks by refugees who were prepared to stay in other cities. It seemed that Memphis would have to be abandoned. There was a sudden interruption when Luke E. Wright stood up and proposed that it be "resolved that Memphis be recreated and rebuilt by the people of Memphis." He was a lawyer, already prominent at thirty-three, who had stayed in Memphis and taken responsibilities for helping fever victims. When he learned the refugees were meeting he went to St. Louis to stem the tide.

Luke E. Wright

Luke Wright was persuasive. The pessimism of the former leaders of Memphis, who were considering seriously surrendering the city to yellow fever, was swept away. His resolution was adopted and enthusiasm took over. Committees were named and responsibilities assigned in St. Louis. Memphis was on its way toward a future many times greater than it had known before the fever.

By the time Luke Wright died the St. Louis incident was only a small part of his obituary. The J. P. Young *Standard History of Memphis* (1912) tells of the St. Louis decisions without special attention to Wright. Instead there is an extensive account of his part in standing off a mob that threatened to take over food at yellow fever relief headquarters when a Negro bully challenged a militiaman, also Negro, and was killed. The passing of many years has obscured his part in the Civil War, his outstanding position as a lawyer, and his several contributions to the building of Memphis, as well as the yellow fever chapter.

Earlier distinctions in his life were diminished in memory, even more than by the passing years, by Wright's own prominence in national affairs. In 1900, when the United States was for the first time finding how to govern a colony, Wright was named to the Philippine Commission. He later became president of the commission, then civil governor and in 1905 governor-general.

Then he was named the first ambassador from the United States to Japan. There were difficulties because of the newness of diplomatic relations between the countries, because Japan had just become a world power by defeating Russia, and because California wanted to shut out Japanese immigrants. His solution was an agreement that certain classes of immigrants be turned back from the United States, and Japan could bar the same classes arriving from the United States. (His military aide in Japan was John J. Pershing, who later commanded the army in World War I.) The ambassador found that the Japanese looked upon us as their oldest friends. He established a basis for good relations.

President Theodore Roosevelt called him to Washington as secretary of war. It was an extraordinary combination of a Republican president and a Confederate veteran, but Wright had been "Good Old Luke" to Roosevelt for years. Wright was a "Gold Democrat," who left the party when William Jennings Bryan and the silver advocates took over.

There was also an unusual situation of an old artilleryman, with a lifelong interest in cannon, being secretary of war just at the time aircraft enthusiasts were claiming that planes would be used in future wars. But he was one of the first public officials to accept the theory and encourage the experimenters.

When Roosevelt left the White House in 1909, Wright returned to his law firm and business interests in Memphis. It was a major law office.

Wright had started fast, as the son of a former chief justice of the Tennessee Supreme Court, with his father as his principal teacher. His father, Archibald Wright, had plantations in Mississippi and had practiced law there before he moved his farming and law offices to West Tennessee. He became a member of the Tennessee high court in 1858 and remained until 1863, when the war brought suspension. He followed his sons to war.

Luke was a Memphis school boy of fifteen when his older brother, Eldridge, joined the artillery. Luke was too young to be a soldier but he went with his brother and in June of 1861 he was enlisted. He became a second lieutenant of artillery.

He was at Shiloh, Stone River, Chickamauga, Franklin, Nashville, and other battles in the western theater of war. He saw his brother killed. He was wounded near Atlanta and regained consciousness in a hospital where another wounded man told him there was gangrene. This so frightened him that he walked out of the hospital and went back to war. With the guns silenced he went to Ole Miss for a literary course and at the same time began to read law under his father. Instead of finishing at the university he turned to the law full time and became his father's partner. In 1869 he married Katherine Semmes, daughter of Admiral Raphael Semmes, hero of the Confederate Navy.

Local fame came to him in 1870. He broke through the ring of carpetbaggers who held city-county offices, following management by the U.S. Army. He became a candidate for prosecutor even though the opposing candidate was a Republican and Irish, at a time when the Irish vote of North Memphis was of high importance. It was a surprise and an abrupt change in politics for the twenty-four-year-old lawyer to win the election. After eight years as attorney general he was ''General Wright'' for the rest of his life.

He turned to private practice as the partner of T. B. Turley, also the son of a Tennessee Supreme Court member. Turley, years later, became a U.S. Senator. The firm was engaged in some of the biggest cases of the times, but Luke Wright also used his talents in public services. He had a substantial part in forming the laws under which the temporary taxing district took charge in place of city government and, years later, in establishing the legal base for returning to municipal government.

A service of the highest importance to the public came in 1890 when horse cars were giving way to electric trolleys, two companies were competing, and both were running down. A. M. Billings of Chicago had loaned some money for Memphis streetcar operation and decided he would take a loss and get out. Wright went to see him, told him how Memphis was growing and obtained a promise that Billings would come to Memphis and see for himself.

Billings came and looked around for several days. Billings saw a future bigger and brighter than those who lived here saw. He said it was the Chicago of the future. He said he would keep his money here and put in a great deal more on condition Wright would agree to be attorney for the company.

This was also the beginning of the Memphis Driving Park, the ''fastest track in the world,'' home of Dan Patch, most famous of all harness race horses, and scene of the Memphis Gold Cup races.

Billings was old and soon died but his money and his son, A. K. G. Billings, moved in strong with Frank Jones in charge of operations. They bought all of the streetcar companies, set up the organizations that prospered as the Memphis Street Railway Company and the Memphis

Power & Light Company, and gave Memphis a popular trolley service ahead of other cities of its size.

When the Mercantile Bank got into trouble, Wright undertook to make good the losses of poor depositors. He put up some of his own none-too-ample money and talked others into joining him. The fund paid in full each depositor with less than $1,000 at stake, and part of the larger deposits. This led to reorganization and reopening of the bank. When Wm. R. Moore wobbled in its early days, Wright took a large part in changes which led to growth of the huge wholesale dry goods firm. He led the campaign which raised funds for building the Y.M.C.A. building.

It was this kind of helpfulness to the city rather than offices he held that caused *The Commercial Appeal* to say in his obituary " . . . he did more for the city of Memphis than any other man that ever lived or died in it."

The opinion was reenforced by the fact that Luke Wright was one of the original investors in the Commercial Publishing Company, owner of the newspaper, and a director. His home was on Jessamine, a block south of Beale, near Lauderdale, until he moved to the northwest corner of Jefferson and Orleans, the residence being restored by his great-grandson. There he fell on the stairs at the age of seventy-six. Although he lingered a month before his death, on 17 November 1922, he knew the end was near and calmly accepted it.

Most Distinguished

War came down hard on Charlotte Moffett Gailor. The conflict was new when she heard the big naval guns booming in the Memphis harbor (6 June 1862) as the Yankee fleet overwhelmed the Confederates and took over the city. She had given up her home in town and moved with two small children to live with friends in the suburb of Chelsea when her husband went to war. He had been city editor of *The Daily Memphis Avalanche,* an ancestor of *The Commercial Appeal.* A few months later some men came to notify her that Major Frank M. Gailor had been killed in the battle of Perryville (8 October 1862).

Less than two weeks afterward her baby girl, slightly more than a year old, became ill with a "congestive fever." Blue-clad soldiers in the picket lines around the town refused to let the doctor through the line at night. The baby died in her arms. Next day she was standing beside the little casket when a squad of Federals pushed her out of the way to get to

Thomas F. Gailor, 1893

the coffin. They lifted the lid to see if weapons were hidden there. She fainted and fell to the floor.

A young woman of ordinary strength of character would have been defeated and the life of her little boy blighted. But there was more, much more, and she kept her chin up as he obtained a superior education and grew into the famous Bishop Thomas F. Gailor. First, she was determined to find how her husband died, and whether he had made any arrangements with fellow officers for disposing of his affairs. Her efforts produced nothing, so she took her boy to stay temporarily with her mother in Cincinnati, and set out by herself to find the answers on the battlefield.

She learned nothing, returned to Memphis, and decided she had to talk to Confederate officials. That required her to make her way through the Union lines to get to Jackson, Mississippi. This was accomplished in a spring wagon, with her son riding on a casket carrying the brother of a friend. The Yankees bombarded Jackson and Mrs. Gailor had to live for weeks in a tent on the bank of the Pearl River. The little fellow had to pick weevils out of cornmeal before they could eat.

Eventually she got back to Memphis and, in the late summer of 1863, she once more set out on a journey to find out about her husband. This time she went by rail to Chattanooga, an attractive young woman accompanied only by a small boy, on a train full of soldiers and roughly dressed men. As the train neared a tunnel at Sewanee a friend, who was a quartermaster, handed her a satchel. He said it held the pay for soldiers and he expected some of the toughs to try to get it in the tunnel darkness. The darkness had hardly closed in when she called for the boy to help. A hand was trying to jerk the satchel away. He reached up, found the grasping hand and bit into the straining flesh with all of the strength of his seven-year-old jaws.

They saved the soldiers' pay. She eventually learned the facts of Major Gailor's heroic death. She even recovered his sword, with the help of a Confederate woman spy. She devoted the same iron determination to rearing her son and getting for him the best possible education.

The high school grades were new to public schools of Memphis then, and Tom Gailor was the first boy to be graduated, in 1872. He was three months shy of sixteen. For a year he worked for W. & S. Jack and Company, learning the selling of queensware, studying Greek in odd moments, and reciting to the high school principal at night. The yellow fever of 1873 struck him down and killed his doctor. He was a little late when he got to Racine College in Wisconsin. But he had saved enough money for first-year expenses and his entrance examinations went so well that he was enrolled as a sophomore.

In 1876 he was graduated, the valedictorian of his class and the winner of the Greek prize, which provided fifty dollars of his enrollment fees at the General Theological Seminary in New York. But he got to New York with barely ten dollars for two weeks of living expenses before the school opened. Walking through the Bowery he saw some men and boys in a big fight, wrote a story about it, and sold his account to the *Evening Telegram* for ten dollars, which pulled him through the emergency.

Studies went well with him and so did his social life. But he was less successful in efforts to give up his pipe. He was graduated from the seminary without examinations, again won the Greek prize, and was ordained by Bishop Quintard in 1879. His first assignment was the Messiah Parish in Pulaski, Tennessee, at $600 a year. As he announced the text of his first sermon, the fire bell rang, and the entire congregation departed. With the fire attended to, the people came back, the young priest read his sermon, and his career was launched.

His parish labors were brief, although remembered with affection all his life. In 1882 he began his many years of building the University of the South, at Sewanee, Tennessee. He taught and was chaplain for eight years, before becoming vice-chancellor in 1890. Three years later (1893) he became a bishop coadjutor of Tennessee, and in 1898, bishop. His title on the Sewanee campus was chancellor from 1909 on.

Sewanee was a young college when he first appeared there. First classes had been held in a log building in 1866. There were only nine students in 1868. Education of all kinds was having a hard time in those years. But Tom Gailor was totally convinced that college education was of high importance, and that Sewanee could be a superior college. He devoted extra effort to building up library service to a university level. Helping the boys gave him real pleasure and he appreciated the view and the air on "the mountain." The affection was returned by the students.

When he brought his bride, Ellen Douglas Cunningham, to the campus in 1885, he had only been there three years but the students met the bridal couple at the railroad station with bonfires and cannon fire salutes. They unhitched the horses so they could push and pull the carriage to their home, a mile away and uphill.

In 1891 he was unanimously elected bishop of Georgia. He was only thirty-five and had been vice-chancellor merely a year. Gloomy foreboding overhung the campus for weeks until one morning he said he had decided to stay and the student body went into a day-long celebration.

He had a summer home at Sewanee and spent a large part of his time there during the long years his duties required him to live in Memphis. He moved when he became coadjutor. As bishop he lived in the official house near St. Mary's Cathedral. The Bishop was a citizen of Memphis and undertook many civic responsibilities, such as serving on the Cossitt Library Board from 1904 onward. Yet when he was in Memphis, or New York, or England, he seemed to be looking forward to his return to Sewanee.

Important as Sewanee was to him, he was still young when he attracted widespread attention for other activities. He drew the admiration of J. P. Morgan, the big money man, as early as 1892. He was a leading figure in the defeat of the revised version of the Bible in the convention of 1904. Bishop Gailor became especially widely known as an opponent of prohibition. When he finally wrote out his attitude, one paragraph said:

> . . . Every community should be left free to decide this question for itself, and my advice would be that the decision ought to be reached by a practical unanimity of opinion, for two reasons, viz:
> 1. Because such a drastic law as Prohibition, imposing a special theory of morals

upon a community, adopted by a bare majority vote, must become a provocation of deception and lying and disrespect of law, which are worse than intemperance, and (2) because intemperate legislation is as bad as intemperate use of food and drink.

The bishop for Memphis became a figure in world news when the structure of the Episcopal Church was reorganized under the Presiding Bishop and Council, the first name for what became the National Council of the Episcopal Church. Bishop Gailor became the first presiding bishop in 1919 and held office until 1925.

As the premier bishop he preached in cathedrals in England, was an outstanding leader in church conferences, and an associate of presidents, kings, and princes of the commercial world. His mother would have had abundant reason to be proud of the man who grew from the boy of her difficult years.

Incomplete details of his life and work are available in *Some Memories,* published in 1937. The book is a compilation of some of his writings and some start-and-stop notations for a diary. He refused to write a book about himself, and directed the destruction of sermon manuscripts. Other details are found in obituaries, appearing when he died at Sewanee, 3 October 1935. (His birthdate was 17 September 1856.)

The Commercial Appeal called him ''Memphis's most distinguished and best loved citizen.'' Bishop Gailor seemed to be taller and broader than ordinary men, partly because he carried himself so erectly. He moved with dignity and spoke with reassurance in an impressive voice. He was eloquent, forceful, and courageous in the opinion of those who knew him well.

His admiration for the English included buying the equipment with which cricket was introduced to the general seminary campus. He wore suits tailored in London. He used ''(Oxon.)'' after his ''D. D.'' His son, Frank Hoyt Gailor, was a Rhodes scholar who went to war in the British army before the United States entered World War I. Ellen, one of the bishop's three daughters, married the son of President Cleveland.

Yet for all of his association with the high and mighty, he was sympathetic and helpful. In the final years of his life Memphis had some churchless and cynical newspapermen with instant doubts about the sincerity of conspicuous personalities. But they gave high marks to Bishop Gailor and some of them, after personal contact, admired him intensely.

Beyond the dates and the details there was an ambience that shines through the words of a churchman recalling the time when Gailor was a young teacher and Sewanee students were just college boys. He wrote:

> When one Lent early in his chaplaincy he announced a daily twilight service . . . the prudent faculty was alarmed. What disorder would not break loose! But nothing of the sort.
>
> Into the dark church the whole student body filed out of the twilight. One could hear a pin drop or a field mouse run. The tall, cassocked figure stole out into the dark chancel, kneeled at his prayer desk, and read by the light of the candle noble prayers in gorgeous vibrant tones, emphasized by interruptions of silence, and after a benediction withdrew.
>
> The most defiant came, the most indifferent. They were not going to be left out. Not they! For this was not a compulsory service, but just Chaplain Tom's private Lenten devotion.

Great and Gracious

Nellie Angel Smith, an outstanding educator for many years, had to overcome extreme difficulties to get her own education. When she was a five-year-old in Horse Cave, Kentucky, her mother died. Her grandfather taught her some reading, spelling, and arithmetic but she was sickly. And she was nine before she entered school at Bear Wallow, Kentucky. She was twenty-two before she won her high school diploma.

She was thirty-nine and had been out of high school seventeen years before she was graduated from college. She had to slowly accumulate college credits in summer school while teaching. Just out of high school her pay was fifteen dollars a month for a five-month year, although the pay improved as she became a high school teacher. Having attained her college degree, she took up graduate studies and won her Ph.D.

She thus was forty-five years old, with white hair pinned on top above a frail but erect frame, when she first stepped down from the train at Normal Station in 1927. She taught until 1952, when she retired to her Kentucky home. She was almost ninety-five when she died in 1976.

She was instantly conspicuous in Memphis. She had the only Ph.D. on the Teachers College faculty. She had been the first woman to win a doctorate at Peabody. She had been the first woman to win the Rockefeller Foundation Award for Advanced Study. She had been awarded a lifetime teacher certificate at Western State Teachers College, at Bowling Green, now Western Kentucky State College. Dr. Smith's activities were diverse, including being dean of women, but she was first of all a teacher, an exceptionally good teacher of Latin. She was

Nellie Angel Smith, PhD

thoroughly experienced in teaching when she came to Memphis, including nineteen years of teaching Latin.

Her grandfather, Angel, an Alsatian, was her first teacher and must have built into her mind a profound belief in the value of learning as well as an unlimited faith in what can be accomplished by determination. With only her high school diploma she first taught a one-room school at Frenchman's Knob, Kentucky. Then she returned home to teach six years at Horse Cave High School. She was then awarded a scholarship at Bowling Green Normal. There followed six years at Madisonville (Kentucky) High School, and four years at Bristol (Tennessee) High School.

This was the teaching she did while accumulating college credits in the summer school at Peabody, where she became a protege of Dr. Charles E. Little. Having obtained her college degree, she taught at the State Normal School, Florence, Alabama, between terms at Peabody in pursuit of her M.A. and Ph.D. The Alabama Department of Education named her an outstanding teacher. Even after attaining her high position on the Memphis campus, she continued to be an ordinary teacher at Peabody during the summer schools. She liked to teach. She was enthusiastic about Latin. She had the ability to make young men and women see what she saw in the Roman world and its language.

Nellie Angel Smith was especially notable for her attitude toward athletes. In place of the common idea that athletes are poor students, she insisted they were all good students if they had the time. She thought it was unfair to expect them to study when they had been worn out in practice or in games. It was her idea that the school, having made extra demands on athletes, should make extra arrangements for them to study and have examinations while they were fresh. During times of high stress in athletics she excused athletes from assignments and on weekends she conducted makeup sessions in dormitory parlors.

Dr. Smith also had a theory that classroom failures were as likely to be due to poor teaching as to dull students. She thought teachers who tried hard enough could usually salvage the slow students, instead of taking the easy road of failing them. She also came to believe that practically any student who came to her from a West Tennessee high school was able to do satisfactory work.

Beyond these special considerations, Dr. Smith was known from one edge of the campus to the other as an "easy grader." One of the results was the unlikely sight of the whole football squad signing up for Latin. The boys liked her and tried to please her. Some of them surmounted the difficulties of Latin so well that they became outstanding students.

Most dramatic of her innovations was a Latin tournament, for which hundreds of teachers she had trained brought their best students to the campus each spring. In 1929, the first year, there were eighty-seven high school students competing in Latin. It was popular, a kind of reunion for the teachers, a trip to Memphis for the students, a chance to win honors and loving cups, displays of recreated equipment used by the people of ancient Rome, as well as the examinations and contest in the use of their language.

The numbers grew until thousands took part each year. The list of prize winners expanded until it required almost half a newspaper page. Then it was expanded into a statewide event with district winners going to Nashville. The state tournament was a victim of World War II, but the Mid-South contest has continued with the help of Memphis public school Latin teachers. It had such a hold that it is almost a tradition already. Dr. Smith is gone but the tournament goes on, now getting the special attention of Dr. Roy Watkins, emeritus professor of foreign languages at Memphis State University.

Dr. Smith also organized a campus Latin club which produced a classic play in costume each year. When she retired Dr. Smith was dean of the department of modern and classical languages.

She was even more widely known as dean of women, which she was for twenty years beginning in 1927. She was old-fashioned and she was strict. Either she or the college president had to know the young men who were allowed to escort her girls. Dormitory girls were forbidden to be on the streets after 6:00 P.M. without an approved escort or chaperone. But sometimes when the rules seemed about to force a girl to stay home, Dean Nellie was known to send for a reliable college boy and slip into his hand the expense money.

A line of dating couples often marched to the Normal Theater, with Dean Smith marching behind as rear guard, to be sure they went to the movie. She often walked with a crowd of girls to the Messick gymnasium, when Normal games were played there. She had a squeaky rocking chair just outside the dormitory parlor. When the chair stopped squeaking the dating girls knew the dean was up and making an inspection. She had a police whistle for summoning the night watchman, and she had strong doubts about the intentions of all young men except those enrolled at Memphis State.

It was her belief that bobbysox and chewing gum must be left behind when a young woman changed from a girl to a lady in her college years. The girls overwhelmed her on those two points. Perhaps she was more popular with the mothers than with the girls, but for the most part Dean Smith had at least the admiration of students. She was a counselor to many, sometimes a confidant, and at intervals a refuge of last resort. Her salary was never adequate by today's standards, but she was accustomed to austere living and she always had a little something available to help a worthwhile person stay in school.

She also had a little extra strength to allow her to be the favorite substitute for other faculty members. She also found time to be purchasing agent for the dining hall. Before she came to Memphis she wrote a book on Latin elements in the Bible and Shakespeare, but she had doubts about faculty members who used part of their energy to write in hope of recognition or a job on a bigger campus.

Her book won the recognition of being used as a text at Heidelberg University, yet her memory is better preserved in several other ways. She had the distinction of a biography with her picture in the *West Tennessee Historical Society Papers* of 1967, done by James R. Chumney, Jr., of the Memphis State faculty. A women's dormitory bears her name. There is a Latin scholarship in her name at Memphis State and there is the annual Latin tournament. She was a devoted worker in Lindenwood Christian Church. She accumulated some very fine furniture and left it to the university. And there are the thousands of students she influenced. When she retired in 1952 a testimonial dinner was given at which the conclusion was that Nellie Angel Smith was a "great scholar, great teacher, and gracious lady."

She Advocated College

At a glance, the great distinction of the life of Miss Willie C. Johnson was her service with the Red Cross in Italy during the First World War. It was a distinction for the Memphis teacher. It also is an almost forgotten item in history, when the people of the United States through the Red Cross moved a mountain of food, clothing, blankets, and medical supplies to aid the people of Italy. Refugees by the hundreds of thousands poured out of the northern mountains after military reverses.

Men, women, children, and newborn babies wrapped in newspapers for lack of cloth of any kind, overflowed the towns near the war front and then the cities. The single idea was to move southward, as far toward the toe of the Italian boot as they could get. Helping them flee was the objective of the government, the mayors, and Italian relief organizations. Most of them were peasants. All were without food, or household equipment, or any clothes except what they wore as they plodded through rain and mud at the side of clogged roads or stood shoulder to shoulder in railroad cars.

A Red Cross report said, "As many as eighty women and children had been packed in a cattle car, and for twenty-four and sometimes forty-eight hours they had gone without a chance to get out to get food or water or respond to the call of nature." When they could, they slept on the stone floors of railroad stations or public halls for a few hours and then moved on southward while another wave of humanity in distress came in behind them from the north.

The Italian front eventually was stabilized and everyone who is old enough remembers news pictures of Prime Minister Vittorio Orlando with President Woodrow Wilson and other peacemakers in Paris. But much of the war in Italy was fought with the unexpected burden of looking after thousands of "profugli" in every town, all the way to Sicily.

Plight of the people from the mountains and hasty Red Cross efforts were published in newspapers of the United States. The urge to help was strong for Miss Johnson. She was especially prepared to be useful by being able to speak Italian. She was a teacher of Latin and Greek. In

Miss Willie C. Johnson, 1918

addition she had spent three months in Rome in 1910 as a student at the American Classical School.

In 1918–19 she was a social worker for the Red Cross (Croce Rossa Americana). She and another staff member were assigned to train twenty-five refugee girls in social work by Red Cross standards. They learned by caring for forty refugee children in poor health at Monte Guiglia villa in the Bologna district.

There was mutual benefit, for Italians displaced by the war and for Willie Johnson, whose life was enriched by the experience. She filled a scrapbook with Red Cross papers and reports, post cards, photographs, and her own accounts of what she did. The scrapbook is still treasured by her niece, Miss Rebecca Young.

But the Italian experience was far outweighed by the impact of her career as a teacher. Miss Johnson was graduated from Vassar in 1895 and became a teacher at the famous Higbee School for girls. She then joined the faculty of Memphis High School, the only tax-supported high school for white youngsters. This is the school that later became Central High. She moved on to the faculty of St. Mary's Episcopal School, which prepared girls for college.

When West Tennessee State Normal (now Memphis State University) was organized she became professor of ancient languages even before the new school had a president. She took a leave of absence from Normal to join the Red Cross. When she returned from Italy she was so exhausted that she never returned to teaching. For twenty-two years she had been an enthusiastic teacher, influencing for life the abilities and attitudes of teenagers in her classrooms.

Miss Johnson had a strong belief in the value of travel as an educational tool, and she had a good deal of experience as a summer traveler, aside from having been a student in Rome and a Red Cross worker. She became an expert on stretching the travel dollar. So she became an organizer of small parties which she took to Europe and Central America. Each first-time traveler enjoyed hours of preparation, anticipation, and detailed planning with Miss Johnson as additional pleasures to the trip itself. From these trips there grew a little Christmastime gift shop in the garage at her home. She was, among her other talents, a good salesman.

For all of the values of her teaching and her tours, those who remember her were most of all impressed by her advocacy of college for girls. She worked hard at it during times when only a few boys went to college and most of their sisters stayed home. There was hardly any financial help available to girls and there were many parents who doubted the value of higher education for their daughters. Miss Johnson undertook both getting more colleges to offer scholarships to girls and getting girls to want the college years.

She had to arouse a strong desire for college because, aside from financial barriers, there were formidable entrance examinations. There were tests on each of fifteen subjects and all had to be passed. When graduation from prep school was past the girls had to settle down to day-long cramming for two or three weeks. Then there was a week of examinations. It was an ordeal. It also was a method of separating the very able from the merely good students. But Willie Johnson was utterly convinced that girls would find that college opened new avenues of life, and that the whole community would be improved by college-trained women. She put thirty years of her life into it.

When she took up the cause she was a conspicuous exception to common attitudes. Then she became one of the founders of the Intercollegiate Association, apparently the first organization for working for college scholarships, and for a time the only such organization in Memphis. Later the Memphis High School Alumni Scholarship Association took up some of the load. Then came the Memphis Chapter of the

American Association of University Women, of which she was a founding member.

She came to have the help of an extraordinary group of teachers, including Miss Ada Raines, Miss Annekay Tharp, and Miss Eleanor Richardson. There were others. Best known among her recruits was Miss Boyce Alexander, who was helped by "Miss Willie C." to win a scholarship at Vassar. Miss Alexander became a teacher at the Cuba school in Shelby County and then at Central High. In 1919 Miss Alexander married C. M. Gooch, who established a big business in lumber mills in and near Memphis.

By 1924 Mrs. Gooch was giving a Vassar scholarship of her own. This interest grew into the C. M. Gooch Foundation, set up in 1943, with a year-round office where hundreds of girls (and boys) used to get grants for the freshman year and loans for higher years in partial financing of the gap between their own resources and college costs.

Today high schools have scholarships for outstanding students and colleges offer student aid as a matter of course. Entrance examinations are taken casually during junior and senior years and brothers expect their sister to go on to college if they want to. The world of higher education is so different that it is probably unrealistic to expect people in their middle or youthful years to understand how rare the college girl was in 1900 or 1905.

Nor is it likely that many modern readers will realize the distinctions of the home in which Miss Johnson grew up. Her father was Dr. William Crockett Johnson, a Methodist pastor who had hoped his seventh child would be a boy. But the baby was another girl, so he made her a namesake anyway, as Willie Crockett Johnson. The birth date was 1 January 1874. The home was in the old Dale Spring area now known as Springdale, so far from town that they rode a commuter train on the Louisville & Nashville to get to Memphis.

Her older sister, Mary, had gone to Wellesley, and returned to teach in the county school at Springdale. At fourteen Willie Johnson enrolled at the Clara Conway Institute, a fine school for girls, where she won a full four-year scholarship at Vassar.

The teaching years came to an end. The Red Cross experience was brief. The travel touring was seasonal. But the crusade to get girls into college carried on through it all. She went on to become eighty-five, living her final years at 1336 Goodbar. Death came on 9 August 1959. As might be expected, her will, after providing for some relatives, gave the accumulation of a lifetime to Southwestern and Vassar.

6

Hospital Heroes

Medical Leader

When Richard Maury had attained the maturity that comes with seven years of living, he announced to his family that he was going to be a doctor. Years later he did—twice. The University of Virginia made him a doctor of medicine in 1857. While he was an intern at Bellevue Hospital in New York, he enrolled in the University of New York and was awarded his second MD. He also took a competitive examination and won an appointment to the Bellevue staff.

His boyish interest had been fastened on medicine when he heard a missionary to China tell of experiences in the Orient. Maury was born (2 February 1834) in Georgetown, D.C., to Fontaine Maury, who had been private secretary to President Monroe, followed by several years as first clerk of the Navy Department. It was a family of Huguenots, with several notable members, including Matthew Fontaine Maury, the oceanographer.

When Richard Brooke Maury was a boy his father had left the government to become a merchant at Fredericksburg. There were three boys, one a baby, when their father died. For a widow to support herself was most difficult in the antebellum South but the former Ellen Magruder did it, and raised three boys too. All were graduated from the University of Virginia. She opened a school for girls, which she taught

R. B. Maury, MD

for nineteen years without missing one day, that did so well she acquired an estate for her senior citizen years.

Richard was the oldest and he thought it would be unreasonable for him to go on to graduate school while his mother was still educating the younger brothers. So he taught in Virginia schools four years and put together the money for his study of medicine. He had begun college courses at sixteen and graduated at eighteen. On his return to the university he worked at his medical studies so hard that he was awarded his MD after one year. Another year in New York produced his second degree. But the grind was too much. His health broke and he was advised to move to a milder climate. He traveled to the South for a short time, then set up in practice at Port Gibson, Mississippi, in 1859.

The Civil War came and Dr. Maury went into a Mississippi cavalry unit as a surgeon. After a year in the field he was assigned to hospitals. He returned to Mississippi briefly before coming to Memphis in 1867. Dr. Maury added teaching obligations to his practice during the first year here. He became professor of physiology at Memphis Medical College, then professor of the practice of medicine. The school came upon hard times and closed. A new school was organized, the Memphis Hospital Medical College, where Dr. Maury became professor of gynecology in 1885. He also wrote on gynecological topics for medical publications. After twelve years of teaching his practice had become so large that he retired from the lectern.

He had become one of Memphis's earlist specialists. After going back to school at Women's Hospital in New York, he limited his practice to women only. He also studied in England and Scotland.

One of the reasons for the high standing of Dr. Maury in the history of Memphis medicine is his part in the rise of infirmaries and the beginnings of hospitals. Less than 100 years ago hospitals were for strangers, travelers, and the destitute. They were in small buildings outside of town to protect residents from unfortunates with diseases of unknown origin. Anyone with a home was sick at home. Sometimes they were sick in the home of a relative, if one was within reach.

This began to change in 1883 when an infirmary was established here by a surgeon who also was head of the medical college. His main objective was to have an operating room with better control of cleanliness.

The next year Dr. Maury and Dr. R. W. Mitchell took over a building at Third and Court. It was an infirmary for women only. It was such a benefit that it was outgrown in three years. In 1886 they built as an infirmary a four-floor structure at 111 Court (old numbering) in which they invested $40,000. This was the building in which the first nurses were trained in Memphis. The first operation for extrauterine pregnancy was done there. Patients of these doctors and their sons continued to use the infirmary until Baptist Hospital was opened in 1912.

Meantime a building that carried the name of "hospital" had been erected, under the leadership of Dr. Maury. He was helped by his son, Dr. J. M. Maury and Dr. E. E. Haynes. They took a home on Washington between Third and Fourth and established the Lucy Brinkley Hospital. Brinkley had donated some funds and the hospital was named for his late wife. Late in the 1880s this hospital became available to women, some of whom paid and some of whom were charity patients.

It was used nearly twenty years. Then the board of directors, all women, built a new and much bigger building at 885 Union, in 1907. This was the building that became Methodist Hospital in 1918, when it was bought, partially at least because it had a school of nursing. In 1921 the Methodists built a much bigger structure on Lamar, but they sold it to the Veterans Administration in 1923 and moved back briefly, while establishing a larger hospital on the Overton home grounds at 1265 Union.

Veterans Hospital has since become the Lamar Unit of Baptist Hospital. The old Brinkley Hospital was converted into the George Vincent Hotel, which remained until knocked down by the Memphis Housing Authority in 1971. The Brinkley name came back in 1927 when Methodist Hospital made its first addition. That is the Lucy Brinkley Pavilion, still in use about ninety years after Dr. Maury practiced in the original Lucy Brinkley Hospital.

Dr. Maury also was conspicuous as the only West Tennessee member of the state's first Department of Public Health in 1877. This was a pioneering outpost in doctoring, which required board members to pay their own expenses, including printer's bills for warnings to the public. Legislators were bashful about using tax money for health purposes in spite of doctors' warnings.

The doctors got more attention and some state money after yellow fever cut short the lives of thousands in 1878. Standard accounts of the Memphis terror list the first case as appearing on Front Street on 11 August. But Dr. Maury had found victims on Second Street as early as 21 July.

Three years later, Dr. Maury as a member of the State Board of Health, wrote in the first report (1880) of that board, a review of the yellow fever epidemics of 1873, 1878, and 1879 here. The title of his paper was "The Sanitary Necessities of Memphis and the Yellow Fever of 1878."

He used scathing words, such as "At the expense of over 1,300 lives and a money loss of many millions, Memphis learned that by her failure to exercise sanitary supervision over the commerce of the Mississippi, she was liable any year to have yellow fever. A properly conducted quarantine would have saved us completely in 1873."

The Maury efforts were used increasingly on behalf of women patients, as state, county, and city funds took up the preventive medicine of public health. Full of years and honors, he retired in 1903, but the very high recognition of the presidency of the American Gynecological Association came to him later, 1906. Still later, on his eightieth birthday, Memphis doctors gave a testimonial and a loving cup.

Dr. Maury was a man with talents and energy overflowing his professional career. He was president of the Memphis Board of Education in 1870–1871. In recognition of this service a fine new building on Bellevue just north of Poplar was named for him in 1908. The school name has been the most frequent reminder in modern Memphis of Dr. Maury.

In his retirement years he was able to encourage interest in birds. He organized the West Tennessee Audubon Society in 1911 and was its president for years. He lectured in schools. He obtained bird protection laws from the legislature. Because of his efforts, Tennessee at one time had more junior Audubon societies than any other state. Dr. Maury was senior warden of Calvary Episcopal Church for twenty years and was its first life senior warden. He was a leader, probably *the* leader of the movement for playgrounds in the days before city taxes went into the recreation department. Citizen donations were collected for equipping the first play areas. The City Club, which had weekly speakers and discussions on local public affairs, was organized in 1907 with Dr. Maury in a position of leadership, president for five years. He was a Mason, and a Democrat. He so thoroughly overcame the ill health of his early manhood that he attained the age of eighty-five before death claimed him on 17 March 1919. He left a family still prominent in Memphis.

First Nurse

Lena Angevine took up nursing when she was eight. On her grandfather's plantation east of Grenada, Mississippi, she had a pet duck whose leg was broken. She bound it up and supervised a complete recovery. When she was older she was a student at St. Mary's School here and learned about Florence Nightingale. The first training school for nurses was opened by Dr. R. B. Maury and Dr. R. W. Mitchell at their infirmary for women. This was a four-floor building at 111 Court (old numbering) which was opened in 1886, before large hospitals had been built, although there was a small hospital on grounds now occupied by Forrest Park for "strangers" who became ill here while away from home.

In this strange medical world before popular hospitals and education for nursing, Miss Angevine became a student nurse in the Maury Infirmary and was graduated in 1887, the first graduate nurse in Memphis, probably the first in Tennessee and, relatives believe, the first in the whole South.

She was associated with Dr. Maury several years and then made history again by organizing the first accredited school of nursing in Tennessee, in 1897. It was in the new City Hospital, on the site now occupied by John Gaston. Miss Angevine had helped design the hospi-

Lena Angevine (Warner), PhD (portrait from the University of Tennessee).

tal. It was as the founder of this school that she has been honored for many years by nursing organizations. But it was neither the first nor the last of her distinctions.

She was Lena Clark Angevine, auburn-haired daughter of Saxton Smith Angevine, who was descended from the Anjou and Plantagenet families of European history. He was a Memphis lawyer who had been educated at Harvard and had moved from New York. However, he became better known as editor of the Grenada newspaper than as an attorney. All of his brothers stayed in the North and took the Union side. He became a Confederate, and his editorials protesting carpetbag rule got Northern attention because of his connections and background in the North.

Her mother was Missouri Jane Mayhew, daughter of Dr. George Washington Mayhew, whose family was prominent in New England history, as well as in North Carolina and Memphis. Dr. Mayhew left the practice of medicine when he became wealthy from farming on 4,000 acres with almost 300 slaves, eight miles out of Grenada. It was on this farm that Lena Angevine was born, 18 May 1869. Her parents took her to Memphis when she was six weeks old, and she was reared among Battle and Turley cousins.

On this plantation her story very nearly came to an end as a child. The yellow fever got to Grenada in 1877 and killed her grandfather and her mother. The fever came back to Grenada in 1878, just before the Memphis epidemic. The family barricaded the farmhouse and boarded up the windows to keep out visitors who might be carrying the fever. The plague came in anyway, and then health authorities quarantined them inside.

An older sister died, their father, the last of five brothers and sisters, then the guests and the servants. A former slave who had become a servant became uneasy about the shut-up house, pried open a shutter, broke the glass and climbed in. Among the corpses was the fly-covered body of a little girl who seemed to have died most recently.

He carried her out into the air and laid her down in a servant's house, with a piece of raw bacon laid across the parched lips. She sucked savagely at the bacon, the only sign of life. Medical skill and patience brought her back from the brink of death from fever and starvation. Her grandmother sent Lena to a boarding school in Memphis.

The year after she had set up the accredited school for nurses brought the Spanish war (1898) and alarming death tolls for U.S. Army men in Cuba, especially because of the yellow fever. President McKinley appealed for volunteer nurses through the Daughters of the American Revolution. The Watauga Chapter in Memphis answered with a team of four headed by Lena Angevine, who was believed to be immune to yellow fever since she had survived the childhood tragedy of her family.

It was less than a hundred years ago but modern readers can hardly believe what they found. More soldiers were dying from the disease than from the war. The cause of yellow fever was still unknown and it was rampant, with malaria, cholera, smallpox, and bubonic plauge. The only hospitals were tents. There were hardly any medical supplies. Rows of tents were put up for soldiers, without camp sanitation. There was nothing for nurses except bunks, army chow, and army clothing.

The principal reaction to illness was to roll the soldier into a huge detention camp where a man who needed help with an ingrown toenail might be in a cot next to a smallpox case. In a prison for deserters she contracted cholera and was consigned to the big camp for all kinds of illness. Her case was severe and she was given up for dead. Day after day she defied her fate and there came a time when she was strong enough to stand. She walked out and into a gathering of doctors and nurses who were so astounded that one of them said there was almost a religious feeling, as though Moses had come down from the mountain.

Another time a doctor diagnosed yellow fever from some strange symptoms and ordered the soldier rolled into the camp for the doomed. But the symptoms said appendicitis to Lena Angevine and she refused. The doctor was firm too and finally told the nurse, "We'll confirm your diagnosis at the autopsy." The nurse went looking for a doctor who would operate but they all refused until she came to one who had never done an operation but was willing. Instruments were so crude that she closed the incision with a darning needle from her sewing kit. But it was a burst appendix, with gangrene, and the patient lived.

She then became chief nurse of the island, and an officer. Relatives believe she was the first woman to become an officer in the Army. She designed and modeled the first official uniform for nurses, a zouave jacket in blue, over a waist of white linen, with a long skirt in navy blue, decorated by a sash of red silk. Light blue was used for the hat, shaped somewhat like the Rough Rider headpiece.

Then the yellow jack struck the medical corps and doctors and nurses died one by one. Lena Angevine survived and, with the war over, came home with the troops, a most conspicuous hero.

A short time later Dr. Walter Reed of the Army Medical Corps and his associates went back to Cuba to make another effort to solve the mystery of the transmission of yellow fever from patient to patient. Miss Angevine was asked to go back with them and she became nurse in charge of the yellow fever experiments that proved the *Aedes Egypti* mosquito was the killer, and that removal of the standing water stopped the mosquitos.

The experiments took the lives of several doctors and volunteer heroes and brought another tragedy to Lena Angevine. She fell in love with one of the doctors, Edward D. Warner from Pennsylvania, and married him. Three months later the fever took him.

She came back to the United States and returned to school, earning a Ph.D. in bacteriology from the University of Chicago in 1904. Thereafter she was usually "Dr Warner," causing some writers to assume she had become a doctor of medicine. Back in Memphis she seemed to settle down to such routine as organizing Red Cross chapters. She set up a statewide survey of health conditions for the Metropolitan Life Insurance Co. She became state chairman of Red Cross nursing services and state chairman of the Red Cross Association. She organized the Tennessee Health Association.

In 1918 University of Tennessee cadets, in training for World War I, were attacked by influenza, and she went to Knoxville to help them. That was the end of her Memphis home. The university put her in the Extension Service and she taught better health for rural homes year after year.

Dr. Warner retired in 1945. She died August 18, 1948. A plot was reserved for her among the nation's heroes at Arlington but she was buried with relatives in Elmwood Cemetery here. Only four nieces and a nephew remain: Miss Elizabeth Cole and Mrs. Josephine Longinotti of Memphis; Frank Elliott Weir and Mrs. Evelyn Angevine Mitchell of Grenada; and Mrs. Lucille Weir Thomas of Sylacauga, Alabama, a retired nurse.

About two months before her life ended, a portrait, painted by Jascha Shaffran, was hung in Gaston Hospital. It now is in the conference room at the College of Nursing, University of Tennessee Center for the Health Sciences. In it she seems to be dressed in man's clothing. Another portrait, in which she models the uniform she designed, dates from 1937. It is in the Nashville headquarters of the State Nursing Association. Copies of one or the other painting are often seen in schools for nurses, hospitals, clinics, and nursing homes of the Southeast, especially in Tennessee—a tribute by professional nurses to their fearless leader.

Worldwide Fame

He is remembered as a tall and gray-haired man with a soft voice. It was a voice that was heard all around the world by doctors who devoted their talent to the eye. He was Dr. E. C. Ellett who practiced in Memphis from 1893 until his death on 8 June 1947. The number of persons whose sight he saved and the number of times he restored sight were countless.

The benefits of his skill were spread to ever-widening circles as a teacher of students who looked up to him with unlimited admiration. He was professor of ophthalmology for the College of Physicians and Surgeons from 1905 until it was merged into the University of Tennessee in 1911, when he became the first professor of that branch of medicine on the Memphis campus. He resigned in 1922.

Edward Coleman Ellett had many distinctions, one of which was that he was born in Memphis on 18 December 1869. His father was Judge Henry T. Ellett and his mother, the former Katherine Coleman. It was a family of prominence, his father having been a member of the Mississippi Supreme Court before moving to Memphis, where he be-

E. C. Ellett, MD (from the S. R. Bruesch Collection).

came a Chancery Court judge. He held other offices, including membership in the House of Representatives, and was highly regarded as a lawyer and judge, yet is most often recalled for his dramatic death. He made the welcoming address to President Grover Cleveland and his bride in 1887, speaking before a vast crowd in Court Square. As he completed his closing words the judge fell dead on the grandstand.

The future doctor was a schoolboy when his father died. He was taught in private schools here and then at Southwestern Presbyterian University at Clarksville, Tennessee, now Southwestern at Memphis, for two years, followed by two at Sewanee. He studied medicine at the University of Pennsylvania and was awarded a medal for the best average in the class of 1891. He was resident for a year at St. Agnes Hospital and for another year was house surgeon at Will's Eye Hospital.

From the beginning of his practice in Memphis it was restricted to eye, ear, nose, and throat. World War I took him away from Memphis again. He became a lieutenant colonel and commanded a base hospital in France, where he earned a citation for "exceptionally meritorious and conspicuous service." When he returned from war he restricted his practice still more, to the eye only.

The first of the nation's specialty boards was the American Board of Ophthalmology and it was organized here. This board conducted its first examination in Lindsley Hall, a University of Tennessee building which stood on Madison adjoining Baptist Hospital. For the original examination in 1916 Dr. Ellett was an examiner and he was a member of the board for many years. He obtained a microtome from Germany, probably the first in Memphis, with which he "sectioned" eyes he had removed, for study of tissue.

In 1926 the Memphis Eye, Ear, Nose, and Throat Hospital at 1060 Madison was opened. It is a three-floor brick building. There were three operating rooms and sixty-five beds, although only about half of them were used by the eye patients. It was the only hospital of its kind in the South, and had the only residency in opthalmology between St. Louis and New Orleans. It is remembered by thousands in the Memphis area because of free clinics every afternoon during the Ellett era.

In this building Dr. Ellett did all of his operations from its opening day onward. Other eye doctors of the time did likewise. He was chief of staff from the opening until his death.

Honors came to Dr. Ellett in profusion. He was president of the Memphis and Shelby County Medical Society, chairman of the section of ophthalmology of the American Medical Association, president of the American Ophthalmological Society, president of the five-man Academy of Ophthalmology and Otolaryngology, and for five years chairman of the American Board of Ophthalmology.

One of his most unusual marks of distinction was "Ellett Day" in 1935 when eye specialists of this area came to Memphis and operating rooms throughout the city were filled with sight-saving procedures done in his honor. Dr. Ellett did some of the operations himself that day, and explained what he was doing to visiting doctors. In 1939 he was awarded the Leslie Dana Medal. The medal of the St. Louis Society for the Blind was engraved to hail his "outstanding achievements in the prevention of blindness." He had been nominated by the Association for Research in Ophthalmology. In 1943, a half century after he began practice, the doctors of Memphis paid tribute with a formal dinner.

His career came to an abrupt end on 8 June 1947, in Atlantic City where he intended to take part in the American Medical Association convention. He was felled by a heart attack, of which the only warning had been a coronary incident a year and a half before.

His name lives on in Ellett Hall, a men's dormitory at Southwestern. His will left the residue of his estate equally to his two colleges, Southwestern and Sewanee.

The hospital in which he worked is again serving medical needs, after some turbulent financing. It had been organized by Dr. Louis Levy at a cost of about $300,000 in dollars of the old fashion. But $220,000 was in bond issues, based on a mortgage. There were second and third mortgages.

There was an unusually large proportion of charity work in the Eye, Ear, Nose, and Throat Hospital. There was even a time when the City Hospital sent all eye cases down the street to the privately owned eye hospital, but the city fathers were unable to find tax money for the free clinic. Another time a group of doctors was organized to take over financial responsibilities, which resulted in unexpected money contributions to the public benefit from the doctors.

Eventually the building was bought by Methodist Hospital for $80,000. Methodist management took over on 1 January 1943, and did extensive remodeling. When the Thomas Wing of Methodist Hospital was completed, the third floor was devoted to the eye work that had been done at the Eye, Ear, Nose, and Throat Hospital. This includes the Eye Bank and the Lion's Club clinic. For a time the old eye hospital was used for Methodist Hospital patients, overflowing the main building. There was a time when eye hospital rooms stood vacant.

Then the old eye hospital became an ear hospital, although some other types of specialists are using part of the rooms. It was bought by Dr. John J. Shea in 1966, for enlargement of space for his ear practice, known as otology in the profession. It is accredited by the Joint Commission of Accreditation of Hospitals. It is the Memphis Otologic Clinic, although the public speaks of it as the Shea Clinic.

Probably the Ellett influence lingers more than anything else in the tones with which doctors he taught speak of their teacher and exemplar. They remember especially that he repeated the old saying, "despise not the day of small things." He said that importance of detail was the most profound lesson of his experiences. The older eye doctors remember that Dr. Ellett had patients who came from Europe to get the advantages of his careful hands and long experiences. Dr. Ellett was, the doctors say, the first to draw international attention to Memphis as a medical center.

Bone Specialist

Writers of the *History of Medicine in Memphis* used more space for Dr. Willis C. Campbell than for any other physician during all the years before 1971. Dr. Campbell was central to the story of Crippled Childrens Hospital, the Hospital for Crippled Adults and the clinic which bears his name, as well as because world famous athletes come to Memphis for care of broken legs, abused knees, and overworked elbows.

His personal story, without the hospitals, would have been lengthy and impressive. He was asked to address medical groups in Europe. Sometimes his cases came from Europe. Some physicians in the United States sent members of their own families to his clinic. His was the remarkable case of a doctor for children who became interested in bone surgery, went back to school and started over.

Willis Cohoon Campbell was a big old Mississippi boy with 270 pounds padding a body of 6 feet, 2 inches. He had a friendly manner and his speech was distinguished by a slight lisp. His grandfather was J. A. P. Campbell of the Mississippi Supreme Court and his father was Charles C. Campbell of the Kosciusko, Mississippi, family. The Cohoon in his name was the maiden name of his mother who was from Suffolk, Virginia.

Willis Campbell was born (18 December 1880) in Jackson. On his way to becoming a Phi Beta Kappa student at the University of Virginia, he was taught at St. Thomas Hall (Holly Springs), and Millsaps, Hampden-Sydney, and Roanoke Colleges. He took his medical degree at Virginia, was an intern in Norfolk and New York two years, and became a Memphis doctor in 1906.

For a short time he had a general practice and did some anesthesia, but he soon limited himself to pediatrics. However, he became doubtful of his place in that specialty. Once, while he was on a house call, a mother motioned for him to sit in a chair of delicate antiqueness. It collapsed under his poundage. He got up from the floor, brushed off his clothes and went to the bedside of the infant patient. But the mother stopped him saying, "Don't touch that baby, you will crush him."

Such a story, known to hundreds of doctors, could only have origi-nated from one source. He probably was the source of another anecdote in which mothers and their extended telephone calls about baby ailments finally wore down his tolerance. It was the day a mother talked on and on about her baby's diarrhea, coming to the detail that the stools had

Willis C. Campbell, MD (AP photo).

turned to "Kelly green." To which Dr. Campbell responded, "I don't give a damn if they're red, white, and blue."

So in 1909 Willis Campbell decided to take up orthopedics. He studied at the Royal National Orthopedic Hospital in London and at the University of Vienna, followed by postgraduate work in New York and Boston clinics. At the time they were the only cities in the United States with centers for orthopedic surgery. He began the clinic which brought fame to Memphis the day after Christmas of 1910. The building for Campbell Clinic near Baptist Hospital was opened in January 1921.

One of his major contributions to the public was his teaching of young doctors who added to the stature of Memphis as an orthopedic center. Young as he was, he had been on the faculty of the College of Physicians and Surgeons. When the University of Tennessee medical campus was organized here in 1911, Dr. Campbell became the first professor or orthopedic surgery and the head of that department, which he remained as long as he lived. He also taught far from Memphis through textbooks that became classics on the subject. He wrote *Orthopedics of Childhood, Injuries and Surgical Diseases of the Joints, Orthopedic Surgery,* and *Operative Orthopedics.*

He was founder and first president of the American Academy of

Orthopedic Surgeons. He was president of the American Orthopedic Association, and of the American Medical Association. He was a member of advisory committees for the National Foundation for Infantile Paralysis, the Georgia Warm Springs Foundation, and the International Society for Crippled Children, and he served many other similar organizations.

Probably the most spectacular part of the Campbell chronicle is the building of Crippled Children's Hospital. He was chief of staff from its opening in 1919 until his death, but he was more than that. He was the originator.

In earlier years this region had thousands of children who were cripples and too poor to pay for treatments that would have helped, or perhaps cured the trouble. Late in 1917 two dozen "King's Daughters" of Calvary Episcopal Church raised $135 at a bridge party. They went to Dr. Campbell and said they wanted to provide a wheelchair for a crippled child. But he startled them by saying, "Ladies, you don't want to buy a wheelchair; you want to found a hospital."

He said a donor was waiting to put in $10,000 if $5,000 could be raised. They enthusiastically enlisted a small group of men and soon had $16,000, without learning the name of the philanthropic woman. They also enlisted an architect, a contractor, and some dealers in building materials with the result of a $40,000 building on ten acres at the edge of town, at Lamar and LaPaloma.

Four little cripples came to this haven of hope the first day. There were twenty-four beds and they were so often full that additions were made until there were fifty-five. An accredited twelve-grade school, a gymnasium, and a workshop became features of this very special place where thousands of youngsters have gone through the medical treatments and the training that have put them on their own feet and back in the ordinary world, leaving behind inspirational pairs of before and after pictures.

Probably it is too much to expect the present generation to understand what a cheerful spot this hospital was in the world before Medicaid, Medicare, hospital insurance, and nationwide campaign funds for medical funds. It was a world in which being poor meant doing without medical care, especially being poor in a county without a large city; for only cities had hospitals, and they were small.

Neither is it probable that anyone except the oldsters remember much about the years before medical scientists drove back the yearly threat of poliomyelitis (often called infantile paralysis) which left hundreds of twisted bodies. It also caused one of the sights of Memphis to be the special Isolation Hospital where distressed mothers climbed on chairs and stepladders outside the windows in the hope of comforting an ailing child.

In the old days before World War I and before Dr. Campbell opened his clinic, there simply were few doctors who specialized in orthopedic surgery, although Memphis already was a medical center and this city was comparatively fortunate in the abilities of its orthopedists. The difference between the days before and after Campbell is illustrated by the special hospital established for those more than twelve years old and disqualified for the children's hospital.

The Hospital for Crippled Adults, next door to the Crippled Children's Hospital, was the only hospital of its kind in the world, doctors say. The only persons admitted were the physically handicapped who could be benefited by orthopedic surgery and treatment but were financially unable to obtain it.

The plan for such a hospital originated with Sam Woods, state supervisor of the Vocational Rehabilitation Service in Mississippi. He had come across hundreds of persons, some of them quite young boys and girls but too old to be accepted at children's hospital, who had to have orthopedic corrections before they could benefit from vocational guidance and become earners.

The Woods efforts to interest hospitals, organizations, or wealthy citizens were unsuccessful until he went to see Dr. Campbell. The doctor had noticed the same need and he offered his services and his clinic for examination, as well as use of his name. The efforts then produced some contributions from Arkansas and Tennessee, as well as Mississippi. They were able to obtain the empty Presbyterian Hospital building on Alabama by agreeing to pay the taxes. St. Joseph Hospital, just down the street, offered use of operating rooms.

There were twelve men and boys for the opening in August of 1923. There were twenty beds on the first floor. Capacity was doubled in 1926 when the second floor was opened to women and girls. At first patents could be accepted from everywhere and they came from nineteen states.

The good news spread fast and within five years the number of operations for Crippled Adults Hospital was causing scheduling difficulties for patient operations at St. Joseph Hospital, and the recuperating orthopedic cases were overloading the old Presbyterian building. In 1928 funds were raised by B. B. Jones of Berryville, Virginia, for a $200,000 hospital, which was opened as the year ended. A large part of the operation funds, from the first, came from members of the Memphis Rotary Club. In 1936 Rotary clubs of Tennessee, Arkansas, and Mississippi united in the Tri-State Association for Cripples, and in 1953 the hospital service area was enlarged to include parts of Missouri, Kentucky, and Louisiana. In the face of these efforts, operating funds were often short. The Depression struck soon after the new building was occupied and half of the hospital was closed.

Dr. Campbell died, but he had provided in his will for the staff of Campbell's Clinic to continue operations for the Hospital for Crippled Adults. More than two thousand persons benefited from its special services. But operating funds dwindled and eventually, on 6 June 1970, the last patient departed. The clinic was replaced by arrangements for an outpatient clinic in the Lamar Unit of Baptist Hospital, where recuperating patients might stay. The building once used for adults is now used by the University of Tennessee for designing and making devices needed for the crippled to take up independent lives.

Modern times also have brought about a change in Campbell Clinic itself. In 1967 it was found that the 80-bed hospital at 869 Madison was beyond renovation. The hospital rooms were closed and replaced by arrangement for 100 beds on one floor of Baptist Hospital. The offices remained in the clinic building and outpatient space was enlarged.

Dr. Campbell had died on 4 May 1941, a year after a heart attack as he prepared to read a paper before the American Orthopedic Association convention in Kansas City. Numerous stories clustered about this legendary hero. One of them was chosen by Malcolm Adams, city editor of *The Commerical Appeal,* to put a fitting close on the obituary of Dr. Campbell. It told of a young mother from Missouri whose baby was crippled by infantile paralysis. She appeared at the clinic one day, asking for Dr. Campbell's help.

She was without funds but Dr. Campbell took the case, treated the baby, and provided braces during months of regular trips from Missouri to Memphis, without a bill for medical services. Then one day a letter came asking for postponement of the next appointment. The mother said she was unable to get the transportation cost. But the mother and the baby, who was about to walk again, made the trip anyway—on money sent from Memphis.

Big Among Surgeons

In July of 1912 the doors of Baptist Hospital were opened, a seven-floor building on the hill beside the new University of Tennessee medical school and across Madison from the City Hospital. It seemed like a big building then—for most of the rooms were empty. Before the year was over, drastic action by the directors had changed that. They went down to Yazoo City, Mississippi, where Dr. Eugene Johnson was operating in two hospitals, one for whites and one for blacks, and convinced him that he should move to Memphis.

He came, and he brought with him his nurses, his office staff, and his patients. Everything was moved to Baptist Hospital for the foundation of a cooperation that continued as long as he lived. When he died, *The Commercial Appeal* estimated he had performed more than forty thousand operations in that hospital. The *Memphis Press-Scimitar* estimated the total number of his operations at more than one hundred thousand. The medical society took note of his demise with a resolution saying he probably did more major operations than any surgeon who ever lived.

When the move to Memphis was made, Dr. Johnson was a man of thirty-seven, of considerable fame in Mississippi after fourteen years of practice. He had been born near Lexington, Mississippi, 13 July 1875, and named Joseph Eugene Johnson, Jr., but he reversed the given names because another doctor had the same initials.

As a boy of fifteen he took up medicine while working in a drugstore at Zeiglerville. He bought medical textbooks and studied at odd hours, dissecting small animals at night by the light of a coal-oil lamp. He then borrowed some money to get to Memphis and enrolled in the Memphis Hospital Medical College which had a three-floor building on the south side of Union, opposite the site on which the statue of General Nathan Bedford Forrest has since been erected. There were about seven hundred students in what was the "hospital" college. What now is Forrest Park was then the grounds of City Hospital, with the charity patients so necessary for student doctors.

He had to pay his own school expenses and support himself. He worked as a nurse and was employed by several doctors. But he was a quick learner and the lectures often were reviews for him, because he had learned what the books said, working in the drugstore. He was graduated in 1897 at the head of his class.

By the time he had his MD, he was an unusually large man, 6'3" tall

Eugene Johnson, MD

and eventually to grow to weigh 225 pounds. Dr. Johnson hung out his shingle at Eden, a lumbermill town in Yazoo County, in 1898. Two years later he moved to Yazoo City.

Legends began to cluster about his name early. He once swam a river and clambered through underbrush to get to a child with diphtheria. He once rode an ox cart and once pumped a railroad handcar until a train needed the tracks in a hurry, and he often rode the caboose. At least once he ran his automobile up to the kitchen window to provide light for an emergency operation. Two barrels and a door sometimes made an operating table. Once he strapped a door to the back of a frightened husband to make a tilted table necessary for his wife's operation.

The standing of the young doctor was more generally known after he was elected president of the Tri-State Medical Association 1907, an event given some attention in *The Commercial Appeal*. At Baptist Hospital he was an instant favorite among nurses and patients. He was heard before he was seen, with a hearty voice and a happy laugh. Then came the big frame, always immaculate in dress. There followed a friendly interest in every person. He stood and prayed at each bedside.

Frightened student nurses quickly were put at ease and addressed as "child." Patients, worried about the price of a famous surgeon, soon were assured that payment meant little to him.

And it really was of small consequence to a doctor who could have been a young millionaire. Instead, he sometimes went beyond operating without a fee, to providing the money that got a patient a train ticket back home. There was a family that came from a distance for eleven operations and five times had their fare paid to get home. Another time a woman from Arkansas was given the operation, her hospital bill, and money for her family to live in Memphis while she was hospitalized. Dr. Johnson once picked up a newsboy who needed an emergency appendectomy and carried him in his arms into the hospital.

Among doctors, he was known for speed. His jovial air was gone when he put on the surgeon's mask. He worked with precision, yet needed only half the time used by ordinary surgeons. In his maturity, he was still a fast learner, being able to repeat an operation he had seen only once.

The devotion of people with whom he came in contact was phenomenal. He had the same anesthetist thirty years. A nurse, whose first assignment was to assist Dr. Johnson, wrote an essay twenty-five years after his death about him as the "bright and shining light" of her nursing career, and about the untold charities she had seen. He seemed to inspire an unusual amount of verse from patients and associates.

He was also noted for his stamina. He was so strong he could stand at the operating table all day, then go back for an emergency ending at daylight, and still take up his normal schedule the second day. He once did twenty-two operations in twenty-four hours. For years the entire sixth floor of the hospital was reserved for Johnson patients, and he was assigned his own operating room. He was surgeon for the Illinois Central Railroad.

Soon after his graduation from medical school, he married Miss Annie Yowell. Ten years later, in 1907, she died, leaving four children, the youngest thirteen months old and the oldest eight. He never remarried but became mother as well as father, and he managed in the face of increasing professional demands on his time to give his devoted attention.

He never took time for the usual sports and social activities, partly because he enjoyed his children and partly because nothing gave him as much pleasure as helping those who needed him. It would be inaccurate to call him a "workaholic," for workaholics are grim. Dr. Johnson was happy and always had time to calm the fearful and bring them into an assured confidence about what was ahead. Thousands left the hospital feeling that they had a new friend with a personal tie that lasted as long as they lived.

But he had a hope for years that he would have a long vacation for a safari in Africa. Instead, on Saturday afternoons of fair weather he went a few blocks to the Memphis Gun Club at the northeast corner of South Parkway and Bellevue and shot clay pigeons. He was considered the champion among local skeet shooters and in 1931 he won the Grand American Shoot.

When illness came to him he resisted being confined to his home at 1521 Vance until a portable X-ray unit was brought from the hospital to show him a lung was affected. Even then he insisted that he had promised to operate on a young wife who had twice been his patient as a child. He was under obligation, and he went back to the operating room. It took two men to get him dressed and into his car and up to the door. But as he reached the door he straightened up, threw his chin out and strode in. (She lived only a short time longer than her doctor.)

He went back to his home but was returned to the hospital as a patient in the constant care of his associate, Henry Rudner; another associate, Robert C. Taylor, who was his son-in-law; Dr. Ike Johnson of Blytheville, Arkansas; and a cousin who had been more like a son ever since he interned under Eugene Johnson at Yazoo City. Dr. Johnson died 18 February 1938. Pneumonia was announced as the cause, but the underlying situation was leukemia. One of his children is living, Mrs. George Treadwell. One of his great-grandsons, George H. Treadwell, III, is an intern on his way to a career in medicine.

He had been hailed in a Methodist publication as "The Christian Physician." When he died, the rector of Calvary Episcopal Church published a tribute including such phrases as "one of the great souls of this community," "Always something of the gigantic about Dr. Johnson and his work," "one never heard anything small about him," and "there was a tenderness in him."

Services were held at Idlewild Presbyterian Church, which was overflowed an hour ahead as mud-caked cars from the backroads of Arkansas and Mississippi took spaces beside chauffeur-driven limousines. Aside from the usual newspaper editorials and medical society resolutions, there were letters from patients and from several doctors. Most unusual of all the tributes was a memorial fund given by ninety private-duty nurses who had admired the remarkable Memphis surgeon from Yazoo City.

More than a Doctor

The name of W. A. Evans was as familiar to millions in the United States and overseas in the 1920s. Yet hardly any of them knew that until 1891 he was simply Dr. W. A. Evans, a physician at Aberdeen, Mississippi. His greatest fame was as the writer of a newspaper column on health. He had become health editor of *The Chicago Tribune* in 1911, where he remained until retirement on pension in 1934. *The Commercial Appeal* published his writings on the Editorial Page under the heading "How To Keep Well." It was the first syndicated column on health and became tremendously popular in hundreds of newspapers. He was a tower of strength in the early campaigning for preventive medicine.

While most assumed that he was a Chicago man, he was a Mississippian both before and after the Chicago years, and he became the outstanding authority on Monroe County history.

He was William Augustus Evans, Jr., but he was known to his friends as just "Gus." His grandfather, Dr. William G. Evans, moved to Monroe County in 1836, from Wilkes County, Georgia, with a background of Virginia and English history. His father also was a doctor and had charge of the Confederate hospital at Marion, Alabama, where he married a nurse. They were still at Marion when their first child was born on 5 August 1865. They returned to the family plantation near Prairie and lived there and in Aberdeen while the famous Dr. Evans was growing up and six other children were being born.

The future writer on medicine was graduated by Aberdeen High School and was a member of the first class, of five, to be graduated at Mississippi Agricultural and Mechanical College, now Mississippi State University. He earned his MD at Tulane in 1885 and took up the inherited practice at Aberdeen.

Leadership qualities showed up early. He was captain of the Aberdeen Guards in the days when militia companies were important and while still a student won the 1885 cup as the best-drilled soldier in the state, the culmination of competition that held intense public interest. His medical degree was barely four years old when he was elected vice-president of the Mississippi State Medical Society in 1889.

William Augustus Evans, MD (courtesy Evans
Memorial Library).

While still very young his interest in preventive medicine had been
ignited in 1888, when there was a yellow fever scare and he was put
in charge of a receiving station at the Alabama line, near Gettman,
Mississippi.

Drastic change came in 1891. He left Aberdeen and went to the
University of Chicago Medical School as demonstrator in pathology. In
1895 he moved to the University of Illinois campus in Chicago as
professor of pathology. In 1903, still a young doctor from Mississippi,
he was president of the Chicago Medical Society. In 1907 he became the
original Chicago health commissioner and was off on a twenty-year
career of cleaning up the milk supply, purifying the drinking water and
other projects, such as the Chicago Drainage Canal, which held the
attention of sanitary engineers and some public interest for years. The
nationwide Public Health Association chose him president in 1916.

His teacher career settled down in 1908 when Northwestern University made him professor of sanitary science. He remained until 1928, and
then became professor emeritus.

He was thus, essentially, a teacher both in the classroom and his daily newspaper column. In his early years he was often downgraded by other doctors for various reasons but attitudes changed when it was realized that he was helping the cause of good health in which they all were enlisted. He was more a persuader than an enforcer, his accomplishments as health officer came from leading the public to demand more healthful milk and water than from using the power of the laws. His was a powerful voice for clean air many years before the environment excitement. Because of smoke from railroad trains, and especially the little locomotives that took commuters in and out of the South Side on the Illinois Central tracks, he took a hand in writing, *The Electrification of Railway Terminals*.

One of his intense interests in public health was protection from tuberculosis. He was one of the original directors of the City of Chicago Municipal Tuberculosis Sanitarium and profoundly affected the efforts in Chicago, and the nation.

Dr. Evans was ready for tireless pursuit of diverse objectives. While in Chicago he researched and wrote a biography of Mrs. Abraham Lincoln. When he retired he went to New Mexico to prospect for gold. He also found reasons for research trips to Mexico, South America, Asia, and Africa with the pleasures of foreign travel added. He explored the Tombigbee River banks in search of the crossing used by DeSoto's expedition, consulted experts, and decided on a point near Aberdeen to the distress of other specialists of DeSoto. He got Boy Scouts to help him find and mark Gaines Trace along the western side of the Tombigbee and wrote about it for *The Journal of Mississippi History*. He was one of the early advocates of the Tennessee-Tombigbee waterway, which is being built long after his death. When Beauvoir, the Jefferson Davis home built on the Gulf, was being abandoned and destruction had begun, Dr. Evans went to the coast and took up a campaign of speaking and writing that led to the widespread efforts which saved it.

In the face of his multiple interests, Dr. Evans carefully answered each person who wrote to him in connection with his newspaper column (1911–1934), more than a million of them. While improving the health of the general public was his paramount concern, when he retired and returned to Aberdeen his other interests had a chance to claim more of his time. His priority went to the early people and events of Monroe County.

He was sixty-eight but his energy seemed to be without limit. He took a special interest in verse written by S. A. Jones, civil engineer in building the New Orleans, Jackson & Great Northern (now part of the Illinois Central Gulf), a major in the Confederate army, and original editor of *The Aberdeen Examiner*. He assembled a collection of the rhymed compositions and published them in the contemporary *Examiner*. He then did a piece on "History of the Original Major S. A. Jones Poem 'Lines on the Back of a Confederate Bill,' " sold it to the *The Commercial Appeal* and gave the money to the Aberdeen library, which thereupon bought its first filing cabinet.

He then did a weekly column for the local newspaper on letters written in 1877–1879 by W. B. Wilkes about the settlement days. He called it "Pioneer Times." Then he undertook to list every gravestone in Monroe County's 153 cemeteries, with help from fourteen volunteers. The list was converted into a manuscript book. These cemetery inscriptions are still used every day by researchers in Monroe County history.

For Dr. Evans they were followed (1936–1939) by weekly bits of regional history, under the newspaper caption of "Mother Monroe." But none of the compilations had been converted into anything as handy as a book until 1979. The Wilkes letters, the gravestone information, and Dr. Evans' writings have been copied by four women and published under the title *Mother Monroe*. They have added an index of 1,400 topics and 2,500 names. The compilers are Mrs. Brynda H. Wright of Amory, Mrs. Helen M. Crawford of Hamilton, and Mrs. Jo D. Miller and Mrs. Patsy C. Pace, both of Aberdeen. They have formed the Mother Monroe Publishing Company (Route 2, Box 50, Hamilton, Mississippi 39746) and sell the book at twenty dollars, plus one dollar for postage.

The book freshens the memories of a most remarkable Aberdeen man, although his name has been very well preserved in the library he gave his hometown and provided with endowed operating funds. Other books he wrote are available only in rare book shops, if at all. Some of the titles were *Notes on Pathology, Yearbook of Pathology, Yearbook of Public Health, A History of First Baptist Church, Aberdeen, Mississippi, 1837–1945*, and *Wyatt's Travel Diary*. It would be easier to find in technical libraries some of the many articles he wrote for medical journals. He also wrote about Chickasaw land sales for *Oklahoma Chronicles of History*, and he wrote several articles for *Chase* magazine about fox hunting and fox hounds.

This man of knowledge in so many fields of endeavor came to a sudden end on 8 November 1948, when his heart stopped. His long marriage had been childless, although he has more than the usual number of persons to call attention to his accomplishments. He has a biographer, Dorothy Nell Phillips, who wrote *William Augustus Evans: Statesman of Public Health*. His life was more briefly summarized in his obituary on page one of *The Commercial Appeal*, which identified him as an ''internationally known physician, health authority, author, and newspaper columnist.''

7
Just for Fun

Eats for the Elite

Memphis was once known—to the upper crust of sportsmen, actors, opera singers, and financiers—as the home of the Luehrmann restaurants. It was a splendid place to dine in leisure. There were 135 kinds of wine. The seafood was especially good because it was so fresh. In fact, Henry Luehrmann bought only live lobsters, crabs, and oysters to be fattened in the basement, where he personally fed them. Yet the Luehrmann fame was more often spread by word of his superior canvasback ducks from Michigan and partridges from the Argentine.

When the superrich who traveled in private railroad cars were here for the Memphis Gold Cup season at the Memphis Driving Park or the Tennessee Derby at Montgomery Park, it took five bartenders, plus two lesser figures, to handle the beer drinkers, and to keep the barroom as neat as Luehrmann demanded, even then the crowds were crushing.

Waiters wore tails. Napkins and tablecloths were thick linen, never marked with ink because they were custom woven in patterns of big roses, with the name "Luehrmann" worked into the pattern.

Memphis men who could afford it liked to eat and drink there, too, even though it had the highest prices in town. Sometimes they brought their wives and daughters to dine. But it was a building of four floors, over three basements, and the three upper floors were a fine hotel with

Above: Henry Luehrman

Right: Luehrman Hotel

only thirty-eight rooms, reserved for men only. Ladies were never seen on the stairs, although some women in fine clothes appeared at intervals. There was one exception, however, Ernestine Schumann-Heink, the popular Metropolitan contralto, was a friend of Mr. and Mrs. Luehrmann, and she was allowed to have a room in the all-male world.

The fortune it took to build and equip this magnificent establishment came largely from beer. Luehrmann became big in Memphis as the bottler and dealer in Schlitz, and later as the bottler only, while he also developed a fine restaurant at another location.

Luehrmann was born 27 August 1841, at Melle, in the Hanover area of Germany. At fifteen he came to the United States and obtained a job as a clerk in St. Louis, while going to business school at night. When the war came, he enlisted in the Union ranks and served on the other side of the river, notably at Pea Ridge. His regiment was mustered out in

August 1864. He then came to Memphis and took a job as clerk to the sutler for a cavalry regiment from New Jersey. With the war over, he returned to St. Louis, and then took a long trip to his old home in Germany.

He came to Memphis a second time late in 1866 and looked up the many acquaintances he had made during the war. He soon had a job as bookkeeper for a brewer, Sweisfel, Hergan & Company. After two years he took charge of the V. Dreisigaker Saloon at 35 Monroe (old numbering). He expanded into much bigger business when he built a bottling plant next door in 1872. He became the Memphis agent for Schlitz and the bottler, transferring the beer from barrels arriving by rail, four days out of Milwaukee. Some was kegged, and Luehrmann had space for 400 kegs under tons of ice. In 1874 he installed the South's first cold-storage plant for beer, which he sold to Schlitz in 1878.

In 1875 he was elected to the City Council, but one year was enough of that. He was the builder of a Memphis brewery and president of the company in 1877, but he sold his stock the next year. In 1879 Schlitz named another Memphis agent, but Luehrmann remained the Schlitz bottler.

Luehrmann made a brief expansion in 1881, still bottling for Schlitz. He opened at 8–10 Union (old numbering) as a dealer in soda water, cider, Boston ginger ale, imported seltzer water, ale, porter, and saloon supplies.

The saloon on Monroe had become a restaurant and had begun to gather fame as early as 1871, especially as a caterer for banquets. Big as he was in beer, Luehrmann shifted more of his abilities into the restaurant business in 1883 when he moved up Monroe to Main and opened the "Terrace Garden" at the southeast corner. It was a great success, while beer wholesaling went into murky times.

John Schorr and his associates came down from St. Louis in 1885 and established the Tennessee Brewing Company. This is the company that produced, years later, the popular "Goldcrest" brand, and their brewery is still standing on the bluff edge. In 1886 Schlitz put its own bottling plant on North Main, in the building still standing north of Auction Square. But the Schlitz agent continued for a while to use the Luehrmann bottling plant on Monroe as his address, even though the horses and wagons were housed on North Main.

Luehrmann's restaurant and bar business at the Terrace Garden flourished. He had been famous for extraordinarily fine food for years, and his fame grew. He was the champion of German cooking against the

French cuisine, longer established in Memphis, of John Gaston in his small but renowned hotel on the south side of Court Square. Both served finer food than had ever been known in Memphis. As long as the generation who ate at Luehrmann's and Gaston's lived, it was often said that none who came after equalled them.

Luehrmann did so well that he built the original Luehrmann's Hotel on the site of the Terrace Garden, at 314–316 Main (old numbering system). It, too, was a great success, briefly, until fire ended that chapter in 1892. He then moved across Monroe a half block and built the well-remembered Luehrmann's. The old street number was 296 Main, the property later occupied by the Bank of Commerce, which has become the Commerce Title Building. Distinctive as the Luehrmann building seemed, it was a rebuilding of a leased building. It was leased as long as he had it.

This was the location patronized by the big sportsmen and the famous names of the theater. Diners at the heavy oak tables covered with thick napery included Joseph Jefferson, Sir Henry Irving, Frederick Warde, Robert Mantell, Otis Skinner, and many others of less luster.

Henry Luehrmann was especially impressed by the actors, but some big businessmen also came, and he sometimes ventured into other investments—as a founder of the Pioneer Cotton Mills, a director of First National Bank, the Home Insurance Company, and other firms. He and Mrs. Luehrmann, the former Louise Correl, had a home on Madison, near McLean, and there were six children.

Some details were left to William H. Otte, manager in later years, who with John Brame, one of the black waiters, was happy to call up memories years afterward. But nothing was too small for his attention. When he arrived in the morning, he first thoroughly inspected the bar to see that everything was precisely where he wanted it, polished and clean, as tested with his silk handkerchief. Then he sat down and coffee was set before him. He poured a half cup and passed it back and forth under his nose, like a highborn lady in a perfume shop. His nose told him instantly if some newly hired minion had tried to get by without scalding the urn or washing the strainer. When that happened, all the coffee had to be poured out and everything done over until the coffee pleased him. Then he went below to feed the oysters.

This luxurious world came apart fast. In the spring of 1904 the Luehrmann building was sold at Chancery Court auction at the corner of Main and Madison, producing only $91,000 for creditors. A few weeks later, Luehrmann's health broke, and he went to Southern California.

Several months later he came back, but his health broke again and he went to the Tate Springs spa and then to a Knoxville hospital, where he died on 18 June 1905. He had been ill about a year with tuberculosis.

His son made an attempt to revive the hotel. But the horse crowd was gone; the legislature had shut down race betting in 1905. Bitter statewide politics split the state on saloons, and the antiliquor forces won a law in 1909, although enforcement was delayed. On 22 June 1909 the hotel, dining room, and bar officially were closed with a sale of fine draperies, carpeting, chairs, and other furnishings at a fraction of their value.

Memories of elegance lingered for decades, as well as respect for a man whose accomplishments are permanently recorded in the Vedder history of Memphis, which called him "honorable and honest in every way, and one who can be thoroughly trusted and relied upon." The book was published while he was still on the corner of Monroe, before he had even built the famous epicurean delight of his widest fame.

Cycle Glory

" . . . Introduction in 1877 of the 'safety' bicycle made it possible for ordinary people to enjoy bicycling. Clubs were formed, and on pleasant Sundays rural areas were invaded by picnic parties on bicycles, and the farmer's horses were scared by the sight of women astride the machines engaged in unladylike exertions. By 1900 there were 10 million bicycles in use, and manufacturers and bicycle clubs were promoting a good-roads movement." So says Leland D. Baldwin in *The Stream of American History*.

The "safety" bicycle is the one with wheels of the same size, replacing the big-wheeled "bone crusher" on which acrobats and daring young men took their chances of dangerous falls. The new design was a plaything of the "gilded age," just before the sporting crowd took up one-lung automobiles. Girls who had ridden sidesaddle on horseback soon gave up the long skirts that caught in bicycle sprockets in favor of bloomers, while men developed a whole new outfit of clothing for cycling. The tandem came on strong for the unmarried set.

In Memphis the cycling fad took hold in full fervor during the '90s. A web of bicycle trails was developed out from the city line in all directions, to Lucy, Egypt, Rosemark, Munford, and Horn Lake. Numerous contests of speed and endurance were set up along the established routes, especially out the Raleigh Road, now Jackson Avenue.

Styles for Cycling in the '90s (courtesy of the Memphis and Shelby County Public Library).

Perhaps the news that more than fifteen thousand had turned out for a national bicycle competition in New Jersey in the fall of 1892 was a spur to local interest. Memphis enthusiasm certainly was increased when bicycle news spread from the sports pages to the social news in the spring of 1893, as it became fashionable for young men and women to put a picnic basket on the rack and pedal into the country. Especially popular were picnics at Billings Park, the half-mile harness-racing track on the south side of White (now Firestone), on property partially used now for Manassas High. (This track is often confused with the mile oval of the Memphis Driving Park, built later and farther north.)

Popularity of the bicycle increased the clamor for better roads, and then for tracks of crushed cinders along the roads especially for cyclists. In an era when everyone who could afford one had a horse, the bicycle allowed escape from the expenses of stables and stable hands.

Road contests were frequent and a few boys who perched on gates and fences to watch the "scorchers" go by are still alive. Yet interest in outdoor events was dimmed in October of 1896 when a bowl with a steeply banked track, under a roof, was built for cycle men—and women—professional racers as well as amateurs. It was on Madison at Tucker, just west of the popular East End amusement park.

Information about this building is sparse because it was miles from Memphis, in the town of Idlewild, or because it was so popular that everyone knew where it was without writing the location. A treasured item in my files is a letter from Nash Buckingham, a sensational performer in several sports, and famous writer about sports. He says: "in the mid-nineties, immediately west of East End Park was built a bicycle racing 'Coliseum' or Vendrome, a steeply banked wooden track, completely grandstanded. Here amateurs and pros pedaled for cash and fame: such figures as Al Weining and the imported sensational midget Tommy Michaels, or Michael."

Both East End and the coliseum for bicycles were made possible by the East End "dummy line" cars hauled by little steam locomotives. They ran on Madison, connecting the downtown loop of street cars with East End and then turning south down Cooper to Young and the horse races at Montgomery Park, now the Fairgrounds. The coke-burning boilers appeared in 1887, later to be replaced by electric trolleys, and still later to become a part of the Memphis Street Railway.

This five-cent ride was popular among those going to the bicycle dome and it was competition for East End. The amusement park attempted to hold the bicycle crowd with an East End bicycle "tournament" 10 September 1896, as the coliseum was about to open. But East End seems to have been handicapped in attracting cyclists riding out from the city by bayous crossing the Madison route. At least the East End Railway tracks had to be lifted on trestles over bayou bottoms at what now is Dudley and again at what is now Willett. Both were outside the city limit.

Cycling was booming here in 1896, even before the "vendrome" opened. On the Fourth of July the Columbia Club of Memphis took part in races at Nashville. They wore new uniforms of pale steel blue, trimmed in white, with sashes of stars and stripes which had been provided by the Pope Manufacturing Company. Memphis club members "covered themselves with glory," it was reported.

A number of bicycle models were available here. The Pope was a well-advertised machine, as magazines of the time will testify. But there was lots of competition. In 1896 the big Memphis dealer seems to have been the Southern Cycle Emporium at 211 Main, owned by C. J. Scherer. The Emporium offered the Victor, the Ben Hur, and the Crescent. Another dealer was Rice & Humes at 258 Second, a partnership of W. Y. C. Humes and Francis J. Rice, who was much better known in later years as Frank Rice, generalissimo of Crump state politics. J. P. Parker sold bicycles at 296½ Second, although he gradually edged into automobiles a few years later. He was once agent for the Ideal, the Rambler, and the Tribune, with a big business in bicycle tires and parts. This was the same Jerome P. Parker who is best remembered as the Packard dealer, although he also sold other automobiles. H. L. Sawyer had a bicycle shop at 308 Second. The Memphis Cycle Company was at 235 Main. Frank Shumann, who had a general business in equipment for sports and athletics, sold bicycles at 414 Main.

The Bicycle Dome had a spectacular event on 19 October 1896 when J. Eaton did an exhibition mile in 1:58. That was a second better than had been accomplished by a famous racer, Tommy Cooper of Detroit. The large crowd was especially thrilled by another comparison, however. Nashville newspapers of the day before had claimed the nation's fastest track because Johnnie Johnson had turned in a 2:02 mile on 17 October. So the Memphis boards were obviously faster. On 27 October about thirty-five hundred persons piled into the grandstands to watch the "Southern Championship" events. Dick Yeates of Memphis did very well but the championship went to Cooper, the Detroit speedster. There were several displays of "fantastic wheelmanship," it was reported. A "bicycle carnival" was announced for 16 November with two cycles as door prizes, the King's Daughters as sponsors, and music by Arnold's Brass Band.

Early in 1897 it developed that Memphis had a bicycle factory. The University was a high-grade wheel at a price within the reach of all, it was announced by R. Kupferschmidt, proprietor. He also sold the Halladay, the United States, the Clipper, the White, and the Aetna. Furthermore, the maker of the University bicycle offered free repairs for one year for any brand bought from him for more than seventy-five dollars during 1897, and that included patching of the frequent punctures.

That was in February. In early March there was a report of dozens of riders and hundreds of fans coming into town for approaching races at the coliseum. Jay Eaton of New Orleans, the indoor champion of the United States, was an early arriver. Henry Bradis and the Terrible

Swede, who may have been the same person, were expected close behind. Jack Prince, coliseum manager, had plastered flaming posters on buildings and lamp posts. For this event there was a tightening of ticket procedure. Bettors had begun to follow the professional cyclists several years before and the 1897 announcement said an "undesirable element" had been frequenting the bicycle tracks.

Something put a deep chill on the bicycle enthusiasm that spring, whether it was betting on the professionals or another development. In July a news story said the southern Bicycle Racing Circuit was practically a thing of the past. However, although the coliseum had been built for those races, it was surviving their decline. The track was about to be "illuminated," meaning electric lighting was to be installed for night cycling. On the night of 15 July women and children with their own wheels were to be admitted at half price.

In early August a crowd of two thousand was seen as a big revival of interest. There was a Halle-Goldsmith cup for amateurs. There was a fifteen mile match in which Zack Oliver of Memphis beat A. G. Bartholomew of Philadelphia, Pennsylvania. One of the wonders of the bicycle world was Frank Frain, the "Memphis Midget," a small man who in later years had a stove business on Second.

Outdoor cycle events went on while professionals on the indoor track were getting most of the attention. On 24 May 1898 the "greatest road race in county history" was held and it was the ninth annual contest. The course was on Raleigh Road from Breedlove almost to National Cemetery. There were fifty-eight contestants and at least two thousand spectators strung out along the way. The winner was F. M. McClintic, telegraph operator on *The Commercial Appeal* staff.

But 1898 brought a sudden end to the glory days of the bicycle here. The bicycle coliseum burned. It was a total loss. After that the Memphis stars of pedal speed, notably Ben Monroe, or Munroe, had to make their news elsewhere. In 1899 Monroe won the National Circuit Meet in St. Louis. Earlier the same year he and two other racers set a new world record for a "triplet" mile. In 1903 he and a partner were the world champions of the six-day race, after winning at Madison Square Garden. His partner, as the "Dixie Fliers," was one Walthour of Atlanta. They clocked 2,318 miles.

But, by 1903 the times were changing. Jerome Parker's catalog that year had pages of automobile parts behind the bicycle parts in the front. He was the only automobile dealer here that was offering a Rambler to those who would send $750 to "Kenasha," Wisconsin, with five dollars for crating, plus freight. The automobile was about to look far more attractive to young people than the tandem bicycle or the buggy.

Militia Entertainment

Less than a century ago one of the popular amusements in Memphis was watching the militiamen drill. In elaborate uniforms of varied designs and colors, the young men of good standing went through drills or competed as individuals. They had to have more than average income, for they bought their own uniforms and they had to have free time at least one evening a week for the drills. They elected their own officers. They paraded and gave fancy balls and banquets. And when they wearied of militia obligations they simply broke up the company, letting the public move on to another unit displaying its drilling skills.

Some of these volunteer local soldiers were the great-grandsons of Tennessee's militiamen of the days when every able-bodied white man between eighteen and forty-five was required to serve. They had to report for a battalion muster each spring and a regimental muster in the fall. Those were two days every man, woman, and child looked forward to. Aside from the drilling formations with drum and fife music, there were stands offering ginger cakes, pies, and cider, as well as a handy barrel of whiskey, foot races, target shooting, and lots of fights.

A lively description of muster days in Tipton County about 1820 is still available in *Old Times in West Tennessee*, thanks to reprinting in 1975 by the Daughters of the American Revolution of Ripley. But records of whatever militia activity there was in Shelby County then have been lost.

Memphis militia made their first mark in the record in the "Flatboat War" of 1842. We then had the Rifle Guards, commanded by Captain E. F. Ruth, and the Memphis Blues. When war with Mexico came in 1846 Memphis suddenly had six companies of militia. Three went to Mexico: Captain Ruth's Rifle Guards, the Gaines Guards with M. B. Cook as captain, and the Eagle Guards, W. N. Porter captain. Eight men were killed south of the border. The other companies were too late to join the overflowing rolls of Tennessee volunteers. The Irish took the name of Jackson Greens, under a Captain Dunne. The Germans had another company. There also was a company captained by one Finley.

None of these companies survived until 1852, when two new ones were formed in the fast-growing city. One was the City Guards, Charles

M. Carroll, captain. They drilled Thursday nights in the first Exchange Building, on Front where the Auditorium is now. The other was the Continentals. Uniforms were like those of officers in the Continental Army; a shad-bellied coat over a long Quakerlike vest, knee breeches, high boots and tricorner hats.

In 1853 the company of Washington Riflemen was formed under Captain F. Ringwald. They were Germans, mostly refugees from the Prussian Revolution. Drill nights were Mondays and the armory was in the Exchange Building. Before the year was over this name was altered to Washington Rifle Company and the armory was moved to the Navy Yard. This was a company that lasted for years, while others dropped from sight. The Young American Invincibles lasted at least long enough to get their uniforms in 1855.

In the winter of 1858–59 the Light Guard appeared, Jones Genette, captain. They paraded in blue coats trimmed in gold and buff. Pants were blue with gold stripes for officers and buff stripes for the ranks. The headpieces were in West Point style, a gold wreath in front circling the letters "LG." This was another company with an Exchange Building armory.

That winter the young Germans again claimed attention by organizing the Steuben Artillery. The company, captained by William Miller, was given four fine brass cannons by the state and the city rejoiced in being able to retire the old iron cannon which had been fired from the bluff for ceremonies. The aldermen almost rejoiced enough to give them a building for storage and for bad weather drills. But on reconsideration the idle Navy Yard was again used for storage, and a drill field for several companies was set aside behind a fire house at Adams and Second.

Two other companies were set up in 1859. The Jackson Guards, under Captain M. Magevney, Jr., had its armory in the Exchange Building. The Southern Guards had an armory at the northeast corner of Main and Monroe. James Hamilton was captain.

When the Civil War came, two other companies had been formed, the Light Dragoons and the Harris Cadets. In honor of Mississippi troops passing through on their way to war in April of 1861, the Memphis militia lined up: the Washington Rifles, the Steuben Artillery, the Southern Guards, the Light Guards, the Light Dragoons, and the Harris Cadets.

Men and big boys of Memphis went to war. While they were away thousands of newcomers came in behind the Yankee army and they formed a militia unit called the Home Guards. David C. Lowenstine, a wholesale dry goods merchant and competitor of a Memphis firm with a slightly different name, was distinguished as captain in this Yankee militia.

When the war was over none of the prewar militiamen revived their companies. The first return to military interests probably was the De-Soto Rifles. But all we know of them is that in 1872 two newspapers bemoaned their passing and the waste of their guns and equipment in calling for a new organization.

Nothing happened until the summer of 1874 when a feeling of uneasiness developed because of Negro "breakouts." There was a proposal to form a military company for protection of the law-abiding community. Some young men, none of them veterans, were gathered by invitation only in a secret meeting. They organized the Chickasaw Guards, by far the most famous of all Memphis militia companies. They paid a twenty-five-dollar initiation fee and they drilled twice a week, sometimes three, in the Criminal Court room, then at Jefferson and Second. R. P. Duncan was the original captain, while Sam Carnes was the captain during its years of fame. They had blue uniforms, which outraged part of them, recalling the recent war. They had plenty of officers, including third lieutenants, fourth sergeants, and fourth corporals.

It was still 1874 and the Chickasaw Guards were less than two months old when they were called up for service at Somerville. A threat of "Negro trouble" had passed when they arrived, but the incident put an abrupt end to carpetbag management of Fayette County. The guards also were credited with holding down the voting power of Shelby County's carpetbaggers.

There followed a period in which militia drilling became a spectator sport. Crowds of gentlemen and their ladies turned out at sundown to watch competitions for small prizes in almost perfect drill routines. The Chickasaw Guards went on to national contests at St. Louis, Indianapolis, Cincinnati, Columbus, Louisville, New Orleans, and other cities. Huge crowds cheered performances that were judged in decimal point scores, and the grandstands moaned when favorites missed the prize.

They became well known when they toured the North with benefit performances which raised thousands of dollars for the Memphis yellow fever fund. In 1882 they won the national championship. West Point officers, in *Harper's Weekly*, named them the best drilled citizen soldiers in the United States. General William T. Sherman went further. He said they were better than anything at West Point.

The Chickasaw Guards had the longest life and the greatest prominence among our militia companies. The Templar Guards, with Jackson
P. Crews as captain, was also organized in 1874. The Bluff City Grays
appeared in 1876 with Captain J. F. Cameron. The name of Memphis
Light Guards returned in 1877, led by E. B. Moseley. The Grays and the
Light Guards merged in 1882 to form the Porter Guards, with J. D.
Waldran as captain. They wore swallowtailed red jackets. The trousers
were buff, with scarlet stripes between cords of gold. They were the
strongest rivals of the Chickasaw Guards. During their first year they
won a $1,000 first prize at Dubuque, Iowa, and came home to a Main
Street parade, with skyrockets, Roman candles and bonfires.

Militia interest spread to the Negro community. The McClelland
Guards were formed in 1875, with James G. Glass as captain. This
company served the city well during the yellow fever of 1878. It kept
order at the distribution of food each noon in Court Square. Control was
thoroughly established when a black militia killed a black bully as a riot
threatened. The McClellands won the national Negro militia championship at St. Louis. Another Negro company, the Zouave Guards,
made its bow in 1879.

The Humes Rifles was a company with a short life in 1878, under
Captain C. E. Waldran. The Porter Reserves helped the city through the
yellow fever of 1879. Artillery came back in 1878. The Bluff City Light
Artillery had two twelve-pound Napoleons and forty sabres. J. S.
Reudelhuber was captain during a brief existence.

On 7 May 1878, there was an outing at the Fairgrounds which drew
3,000 to a program of which the big event was a drill competition
between the "Chicks" (Chickasaw Guards) and the Bluff City Grays.
The crowd paid seventy-five cents at the gate and most of them paid
another twenty-five cents to ride cars of the Memphis and Charleston
Railroad for the four miles from city to fairgrounds.

In 1881 the Light Guard name came back. Willis Cole was captain of
this company, which had a Main Street armory and gave a ball.

Parade grounds were moved to the bluff. By 1881 there was a militia
drill almost every night. Crowds were so big police had to be called to
keep spectators from overflowing into the line of march. When electric
lights came to Memphis (from a company founded by Sam Carnes of the
Chickasaw Guards) in 1884 some of the earliest lights were installed on
tall poles at corners of the parade grounds.

The Waldran Guards, under Capt. L. V. Dixon, came in 1882, but
lived only a year, maybe two. That year was more notable for the girls
who joined the militia. They called themselves the Broom Brigade, and

drilled with brooms as though they were rifles. A few weeks later Negro girls did likewise, forming the Broom Rangers and drilling in the Zouave Armory, at least long enough to make a newspaper story. The Light Infantry came on the scene briefly in 1885, with B. F. Hollenberg as captain. In 1886 the Memphis Zouaves was organized under F. K. Deffry. It was an active company for more than twenty years. Montgomery Guards, Abe Frank, captain, was organized in 1889. The name honored H. A. Montgomery, businessman and president of New Memphis Jockey Club, for whom Montgomery Park was named. There was a company of Schorr Zouaves which was reorganized as the Bluff City Zouaves in 1890.

Applause for the best drill teams was abundant on 27 July 1897, when the Neely Zouaves came back from the national competition at San Antonio bearing the first prize. There were fireworks and bonfires and 15,000 lined the curbs from the Iron Mountain station to the Court Square. The fireworks fell "like rain" as the parade of red fezzes marched in triumph.

Then the National Guard began to take over. The word "militia" slowly faded out of common use. The tradition of local management was weakened. The Hibernians and the Schorrs became National Guard units. So did the Governor's Guards and the Frazier Light Guards, and eventually the Chickasaw Guards. The National Guard is a stronger peacetime army and yet it is different—how very different—from militia companies in which the men chose the design of uniforms and the bright colors they wanted, bought their own uniforms, built or rented armories with lockers for their gear, elected their officers, drilled at least one night a week and strutted before cheering crowds of girls, uncles, and neighbors.

Lyric Quality

In September of 1908 the theatrical menu of Memphis was enriched by the opening of a new theater on the south side of Madison, just west of Fourth. It was the Jefferson, named in honor of the theatrical Joseph, rather than the political Thomas. In 1911 the name was changed to "Lyric" and it is as the Lyric Theatre that is best remembered. There were about fourteen hundred seats, of which a few were boxes. The cost was $150,000.

The opener was *If I Were King,* starring the handsome young matinee idol of the highest rank, Sidney Toler, who attracted another following many years later as the rotund Charlie Chan. Another favorite, much later, was Lyle Talbot, who had a second surge of popularity in a stock company with a new drama each week on another stage, the Lyceum. He also had a long career in Hollywood. Sarah Bernhardt was seen on the Lyric boards, as was Maude Adams.

The best of music was presented there. The magnificent tones of Galli-Curci flowed over spellbound audiences. Kreisler's violin thrilled even reluctant husbands among the music lovers. Rachmaninoff's keyboard chords brought rounds of roaring applause. Scotti was heard at the Lyric, and Martinelli. There was a remarkable program in 1921 with Alma Gluck and Efram Zimbalist together on the stage. The Cortese brothers brought in the Creatore Grand Opera for three nights and a matinee.

Deep pathos settled on the Lyric stage on 5 March 1915. The original "Kathleen" of "I'll Take you Home Again, Kathleen" lived here. Her real name was Jane and she was called "Jennie," even during the long years after the famous song was first heard in 1876. A touring musical company knew she was here and when it got to Memphis put the song about "Kathleen" on its program. A special box was prepared for her and for her composer husband, Thomas Paine Westendorf. A chauffeured limousine was sent for them. But it came back empty. "Kathleen" had died a few hours before the curtain. The show went on—with the box occupied only by flowers.

The Lyric was the center of an extraordinary event in early radio. From that stage came the best broadcast of opera heard in Memphis up to that time, which also was one of the worst opera broadcasts ever on the air. It was the best because it was the first. WMC was the only radio broadcaster in Memphis, having come on the air 19 January 1923, with a test program in which The Community Melody Makers played dance tunes. It was a roaring success. So the elaborate opening program was presented on 20 January. On 21 January the WMC crew surmounted the difficulties of an experienced concert singer silenced by mike fright. They got prima donna Anna Fitzui back on her feet by hiding the microphone in a floor lamp.

Thus emboldened, they undertook on 22 January to broadcast The San Carlo Opera Company singing *Aida* from the Lyric stage. There were only a few radio receiving sets then and those who had them invited guests for opera parties. WMC then had exactly one microphone. So they took it from the studio, on the top floor of *The Commercial Appeal* building at Second and Court, and put it on the stage. Trying to pick up a stage full of singers on the move was enough to guarantee a poor production. More than that, the broadcast faded into silence after about two hours.

The transmitter had overheated and the opera was long over when it cooled down. In the beginning there was programming with numerous periods off the air and long sustained transmitting was unimportant, but after extensive puzzlement about the heating it was found that the transmitter, originally in a closet without air, did fine when ventilation was installed fore and aft.

There had been a period of good vaudeville at the Lyric. It was when the Shubert and Erlanger partnership in New York broke up. Erlanger, after setting up the new firm of Klaw & Erlinger, came to Memphis with his acts at the Lyric. The Shubert acts were booked at the Lyceum, and they both had to be good because of competition at the Orpheum.

Then there had been a period of big moving pictures at the Lyric. It was on the Lyric screen that Memphis first saw "The Big Parade" and *The Covered Wagon*. An incident at the Lyric in 1929 brought nationwide attention to the Memphis Censor Board and its chairman, Lloyd T. Binford. The film version of the life of Jesus, *King of Kings,* added some chapters to the Gospels. After a previous screening the censors ordered the variations cut. The manager refused. The film was barred from Memphis, and the producer went to court. The censors won.

By that time the Lyric had come upon hard times. During its first two years, as the Jefferson, it had been a great success. The beautiful SRO sign bloomed in the lobby almost nightly. The original manager was A. B. Morrison, who either was one of the best theater men in Memphis or had the largest number of admirers, or both. He brought in top names. But he was hired away to Main Street.

In 1921 Memphis suddenly had three big, new, and fine movie houses, the Pantages, Palace, and State. They were luxurious while the Lyric was a plain building of yellow brick. They were convenient to patronage on the main street, while the Lyric was a bit out of the way.

The Lyric became available for prize fights and wrestling shows, political rallies, and revivals. In 1921 the American Legion held a minstrel show there, hoping to lure ticket buyers with a street parade led by Mayor Rowlett Paine, and a brass band. The Ku Klux Klan, which usually assembled outside the city line in Bethel Grove, once rallied in the Lyric, and packed it to the rafters.

Perhaps name confusion has contributed to the obscurity into which the Lyric has fallen. In its early years there was competition from another Lyric, a variety house of 1,000 seats on Adams, between Main and Second. There was also the shift in names from Jefferson to Lyric. And there has been a modern Lyric, the summer music program at Memphis State. Finally, in its old age, the name was changed again to the Mazda. Most of all there has been an unreasonable, but continuing, confusion of young people of the Lyric, on Madison, with the Lyceum, a beautiful piece of architecture at Second and Jefferson.

Renaming the Lyric the Mazda was an attempt by the Mazda Grotto, a fraternal order, to organize a recreational center. It was unsuccessful and the Junior Order of United Mechanics took over in 1932. This organization used one room and paid neither purchase notes or taxes. The courts ruled that it was only an attempt by the owners to escape taxes. The city and county took over in 1940 for almost thirteen thousand dollars in unpaid taxes from 1928 to 1938. Empty, abandoned, almost forgotten, the old Lyric was wiped off the map on 23 January 1941 by fire, probably the victim of a lightning bolt. The local governments had even neglected to insure it.

Beale Street Rambles

There is a slice of life in Memphis that should be put into the record before the last of those who were there are gone beyond recall. It was known here and for many miles away as the "Midnight Ramble," although it was advertised by the Beale Street Palace as the "Frolic." It was an added showing starting an hour before midnight for a white crowd to see the song and dance acts running that week for blacks. The regular showing for the black audience was held at the regular hour, but on Thursdays it was repeated as a midnight special. White couples came, and so did crowds of young white men, and sometimes groups of women. They came in profitable numbers for years.

George W. Lee, black author of the famous *Beale Street: Where the Blues Began,* was greatly impressed with the Rambles. He described the block of Beale between Hernando and Fourth as the center of night life and said, "On Thursday nights the block belongs to the white people. They come in evening dress in high-powered cars, in overalls and Fords, to see the scantily clad brown beauties dancing across the stage in the midnight show at the Palace."

Years after W. C. Handy had moved his music publishing business to New York, he came back to Memphis with his famous band in 1936.

Bessie Smith (from *Black Magic* by Langston Hughes and Milton Meltzer).

Handy's Band was the attraction at the Palace on Beale for a week. That week the midnight show for whites was offered two nights. Handy had been back before. In 1922 a Handy show was staged in the Lyric Theater on Madison near Fourth by Doc Hottum. There was a night for blacks and another for whites, who packed the big house to the rafters.

Municipal law required racial separation. Furthermore, the Midnight Ramble was only a few years old when Lloyd T. Binford became chairman of the city censor board. Most of the Memphis population at that time probably agreed with segregated audiences, although part of the public would have been less drastic than the censors in snipping Lena Horne out of a Ziegfeld Follies film and lifting Pearl Bailey out of the movie, *Variety Girl*.

In this atmosphere, going down to Beale Street at midnight was an offbeat thing to do. Those in search of the unusual swelled the crowd of ticket buyers who enjoyed the moaning blues and the beat of jazz of the kind now known as Dixieland.

In the Midnight Rambles on Beale Street, Memphis had something special. Advertising appeared among the downtown motion picture displays in Thursday editions of *The Commercial Appeal*. For instance the issue of 13 October 1927 showed: "Palace—Frolic—Tonight 11 P.M.—White People Onil [a misprint for "only"]—The Get Happy Co. in Musical Comedy—presenting William Benbow—One of the big hits of the season."

A week later on 20 October the advertisement said: "Frolic—For White People Only—admission 75¢—(There was then a closely trimmed picture of a black woman, followed by words.) Mamie Smith—Originator of the Blues and her gang—A perfect riot of fun from start to finish—a Black Diamond chorus that has no equal— Palace."

The "originiator of the blues" phrase refers to the fact that Mamie Smith was the first to make records. "Crazy Blues" was one of her best sellers. She was unrelated to Bessie Smith, who later became a favorite of the Memphis audience.

Bessie Smith came along after Ma Rainey. Her gold mine was "Down Hearted Blues," which came out in 1923. It was written by Alberta Hunter, who recorded it first but attracted comparatively feeble attention. Without theatrical staging or showmanship, Bessie Smith simply took stage center and shouted her blues. The applause was a tumult when she appeared on the Palace stage in Memphis and other black theaters of the South, or in Harlem, or on the South Side of Chicago. But when she made a venture into the world of New York night clubs, the white public turned such a cold shoulder that her act was closed after three nights.

Then she came upon hard times. Record companies united in shutting her out because they thought she asked too high a fee. One story was that she wanted fifty dollars a side. She was barely making it on the black theater circuit in 1937 when an automobile crash on Highway 61 near Clarksville, Mississippi, killed her. (There was a false story in the East of her dying because a white hospital kept her out of the emergency room. This became part of an off-Broadway play. The fact is that everything possible was done for her on the roadside by a young white Memphis doctor, Dr. Hugh Smith, who happened by on a fishing trip. She was too badly injured to be saved in any hospital.)

It is Bessie Smith's name that first comes to mind when Lee Hoffman of 1437 Central tells of the numerous Rambles he saw. Hoffman says she drew bigger crowds than anyone else and, in his memory, popularity of the midnight show declined when she was gone. Expert opinion seems to agree with him. She made a deep impression that lasted long after her death. In 1967 the book *Black Magic* by Langston Hughes and Milton Meltzer came out with a section on the blues which opened with some words and a small picture of Handy facing a full-page photograph of Bessie Smith.

But it was Ethel Waters who was favored by Beale Street ticket buyers, white and black, in the memory of Frank Liberto. She was at the Palace at least twice, and her big song was "Am I Blue?" When the Rambles were new, Liberto had the Cadillac Inn at 320 Beale, next door to the Palace, an all-night lunch room with a good view of what was going on along the street. He later became, and still is, an automobile dealer.

In George W. Lee's book he seemed to be especially impressed by the career of Louise Cook, "exponent of the snake hips." She was discovered by Irving C. Miller on an amateur night at the Palace in 1924. He promptly put her in the chorus line of his *Brown Skin Models*. In 1928 he built the show *Tokyo* around her with a Japanese band and his star renamed "Joda, the oriental dancer." She was the top attraction of the later show, *Hot Chocolate*.

A newspaper clipping from January 1934 shows Miller bringing his *Brown Skin Models* show with a "ramble for whites" Thursday night at 11:30 P.M. This was a company of thirty-five. It included Harry Schoolfield and his ten "New Yorkers," who had been heard on national radio. There was also George Bias, whose records were on the market, and Alta Gates, a blues singer, as well as Blanche Thompson. The dance team was Teddy and Estelle. Comedy was in the hands of "Cut-Out" Ellis and "Rags" Cole, who had been seen on Broadway in *Hot Rhythm*.

Another clipping from 1934, in September, shows A. (for Anselmo) Barrasso, the manager, looking forward to the Silas Green company of sixty-five, with twenty singers and dancers, twenty girls and twenty musicians. Such a large touring company has been unheard of for many years on any modern stage. In fact it was a risky venture in 1934 for the Palace, which had it booked for one day only, a Monday; but for that special occasion the whites got a chance to see it on a Monday night ramble. The company included Silas and Lilas, for comedy, and Charley Rue, Frank Keith, Joe Sheftill, Billy and Bing, Cleo Mitchell, and Edna Young. The manager was looking forward to a return of the *Brown Skin Models* with the new 1934 show, to Mamie Smith & Company, to the *Ebony Follies,* as well as S. H. Sooley, Blanche Calloway, Bessie Smith, and Ethel Waters.

Origin of the Rambles, and of the Palace Theater itself, is a bit murky. George Lee's book says the original Beale Street theater for blacks was the Pastime, opened in 1909 by Sam Zerilla, clarinet veteran of the Italian Army band and of the John Philip Sousa band. The 1916 directory shows Zerilla still owning the Pastime at 324 Beale. That is the street number of the Palace. But the 1927 directory shows the Palace name and a new owner, Lorenzo Pacini. George W. Lee thought it had been built by "Barasso and the Pacini brothers." (This Barasso was Anselmo, known as "Zelmo." There were several Pacini brothers, including Joe and Nello and the best known, Lorenzo.)

The name of Pacini brings in the most famous of all Beale Street establishments, the P-Wee Saloon, across the street from the Palace. (Photographs clearly show "P-Wee Saloon" painted on the front of the building, although writers usually give another spelling to "P-Wee." The name "Lorenzo Pacini" also was painted on the building at 317 Beale.) The original "P-Wee" was Vigello Maffeei, who went back to Italy, leaving his partner, Lorenzo Pacini with the business. There is some false folklore in which Handy wrote the "Memphis Blues" while standing at P-Wee's cigar counter. There were amateur shows, with white patrons admitted one night a week. This involved quarters and half-dollars thrown from the audience to the stage as added applause for an attractive number, or at the end of the show for the entertainers to scramble for.

There also was a time when the whites were admitted only to the gallery, but that must have been brief. Luke Kingsley, later widely known as the announcer of fights and other sports events, liquor store owner on Union near Front, and operator of a cigar store and ticket agency, remembers the balcony for having only thirty to thirty-five seats. The Rambles became popular and packed the whole theater with whites. Only a few were in evening dress. Most wore ordinary clothes, with the underworld well represented, including some fancy outfits on fancy women. Kingsley is ninety now, without strong memories of the stars, although he remembers Bessie Smith when asked. The Kingsley memory is sharp for numerous events of sports, politics, and the stage, but he had little reason to mark the first year of the Rambles—or the last. Memories of other oldtimers conflict on these years.

But they all agree that when the Rambles closed at 1 A.M., the thing to do was to go to Johnny Mills's for ribs. He was just around the corner at 150 South Fourth. He was already known to some of the night life crowd, having worked for Liberto at the Cadillac Inn. He borrowed fifty dollars from Kingsley when he opened his rib restaurant. The ribs he served were superior and his fame was spread across the land when orchestra men from the Peabody found him during dance breaks. There once was a band in New York that got to talking with such enthusiasm about how good those ribs tasted that they telephoned for a big order to be airmailed.

While the Palace had a segregated night for whites Johnny Mills obtained segregation with a partition down the middle of the restaurant. In the late night hours the white half overflowed with whites milling around the sidewalk waiting for space inside. It was a very different world and it is poorly recorded.

Sweet Summer Nights

There was a time when sundown on a hot summer day in Memphis brought a chance to put on fresh shirts and dresses and go to Overton Park for an excursion into the tuneful tinsel of the operetta world.

Cool breezes of dusk, constant buzzing of locusts in the trees, violins tuning up and teenage ushers scurrying up and down the aisles built an air of happy anticipation night after night. The ticket buyer might have seen the show a dozen times on other stages in other cities, or have seen the Memphis version earlier in the week and come back for a second helping. Or there could be a boy or girl from down the street right up there in the floodlights with professionals from the East.

Latercomers had to park at the zoo and walk, unless they joined the hundreds who rode street railway buses to the entrance. A line of buses waited for the final curtain. The audience could be pretty sure an airliner would go over during the featured number of the second act. There were frequent threats of rain—but few rains. Still they came, often by chartered bus from Forrest City, Arkansas, or Dyersburg, Tennessee, or other towns.

It was the Memphis Open Air Theatre, which usually was known by its initials, the MOAT. The last curtain call was taken in 1951, after fourteen seasons in which eighty-nine productions were staged, each for a Monday-Saturday run.

When the MOAT opened in 1938 it was a somewhat delayed response to music in the park in 1932 and 1933. Three shows had been offered each season, on the dirt stage at the foot of the slope where the Overton Park Shell was built later. Producers were Ralph Dunbar and his wife, the former Jocleta Howe, each thoroughly experienced performers and

Frances Greer

show producers. They had the support of the Beethoven Club. But they had very little money and it was the bottom of the Depression. When they seemed to be at the end of the money, Mr. and Mrs. W. R. Herstein picked up the expense account. The shows were good enough and public response was strong enough to encourage hope of more. Joe Brennan, Park Commission chairman, undertook to get businessmen as guarantors.

But the stage in the park was silent until the Junior Chamber of Commerce signed up underwriters for the 1938 MOAT. These energetic and enthusiastic young men enlisted support from Harry Martin, amusements editor of *The Commercial Appeal,* and Robert Johnson of the *Memphis Press-Scimitar.*

The MOAT took off with *Desert Song,* followed by *Sally, My Maryland, Katinka,* and *Firefly.* The cost was $30,000 for the five-show season and guarantors were hardly nicked. Tickets sales came within a whisker of paying the bills. Enthusiasm glowed for the 1939 season. Reginald Hammerstein—a big name in New York shows—and his staff were brought in. The new producer offered *New Moon, Roberta, Babes in Toyland, No! No! Nanette,* and *Vagabond King,* all well received. But ambitions and expenses ran ahead of attendance.

For the third season some new guarantors were found, Hillsman Taylor, an attorney, became MOAT president, Joseph Cortese became general manager, and remained throughout the MOAT era. Taylor was returned to the presidency each year except the last. They were behind the stage. On stage the 1940 season was very big because it brought Frances Greer to the shows under the stars.

Memphis singers delighted the crowds. Ethel Taylor (Mrs. Early Maxwell) was a favorite. Helen Parker (Mrs. Watkins Overton) won generous applause. Barbara Walker (Mrs. John Hummel) stepped out of the chorus into a leading role and brought a flurry of ticket sales before becoming Miss America. Leonard Graves and Bill Ching went from the MOAT to nationwide applause.

There was some neighborly feeling about Frances Greer since she was from Helena and had been a sensation in Louisiana State student musicals. She had a fine voice which had carried her to the Philadelphia Opera and was about to take her to the Metropolitan. Beyond her voice she had a pert and happy stage manner that caught and held the MOAT crowd with her first step out of the wings.

Her 1940 show was *Naughty Marietta.* Her 1946 show was *Rose Marie.* It brought out the biggest crowd the MOAT ever had. There are 3,251 seats at the Overton Park Shell, but the ticket buyers kept right on paying for the chance to sit on the grass at the side or stand in the back until 4,459 were crowded in on 23 August. In 1948, the Greer *Rio Rita* attracted the biggest week of the MOAT record, 18,715. That was also the biggest season, with 105,498 for eight weeks.

Another favorite was Eddie Roecker, a fine baritone who first appeared here in 1945. He was brought back each year and, after the MOAT was gone, appeared several times in the free summer concerts on the same stage. He always sang from his MOAT repertory and stirred up talk that there must be a way to bring back to Memphis the old shows in which Roecker continued to sing at St. Louis and other cities.

Marguerite Piazza acquired an ardent Memphis following when she sang *Rose Marie* at the MOAT in 1950. She was on her way to the Metropolitan and television fame. Dorothy Kirsten, Mack Harrell, and John Guerney, all from the Met roster, sang at the MOAT.

A special favorite was Frank Hornaday and his specialty was *The Student Prince.* His tenor lead in the Serenade number stopped the show. The audiences would have been happy if they never heard the final scenes just so they could hear the Serenade again. On at least one night they got it eight times before the show moved on.

From the benches the MOAT was a great success, a sweet bouquet of music fondly recalled ever since. Attendance climbed from a low of 50,780 for the 1940 season to more than 105,000 for 1946, 1947, and 1948. In the treasurer's office the odor was sometimes sour. The hopeful start was possible because Musicians' Union men worked for $25 a week, without pay for overtime or rehearsals, even though dress rehearsals sometimes lasted all night. Boys and girls in the singing and dancing choruses worked for the experience. After two years they began to get the experience plus $4 a week. The Park Commission provided the shell, lights, and water, without charge. When Cortese became manager he was offered $1,200 a year—on the condition he produced a net big enough to pay it. A rehearsal hall at the auditorium was provided free. The Words & Music Shop gave space for a downtown ticket office.

This was the atmosphere in which the first season ticket sales lacked only $1,147 of paying the bills, which produced the splurge of 1939 and a net loss of $21,664. Then Cortese took over and there was a margin of $1,898. There were margins in 1941 and 1942, but lower, followed by a loss of almost fifteen hundred dollars in 1943. Four consecutive years of margins, 1944–1947, were the prosperous years, reaching a pinnacle of almost twenty-one thousand dollars. Losses returned in 1948 and climbed past thirty-nine thousand dollars for the 1951 season. During those years attendance sank from the 1948 peak to 49,485 in 1951.

By that time some of the favorite shows were beginning to lose their flavor. There probably was a factor in the arrival of home air conditioning. There was very little of it when the MOAT began but gradually room air conditioners were bought. They provided even cooler air than the park and the installments had to be paid. Television got to Memphis late in 1948 and some families added those installments to the household budget for a form of entertainment that was novel, available regardless of rainy nights, with cushioned chairs in place of bench planks, and much less trouble than changing clothes for a trip to the park.

Underneath these considerations was a weakness in financing. To make it available to a broad part of the public, the MOAT opened with the best seats at one dollar, and others at seventy-five cents, fifty cents, and twenty-five cents in the rear. A book of six of the best seats could be bought for five dollars. But it is probable that higher prices would have produced less income for there were some empty benches for unfamiliar shows and on nights when the clouds hung low.

There never was an undergirding of sales of big blocks of tickets to business houses, such as carry the Forest Park shows in St. Louis. In a way, however, all Memphis taxpayers were taking part by providing the stage and arena, the utility bills, and similar expenses of commercial entertainment. For all except the last season the MOAT used a stage built by Works Projects Administration (WPA) with which the New Deal made jobs. In time for the 1951 season the Park Commission built a much better stage, used for one season by the MOAT and ever since for free concerts. The city used $50,000 to improve the shell.

Park Commission use of tax money for the MOAT may have been the fatal flaw. E. H. Crump was unofficial manager of city-county business and someone got to Crump with the story that while taxes were being put into the MOAT, Joe Cortese and his relatives had a good thing going. Aside from Joe as general manager, there was Robert as associate manager, Tom as operator of some concessions, and John in charge of others. That is what Crump told me. As we remember it, nothing was made public about the Crump attitude. Perhaps it should have been. Then someone else, who knew the value of the Cortese services, might have gotten to Crump's other ear.

What happened in public was that Hillsman Taylor was replaced as MOAT president. The new president wrote a doom and gloom message which greeted every MOAT patron during the 1951 season from the inside program cover. When the MOAT season was over in the fall, Taylor was restored to the presidency, and some plans for another year, without Cortese, were made. But the fire had gone out. Miss America (Yolanda Betbeze) had been brought in to sing the lead in *Miss Liberty*. It was intended to be only the finale of the 1951 season. Months later it developed that those closing curtains had sent the MOAT over the hill into memories of another era.

Elvis's Home Town

Memphis was suddenly and unexpectedly overwhelmed by hordes of visitors on 17 August 1977. Elvis Presley had died the afternoon before. The town had known for years that Elvis was big in the entertainment world. Before he was graduated from Humes High School in 1953 he had hinted at the future by outshining all others in a show of student talents.

In 1956 the word was spread more widely around town with stories of the lawn of his home near Audubon Park being scalped by admirers. The

young people were driving out to see his house with the musical notes on the iron fence, parking, peeking in the windows and, for lack of any other memento, pulling up a few blades of grass. When the last grass was gone, there were so many parked automobiles that driveways of his unhappy neighbors were blocked. They were shut out of their homes and so were Elvis and his parents.

It was the grass that caused some Memphis newswriters to begin keeping notes on Elvis and the phenomenal sales of his recordings, his movies, and his tours. He soon removed the pressure on his neighbors by buying, in 1957, a big place on a Whitehaven hill already known, for an owner years before, as ''Graceland.'' Elvis had over twenty years at Graceland—twenty-three years of tumult and applause that began the night one of his records was first heard on local radio. His death was automatically a major event for Memphis newspapers. There were large headlines and plenty of pages for long stories.

Yet, newsmen had only a foggy notion of how big Elvis had become. There was surprise at the great number of persons at a distance who had intense feelings of personal loss. The breadth and depth of this interest began to unfold when hotels and motels overflowed the night of 16 August with newsmen from faraway places. Then the wire services began spilling out stories of huge headlines in London, Berlin, and on around the globe.

Thousands stood in the street in front of his home and its gates with guitar designs on the iron bars. Many of the parked automobiles bore license plates from Michigan, New Mexico, or Maine. Some cars were driven by tourists who heard the news on automobile radios, abandoned other vacation plans, and turned to drive all night to Memphis. One visitor told of cashing his savings account to buy an air ticket and get to the funeral. Strange items came in on the news wires about ten dollars and fifteen dollars being paid in distant states for the issue of *The Commercial Appeal* telling the Elvis death story. There was even a report of a twenty-five dollar price.

Responding to this far away interest in what his hometown newspapers said about Elvis, all stories published in the first five days after his death in *The Commercial Appeal* and the *Memphis Press-Scimitar* were put together in a special edition of twenty-four pages. Still unable to see how wide the interest was, it was estimated that about three hundred thousand copies would be sold. By the time it came off the press the plain announcement that it would be available had brought in stacks of check-bearing envelopes. Another printing had to be made, and then another. Extra clerks were hired. Eventually there were eight press runs and thirty-five extra persons were employed.

Dealers from Memphis bought by the thousands, and resold at $1.00 a copy, or $1.50, rarely $3.00. Elvis had been in his grave more than two months on 27 October when it was announced that the extra crews still had hope of catching up with the mail. They were only 114,000 pieces behind and mail had dwindled to 5,000 letters a day. When they finally caught up, more than 1,600,000 had been printed. The fifty-cent price turned out to be a fraction more than cost, so the Memphis Publishing Company added $25,000 to its United Way contribution.

By that time Memphis had begun to understand what an impact had been made by this young man who had been born at Tupelo, Mississippi, 8 January 1935, and lived here since 1948. He was the "most enduring and successful show-business personality ever known," *New York* magazine said.

In record sales a million dollars from one record is both the badge of success and the door to wealth. Elvis had scaled that height forty-five times. He was most often called the "King of Rock and Roll," which he was and which accounted for a large part of his popularity in record shops. Yet some of the most popular records were far from the rocking beat.

In contrast are the love ballads. While the Elvis legend was being built, before there were any movies or the fabulous concert tours of the final years, his blockbuster record was "Heartbreak Hotel." Later it was joined by "Are You Lonesome Tonight?" And both almost always are chosen for résumé programs—songs for the lonesome in a world that has lots of lonesome souls.

Another often-mentioned part of the Elvis show is knee-twitching and pelvis-throbbing. Whatever the attraction in his later career, most of his followers were drawn by his records before they could see him. His record-selling explosion was in 1956 when his records held all five top spots on the best-seller charts. All records were in the shops in September. His first motion picture, "Love Me Tender," came out in November. The well-remembered road shows of his last years were suspended while he made movies, and his earlier television appearances had been few, and some of them poorly managed. Most of his public listened to records and formed in their own minds ideas of Elvis, varied as the endless variations in human personalities.

Underlying all the specifics of the Elvis style was the great attraction of a very young man suddenly very wealthy, a living demonstration that the Horatio Alger fantasy might come true, in happy contradiction to the long years of preparation and slow advancement of ordinary persons. Here was a boy from a public housing project handing out Cadillacs to friends as though they were boxes of candy, and still saying "sir" and "ma'am," as his grandparents had.

As to the pictures, Hedda Hopper wrote in 1965 that he had made eighteen pictures in nine years, yet kept Hollywood at arm's length. She said he was never seen in the famous restaurants, nor in nighhclubs, nor at a party, nor even a premiere. He was "the shyest soul I ever met," she said, while he was, a moviemaker told her, "the only sure thing in show business except the Disney pictures." The next year, when Metro-Goldwyn-Mayer signed him for six more pictures, she wrote, "Every film makes money. He has never been in a scandal; never married, although half-a-dozen stars have run after him . . . and nobody calls him 'swivel-hips' anymore."

Elvis was married (1967–1973) to Priscilla Beaulieu, and their daughter is Lisa Marie. Aside from the divorce, there was some other unhappiness, although it usually is forgotten in looking back over his fast rise. But there once was an official of WHBQ who ordered all Elvis records off the air. And there was once a Grand Ole Opry factotum who turned him down and suggested Elvis go back to truck-driving. A companion says he cried all the way back to Memphis.

Although the movies were moneymakers, several of them at $1 million and fifty percent of profits for Elvis, they came through an assembly-line process which bored Elvis and eventually jaded the ticket buyers. There were thirty-two movies, and while they were being produced the concert tours stopped for nine years. Television appearances were held back, too, in the hope of avoiding overexposure.

With the films stopped, Elvis went back on the road in 1969 and began writing new pages in the record books. A mere announcement of a show date was enough to sell out the tickets. Sometimes they were all bought by mail before the ticket counter was opened. In addition to his roving performances he became the biggest drawing card in Las Vegas, the top spot of show business. It has been written that he never played to an empty seat, which may be true, leaving out his earliest years. He was about to begin another string of sold-out dates, with all tickets gone for the Memphis show and a second concert added for the overflow, when death came.

The funeral was hardly over when a flood of national magazines came out with his name and picture on the covers. Then came the books, each hoping to catch some of the overflow from *Elvis: A Biography,* by Jerry Hopkins. It had been written seven years before and had nothing about the final years, but it was a best seller among paperbacks month after month. By February one chain store in Memphis had a revolving rack with nothing but Elvis books, eleven of them. For months classified advertising in *The Commercial Appeal* was sprinkled with such items as the offer to sell ''sheets, unwashed'' on which the famous singer had slept in Sioux Falls two years before and ''an original copy of Elvis' eleventh-grade report card.'' Display advertising in January offered titles to fractions of a ranch he once owned across the state line, at ten dollars per square inch. In June, ten months after his death, Elvis's home drew as many as ten thousand visitors a day, including a New York postal worker making her third trip to the shrine. The Fourth of July was a broiling hot day, but about fourteen thousand persons stood in line at the famous gates of iron guitars.

Ties between Elvis and his hometown are a conspicuous part of his story. While it is customary for an entertainer to score poorly in the box office of the town that knew him as a youngster, Elvis appeared at the coliseum seven times and every ticket was sold. For the show scheduled in the near future when he died, refunds were announced but thousands kept their tickets for keepsakes.

His associates before fame struck continued to be his friends: Eleanor

Richmond of Humes High School; James Tipler, who hired him as a truck-driver; Bob Neal, his manager in the early days; James Blackwood, the quartet singer; Marion Keisker, the Sun studio receptionist who kept an Elvis tape and kept proposing him for some studio need; Sam Phillips, the Sun studio man; Scotty Moore and Bill Black, musicians who joined him early. All of them were still friends and boosters when the end came. So was Tom Parker, carnival veteran who was his manager for years.

Aside from those who had personal contact, thousands of Memphis people had become accustomed to telling strangers how to find Graceland. The name of the street past Graceland, previously Bellevue, was changed to Elvis Presley Boulevard in 1971. For the Chamber of Commerce, the Presley home had long been the most popular tourist attraction with the exception of the Mississippi River, and there was a question about which was first.

Beneath all of these signs of mutual affection there is the recollection of the night when Elvis was first acclaimed by the spontaneous applause of Memphis. That was the summer night of 1954 when "That's All Right (Mama)" first went on the air. Dewey Phillips used it on WHBQ. The telephone jangled with listeners asking that it be played again and again and then again. It was the first Elvis record on the air anywhere, so new that the master record had still to be cut, and, before it could be made, five thousand orders were stacked at the studio. Without waiting for an opinion from any chart or any other source, Memphis had heard the Elvis sound and liked it. That Memphis enthusiasm was the foundation on which the towering image of Elvis was built.

8

The Politics of It

Senatorial Power

Kenneth McKellar of Memphis went to Congress in 1911, moved up to the Senate and stayed until 1953. His continuous service was the longest in history at that time. He acquired massive power by seniority, especially as chairman of the Appropriations Committee. He became President Pro Tem of the Senate in 1945 and again in 1949, that is a substitute vice-president who might have become president.

As a boy he had a hard time in Alabama. His only teachers were his father, mother, and sister, and he had to support himself at eleven as a farm worker and store clerk. But he managed to learn enough and earn enough to get to the University of Alabama, where he did well in his studies. He was graduated in 1891 and stayed to take his law degree.

He started for the golden opportunities of California, by way of Memphis. He got here with twenty-five cents but he had two brothers with railroad jobs here and they expected to arrange a pass to the West Coast. Instead, he liked it here, stayed, and became a Memphis lawyer while his law degree was hardly six months old. He was soon earning good fees and acquiring property. His name began to appear in politics, as a Democratic presidential elector in 1904, and a delegate to the party convention of 1908.

Early in 1911 the name McKellar was put before the legislature as a

Kenneth McKellar about 1925

candidate for the Senate. So was the name of Guston Fitzhugh, a widely known Memphis attorney. The legislature struggled through twenty-three days of voting, from which Luke Lea, Nashville newspaper publisher, emerged as senator. Later in 1911 death removed George Washington Gordon from Congress. He had been representative for the Tenth District, which then included Tipton, Fayette, and Hardeman counties as well as Shelby.

The principal candidate was Thomas C. Looney, member of a family prominent in Memphis for generations, who had lost to Gordon. It was of small interest to McKellar, who was on a vacation trip, until he learned that Looney had said McKellar ''would not dare to run.'' So McKellar came back to town and announced. It was an uphill battle. E. H. Crump, mayor less than two years, announced it was ''not my fight'' and stayed out. In a special primary on 7 October, McKellar won with 6,356 votes to 4,624 for Looney in the preliminary count reported the next morning. Looney had carried Tipton and Hardeman counties. In Memphis precincts the McKellar vote was 4,152 against 2,788 for Looney.

McKellar was reelected to the House until he became a candidate for the Senate in 1916, the first primary after election of senators was taken away from legislatures. The big candiates were Lea, the former senator, and Malcolm Patterson, former governor. McKellar was definitely the third man. But Lea and Patterson said bad things about each other and some of the voters believed them both. They knocked each other out. In the primary of November 1915 McKellar slipped in between them and came up with an election night total of about 42,500, while the Patterson vote was about 40,000, and the Lea count was 32,000.

In a second primary McKellar came in ahead of Patterson again. In the November 1916 election, a full year after the decisive primary, McKellar overcame a strong bid from another former governor, Ben Hooper, a Republican candidate. McKellar got about 144,000 and Hooper 118,000.

At the end of his first Senate term McKellar was vigorously challenged by Fitzhugh, who was closely associated with *The Commercial Appeal*. Fitzhugh was endorsed by Patterson, a major figure in the Democratic Party. McKellar had become a spokesman for labor. He was opposed to compulsory arbitration of union contests with owners. He advocated collective bargaining, a minimum wage, an eight-hour day for women and children, unions for government workers, and he publicly considered federal ownership of railroads. He denounced lobby efforts of coal mine owners.

Fitzhugh said McKellar had socialist views and said McKellar dallied with the doctrine of "sovietism." *The Herald* of Columbia, Tennessee, said "McKellar was rapidly becoming one of the most dangerous radicals in the Senate." Aside from what *The Commercial Appeal* did to McKellar in editorials and cartoons, it spoke in a news story just before the election of his "socialist answers" to a widely circulated questionnaire. McKellar campaigned as a "progressive" and as a senator whose efforts had benefited Tennessee, especially its farmers. He closed the campaign with a speech in Court Square and a brass band.

The Democratic primary was a clean sweep for McKellar of every congressional district. After two days of counting, the Shelby County vote was 12,299 for McKellar and 3,279 for Fitzhugh.

When his second term was about to run out, McKellar had a challenger who attracted even more attention in distant newspapers. The voice of conservatism this time came from Finis Garrett, a Dresden lawyer who had been in the House since 1905 and risen to minority floor leader. Garrett stood for states' rights and opposed the child labor law as federal interference in the home. McKellar won with a majority of more than 55,000.

It is likely, however, that the McKellar stands on political issues were less important to his power at the ballot box than his personal service to voters. His first order of business was helping residents of Tennessee when they wrote to him or went to his office with passport troubles, Washington red tape, or bureaucratic blockades. They each got prompt and courteous letters and they got help if it was within his reach.

He considered that any federal job in the state could be filled by a Tennessean, in fact by a Tennessee Democrat. He felt it was his duty to see that Tennessee got its full share of jobs and government projects. Being a senator was both his job and his pleasure. He went to his office every morning, including Saturdays and Sundays. He wrote so many letters that at one time it took six secretaries to keep up.

Each year in Washington added another layer of grateful persons, with personal bonds with Senator McKellar, to the thousands of others in every county of the state. This personal service was the basic strength he accumulated among voters. His first interest in legislation was in getting federal income tax money for roads. His theory had been that states should build the roads. But in 1911 he bought a Packard and set out to New England. Roads were so bad he had to give up driving to Washington and ship the car by rail. The best roads he found were between New York and Albany, where he could drive twenty miles an hour. Four days after he took the oath as a member of the House he introduced a bill for federal aid. It was years before the importance of federal aid for highways became obvious.

Much more obvious was his obtaining of authorization for a second bridge at Memphis. He became known in Washington because he defeated Oscar Underwood of Alabama, one of the most powerful men in politics, to get the bridge and to add to it roadways for automobile traffic. He became a hero in Memphis where, until the Harahan Bridge was opened, the river crossing by automobile was made by ferry. When he had been in Congress less than a year the bridge victory won him the all-out approval of *The Commercial Appeal* in an editorial in 1912. It said he was "equipped with all of the necessary qualifications of a successful statesman." It said "no new member of Congress has accomplished in recent years so much for his constituents."

It was McKellar who introduced in 1916 the original bill under which a dam was built at Muscle Shoals to provide electricity for a nitrate plant. It was part of the war effort because the United States had to import from Chile, in ships exposed to submarine dangers, the nitrates for cannon shells. The dam flooded out rocky shoals which had blocked Tennessee River boats. Senator George Norris introduced a bill in 1922 which was modified to become the act creating the Tennessee Valley Authority in 1933. McKellar got behind the Norris proposal in 1924. When the first TVA directors were satisfied with three dams and a "yardstick" demonstration of electricity prices, McKellar demanded five more Tennessee River dams and got appropriations for them.

In 1942 he got a letter signed by all twenty members of the Senate Appropriations Committee saying the TVA dams would never have been built without McKellar's efforts. Congressional opinion turned against TVA but appropriations kept on coming.

I have heard Representative Jere Cooper, who saw it from the inside as a member of the House Ways and Means Committee, tell how McKellar did it. As chairman of the Senate Appropriations Committee he listened with sympathy all year to other senators who had to have McKellar approval to get such things as irrigation dams or harbor dredging. But nothing happened until each of them had delivered a vote for TVA money. McKellar has been called "the rich uncle of TVA" but he objected to some TVA methods, he vigorously fought building of Douglas Dam, and he was often at odds with David Lilienthal, TVA chairman. So he frequently is remembered for his attacks rather than for his support.

Memories got farther off the track about McKellar's association with Crump. It was easy for those opposed to McKellar or Crump to shrink McKellar to a puppet handmade by Crump. This was especially handy for visiting writers making a hasty survey. In fact McKellar was an ally whose statewide influence and Washington connections were as important to Crump as Crump's votes in Shelby County were to McKellar.

McKellar was older than Crump. He had some prominence in the politics of reform before Crump, and his associates joined the movement that put Crump into the mayor's chair. Crump could hardly have done much for McKellar's move from House to Senate, for the crucial primary of 1915 came in the very weeks Crump's hands were full of ouster proceedings.

Crump and McKellar were mutual admirers and they usually worked together. Yet Crump was opposed to McKellar making his brother, Clint, postmaster, and Crump did his best to keep McKellar's choice, Bert Bates, from becoming U.S. Marshal. McKellar went ahead with both, as he did in supporting Burgin Dossett for governor in 1936 against Crump's choice, Gordon Browning.

Fact varied from common belief in another way. Except for close associates, it was assumed that McKellar had earned his "whiskey nose"—long, bulbous, and red. He was a teetotaler, because as a boy he had watched a relative in bottle trouble. His entertainment was usually the movies, especially Roy Rogers sagas of the West. There were times when he saw a movie every night. He was an eligible bachelor who enjoyed the company of beautiful women and was a good dancer. But he defied Washington protocol by leaving parties when his bedtime came, and going back to his hotel. He usually read histories or mysteries.

Apparently he never recognized old age creeping up from behind. Stories of senile failures were often heard by word of mouth in Tennessee when he announced for one more term in the elections of 1952. Albert Gore, a member of the House, became a rival candidate, carefully avoiding any mention of the McKellar infirmities, and won the nomination. McKellar took an apartment in the Hotel Gayoso, with a student doctor to live with him. He died on 25 October 1957 at eighty-eight. He had neglected his property and $15,000 gifts to each of his fifteen nieces and nephews used up most of his estate. The new generation finds his name on the lake formed in the development of Presidents Island, and on a large city park, while his official papers wait in the public library for researchers to weigh the values of his extraordinarily long congressional career.

The Generalissimo

When Frank Rice was fourteen he was suddenly faced with a choice between forty lines of Latin and a beating from his schoolmaster. He had copied the lines once, but his penmanship was poor and he had copied them a second time. Now the teacher was demanding that he write them a third time, in a neater hand. He was a large man, who seemed huge as his menacing face came down the aisle. Frank turned down both the Latin and the whipping. He left school—through a window—a second-floor window.

Years later Rice became the master of the school of practical politics, the man who should have "written the book." He was second in command of the fabulous "Crump organization." He was the top man for hundreds of city and county jobholders with a street-by-street card .

Frank Rice in 1935

index of voters. They saw to it that every "friend" was registered as a voter before the lists closed, which was weeks before election day, and before some rival candidates had an organization. He was the man to whom campaign money flowed from all directions, some of it to be used to pay poll taxes for friends.

Most conspicuously, he was manager of the Shelby delegation in the state legislature. There were eleven of them, but they swung far more power in General Assembly actions than the leaderless herd of twenty-five does in modern times. They had expert legal advice on exactly what each proposal would do before they voted. They met every morning in Frank Rice's room at the Hermitage Hotel, even when he was sick and they had to stand around his bed.

Out of the public view, he was also a kind of teacher, introducing dozens of young men to political methods and, at the same time, grading their performance for possible advancement to higher positions in the organization. Sometimes they failed to pass or, rarely, decided other things interested them more than politics. Whatever the aftermath of the winter in Nashville, they were admirers of Frank Rice as long as they lived.

Such a man probably fits best the description of "generalissimo" of the Crump forces, but in fact he was simply Frank Rice, an individual unlike anyone else. He spoke of himself as a "politician," a most unusual attitude in a profession in which most men call themselves lawyers or farmers, or "attorney at law and plantation operator." Frank Rice even said he was a "politician" in court before a doubtful judge, when he was helping his barber become a citizen.

Rice had been born soon after the Civil War (11 November 1868). His father was was Dr. Frank Rice and his mother the former Isabel Fransioli. His father's war service was as surgeon general to General Benjamin Cheatham. His prominence as a physician was enhanced by his becoming city health officer after the yellow fever epidemic of 1873, the worst Memphis had experienced at that time. In 1875 Dr. Rice and the president of the Board of Health resigned in protest when aldermen failed to take sanitation precautions.

The family lived on the south side of Poplar, between Second and Third, then a good address, when Frank was born. His widowed mother later bought a home on the south side of Poplar, opposite the present site of St. Mary's Cathedral, which was a better address.

The great yellow fever epidemic of 1878 struck Frank when he was nine, although the family had fled to his uncle's farm on Benjestown Road. When he recovered the boy was delegated to make the first trip into town for supplies, where scenes of desolation were burned into his mind.

He had two years of public schooling, followed by the advantages of five years in a school operated by Lyon G. Tyler, son of President John Tyler. But the Tyler school was closed when the headmaster became president of William and Mary. Another private school was the one he abandoned so suddenly. For some forgotten reason, he acquired the name of "Roxie" as a boy.

Several years later, when he was nineteen, Frank went to the University of Virginia to study law, but found he was unprepared. His brother, Stephen, stayed in school and became a doctor. Frank got a job as a bank "runner" before his mother knew he was out of school. He was a teller at the Manhattan Bank after his effort at Charlottesville. For a time he became an insurance man and took a hand in real estate. During the bicycle boom he became an expert cyclist and opened a bicycle shop downtown.

In 1898 he went to war in Cuba as a lieutenant. He wound up at a quartermaster depot, supervising the turning in of government property.

When it was over he had $600,000 more property than he was charged with. Years later he explained that an old Army sergeant had taught him to "always take a receipt but never give one."

He was tighter than that about writing letters. Hundreds of letters were written to him. But the answers came by telephone or in personal contact. Senator Kenneth McKellar said he wrote to Frank Rice for forty-five years, and he never got but one letter from him. That had something to do with one of the Rice daughters. In 1903 Rice married Miss Patte Walker Jones. Their daughters were Mrs. Elizabeth Gildart and Miss Frances Rice. A son, Stephen, died at fourteen. Rice's devotion to his family—and the family's devotion to him—was utter.

He was barely twenty-one when he first sampled politics. He was a minor figure in the organization of Mayor Joe Williams, the leading figure in local politics, for more than fifteen years. Williams spoke for conservatives, who were the natural associates of a young man with the Rice background. The opposition was a reform movement, including such men as Walker Wellford, A. S. Caldwell, and Kenneth McKellar, and several young men such as Ed Crump. In 1907 Rice switched to the reform side as campaign manager for Crump when Williams was defeated as commissioner of fire and police.

In 1908 Rice might be said to have returned to the conservative side as county manager for Malcolm Patterson. In a sensational campaign, Patterson turned back the effort of Edward Carmack and retained the governor's office for a second term. The popular Carmack issue was a rural protest against the saloon and political power of saloon keepers.

The politics of 1908 also included a sample of things to come. Crump and Rice tied together Memphis government and a ticket of state legislators pledged to try to get a law allowing the commission method of city government here. They won and Memphis set up the reform method.

Then came the turning point, the campaign of 1909. Williams ran for mayor, supported by *The Commercial Appeal*. Crump ran against Williams, with Rice as his campaign manager. 1 January 1910 became a red letter day in local politics. Commission government began; the Courthouse, which included City Hall, was first used; and the years of Crump power were launched. A few months later, in April 1910, Rice was a candidate for county register (of deeds). He knocked out a long-time political power, Squire Jim Barret. (Years later Barret's son, Squire Paul Barret, became a big wheel in the Crump machine, turning in sensationally lop-sided votes for Crump candidates at the Stewartville box.)

In 1918 so many young men in the legislature had gone to war that Rice had to fill out the list himself, by going to the senate. After six months of a two-year term, he resigned to become state revenue agent, which he was until the office was abolished in 1923. He then became back tax collector for Shelby County, an appointive office, which he held for many years. For a few weeks at the end of his life he was the collector of customs in the Federal Building.

The title he held had little to do with the way he used his energies. During the long years as back tax collector, the routine of that office was handled by Gene Condon and other staff members. Frank Rice had office space that only insiders ever saw, on an out-of-the-way courthouse corridor, without a door sign. In it were a plain table, some leather chairs, and a couch discarded from some other office, where Rice stretched out on days he was ill—but continued to see visitors. He had a barbershop shave every day, and he wore good, but usually rumpled, clothes. It took countless cigarets and endless Coca-Colas to get him through the day.

He was Frank J. Rice, but he told anyone interested that the "J" stood for nothing. He had added it to avoid confusion. Rice lived in a fine home on East Parkway at Jefferson. He was register and back tax collector under the old fee system which provided him with a splendid income and some surplus he usually invested in real estate. The income in 1933 was so far out of line with Depression joblessness and empty local government treasuries that Rice and John Brown, back tax attorney, turned back $250,000 of their fees. He was a member of the Tennessee Club and the Hunt and Polo Club. His favorite sport was the rich man's pleasure, horse racing.

Yet he was a contrast to some of his companions in the upper level of politics because of the frequency with which he spoke up for "the little devil," the underdog. He had little time for political theories from college professors, nor was he interested in ideas from the country club front porch. In Nashville he led the forces that held back the first sales tax, because of its burden on the poor. He was always "liberal" and sometimes he talked as though he was impatient for the revolution to start so he could join up and throw some bombs where they were overdue.

His general theory was that good government was the best politics and that anything that advanced the welfare of Shelby County was worthy of support. He was strong for a good twelve-grade school system, but doubtful about tax-supported college for all, except that he wanted more state money for the University of Tennessee medical campus in Memphis.

He was conspicuously enthusiastic about the "syncrotax" theory of removing all taxes—federal, state, county, city, school, drainage district, privilege, inheritance—and replacing them with payment of two or three percent every time money was received by anybody. But he renounced it quickly, when the holes in the idea were shown to him. When the Crump ally, Senator McKellar, supported Burgin Dossett for governor in 1936, Rice would liked to have gone with them. But he kept his silence when Crump went into a short alliance with Gordon Browning.

The organization of which Rice was so important a member had many enemies with loud voices and numerous protests about methods, but there never was any question raised about the personal integrity of Frank Rice.

He told me once that the only time he ever attempted to take advantage of inside knowledge was when preliminary arrangements were being made to build the Hotel Peabody. He bought Second Street frontage, expecting a sharp rise in prices. Third Street then ended at Union. When the new hotel was built some old buildings were removed to allow Third to be extended southward. That made more frontage near the hotel and smothered the Second Street boom he had expected. (Many years after his death I found that his inside knowledge probably came from his mother's family instead of his political associates.)

He was an unusually accurate judge of voting trends, with friends in every corner of the state, and in Washington. But he was glaringly wrong once. As a reporter, I had stayed in the "hole," the subbasement Courthouse room where ballots were tallied, all night of the November day in 1928 when Al Smith was defeated. In the gray of the morning he offered to carry me home. He was tired and he was discouraged. He thought the Democratic Party might never win another presidential election. They won the next five.

He was brusque with strangers, but he seemed to be more abrupt than he really was, because he always spoke in plain language, without slanted phrases or shaded meanings. He often flatly declined to talk, or drew a specific line as to what he would talk about. What he said was true, exactly. What he promised was done, completely. Sometimes he

was angry, especially about misguided newspaper owners and sometimes about poorly informed editors and reporters. But he blew it all out,
leaving nothing pent-up to spoil and erupt another day. When he died in
a New York hospital on 29 December 1938 the number of mourners was
extraordinarily large, including some newspapermen who knew they
were unlikely to ever again know anyone so frank.

The Walsh Brothers

During the first quarter of the century the biggest name in North
Memphis was Walsh, a name of first-rate importance to the whole city.
John T. Walsh and his younger brother, Anthony P., had the biggest
store in the north end, a brick structure that loomed over the neighborhood at the northeast corner of Main and Commerce, with business that
blanketed Pinch, Chelsea, Frayser, and part of Tipton County.

They did so much banking at the store that they organized the North
Memphis Savings Bank. For the bank they built a six-floor building on
North Main, at the northeast corner of Main and Adams. At the south-
west corner of the same intersection they took a hand in financing the
Claridge Hotel, with J. T. Walsh as president of the Tri-State Hotel
Company. He was one of the commissioners who built the courthouse,
and of the commission that built the Auditorium. Then there was the
political strength that came with such prominence.

The Walsh Brothers had to scrabble their way up. They were born in
the outskirts of Chicago, John T. in 1854 and Tony in 1856. The family
moved to Memphis in 1859. Their father died in 1861 and their mother
had to face alone the perils of the Civil War and Reconstruction.

At fifteen John dropped out of school and took a job at the cigar stand
at the Worsham House. Tony left school at thirteen and worked in a
grocery a year, until John arranged for him to have the cigar stand job.
John then went to work for another grocer, but after three years took a
job with the Louisville & Nashville Railroad as a brakeman, then a
baggageman. He saved some money and in 1874 bought the cigar stand,
which Tony operated while John continued with the railroad. Their
mother and twelve-year old sister died in the yellow fever of 1873.

In 1877 the Walsh fortune began to move up fast. The brothers had
saved more money and organized J. T. Walsh and Brother, a grocery at
Main and Overton. They later moved two blocks south with a much
bigger building. The business was started only the year before the
disastrous yellow fever of 1878–79. Their business survived the storm

John T. Walsh   Anthony P. Walsh

that almost wiped out the city. It grew into the cornerstone of their other activities. They added wholesale groceries and produce. They financed the crops as far north as the wagon travel allowed, and then sold the cotton. Tony was the cotton man at the Walsh store.

When farmers came to town they drove into the Walsh wagon yard, unharnessed their horses, and left them to be fed and watered while the men did their business and wives and children did their downtown shopping. The loading dock at the rear of the store formed one side of the wagon yard. The other sides were horse stalls. Joining the loading dock was a hay and feed barn so big that years after the store burned it was converted into an arena where weekly fight cards were promoted.

It was said repeatedly that the Walsh brothers "knew every man, woman, and child in North Memphis." Many of them were customers. Hundreds had a special feeling for the store because of groceries delivered to the door when hard luck struck, or cash for the rent that stalled off eviction. The money rolled in and the Walshes began to buy land north of town when prices were low and suburban development was in the far future. When financing overflowed the store the Walsh brothers set up their bank in rented space on the west side of Main just below Poplar, opening on 4 April 1904. In 1908 they erected the bank building, with office space for rent.

Tony was president until his death on 11 June 1912. Then John T.

took the office. It started on $50,000 capital, had deposits of $250,000 at the end of the first year, and grew until deposits were about $6 million.

In 1923 the North Memphis Savings Bank was merged with Union Planters, of which John T. became a vice president. But it continued to be the North Memphis bank, with its own check books for many years. (A Memphis automobile man once paid his considerable bill at the Waldorf in New York with a North Memphis check. There was nothing in the hotel's copy of the bankers guide to show there was such a bank, and the hotel sent for the law and had the auto man and his wife pulled off a departing plane.)

There must have been extra pleasure in the sight of steelwork for the million-dollar Claridge. It was built on the site of the Worsham House, where the cigar stand was their first venture in business.

Then there was politics. Tony never sought office, although he was elected to the school board in 1881, and he gave a helping hand to many friends. John T. was elected to the board of Public Works, somewhat like a city council, in 1893. He became police and fire commissioner in 1904, and vice-mayor in 1906. Any account of the politics of those years seems to be confusing. There were fast changes and shifting alliances.

Walsh friends could make a case for them as reformers. John Walsh was on the committee that built General Hospital (now Gaston) in 1898, a considerable improvement over the small old institution on grounds that have since become Forrest Park. He was a member of the city council that established the municipal water system in 1903, after decades of previous efforts. He supported it, and the purchase turned out to be a fundamental change for the better in city affairs. He was one of the five members of the Court House Commission that built the courthouse, and for many years the City Hall, which was opened in 1910. It was a triumph of design over all previous housing of local government and is still considered an architectural jewel. He was chairman of the Auditorium and Market House Commission that produced a building in 1924 after years of frustration.

In these ways the public good was advanced, with clearly seen results in the North Main Street area. In fact the winners of the 1905 election, James Malone for mayor and John T. Walsh for vice-mayor, were known as the ''Reform Ticket.'' Yet these were years when younger men with a program of more sweeping form were rising, especially E. H. Crump, who became mayor in the 1909 elections.

There was a third group of older and more conservative men in politics, headed by J. J. Williams. It was Williams who usually had the support of *The Commercial Appeal*. To the morning newspaper Walsh was anything but a reformer. For a time he was battered daily in news stories, editorials and cartoons.

When the Malone-Walsh ticket won, *The Commercial Appeal* wrote of switched and stolen ballot boxes, "unprecedented frauds," and a "brazen attempt" to debauch the election. The *News-Scimitar* read the same election figures as the victory of a people's reform, and observed that the "people can be trusted at all times to do the right thing at the right time." There are numerous details of Walsh-Crump-Williams politics in *Memphis During the Progressive Era* by William D. Miller. It was a time of open gambling and prostitution, with *The Commercial Appeal* attacking the hiring and firing of police and firemen. The newspaper once cried out that policemen were hired or fired according to their usefulness as politicians. It said the "Walsh philosophy" had made the police force a platoon of ward heelers. Several years later Crump obtained civil service protection for jobs and often looked back on it as a basic victory.

There came a time of quieter elections in North Memphis. An alliance between Crump and Walsh was formed. J. T. Walsh, Jr., went to work for the Crump mortgage and insurance company. Crump business offices expanded into the Walsh bank building. When John T. Walsh's health was declining he defied his doctor to go to the polls and vote for his son, named like his brother A. P. "Tony" Walsh. The younger Walsh was elected on the Crump ticket in 1927 and went from the bank to be city finance commissioner. The senior Walsh died on 28 January 1929. He had seen branch banking coming and had merged with the biggest bank in town. He likewise saw the future of chain groceries and moved out of the grocery business.

One thing that remained in its accustomed place was the big Walsh home at 686 North Seventh. The brothers were so closely in tune with each other that they worked out of one purse and shared the same broad roof. There eighteen rooms sheltered three generations. The brothers and their wives, the children and the grandchildren ate together at one long table. A chauffeur, a cook, maids, and other help looked after a household that varied in size from one meal to the next, and got them ready for mass at St. Brigid's. The house is still a landmark on Chelsea, now used by the Girls' Club.

Two grandsons from that household were making news in the 1970s. William M. Walsh of the law firm of Hanover, Walsh, Barnes & Jalenak is the son of J. T. Walsh, Jr. A veteran assistant city attorney is Art Shea, son of Elizabeth Walsh who married Arthur Shea, a contractor who died long ago.

Decades after the Walsh brothers were gone, while the neighborhood and the world changed, their home stood firm. Finally another daughter of John T. Walsh, Margaret, gave it up for a retirement home. But she kept the Walsh home alive until 1964.

Crump Under Fire

E. H. Crump's terms as mayor came to an abrupt end late in 1915. He had been elected with a narrow margin in 1909, reelected with a substantial edge in 1911, and returned to office for the third time in a quiet election early in 1915. Ever since there has been a division in Memphis politics between those who think Crump was removed from office by the courts for refusing to enforce state prohibition laws and those who believe the ouster law was used as a weapon to protect the electric light company from a mayor who intended to put the city government into the light business.

This happened more than ten years before I came to Memphis. But I heard a great deal about it. I worked for the *The Commercial Appeal,* which had taken a substantial part in the ouster proceedings, and a few veterans of the ouster days were still on the newspaper staff. As a reporter assigned to city and county offices I heard the other side at length from Crump and his associates. Gradually I came to accept the Crump version of what happened, although there was rarely anything to write about it until the TVA fight years later.

Nor was there a basis for writing. There were only attitudes and bits of remarks on the Crump side. On the other side there was a record, a bit confused, but a record in which Crump had been denied a jury in Chancery Court. He had been advised by his attorney to rush the case to the state Supreme Court for a sure reversal on this ruling against a jury and other procedural points. But the speedy way to appeal required Crump to concede that allegations of nonenforcement of the law could be proved, and to waive trial. Chancellor Frank Fentress then ruled Crump out of office and the Supreme Court agreed. Crump resigned on 2 February 1916 after picking his successor.

Looking at the court record is impossible. The files disappeared years ago and it was publicly charged that a Crump sympathizer had destroyed them. But the docket shows the papers were taken out by an anti-Crump lawyer. However, I saw one of the papers many years ago. While the general idea is that Crump failed to shut down saloons, gambling and prostitution, the paper I saw told of Crump efficiency carried to the extreme.

The complaint was that, instead of shutting down the underworld, the Crump city administration had a quiet cafeteria system of paying fines. It was charged, as I remember, that the whole population of saloonists, madams, and gamblers marched into City Court each Monday, pleaded guilty, paid their fines, and went back to work. The fine was fifty dollars, which was the maximum penalty of the court without the power to send anyone to jail, except to work out an unpaid fine. The income to the city was considerable and it was a contribution to the expense of law enforcement. But the petitioners wanted the city to stop the illegal businesses, rather than merely collecting fees and turning the fine system into a kind of weekly permit method.

There was ample reason to lean toward the power-plant theory for the ouster proceedings because of the timing. The ouster was brought to a climax just weeks before the franchise was to end, giving the city the opportunity to get the plant. But it came after Crump had obtained a change in the election date to the spring. He and his ticket of commission members had run on an announcement that they would use the opportunity to go into the municipal electric business.

The power plant issue was a change in local politics, while lack of enforcement of prohibition in Memphis remained unchanged. Crump had announced publicly that he would leave it to the state to enforce the state law and had been reelected. Malcolm Patterson, a Memphis lawyer, had won election as governor as a ''wet.'' *The Commercial Appeal* had scorned the ''dry'' side of politics. The majority of the big city vote was still against prohibition and in several Tennessee cities the saloons ran on.

But former governor Patterson had a dramatic conversion. Suddenly in 1915 the newspaper took the ''dry'' side of the road. When the quick appeal from Chancery Court to the Supreme Court backfired on Crump, Memphis businessmen even took a trip to Nashville to offer Governor Tom Rye a law-enforcement effort by Crump if the governor would withdraw the ouster case. But Governor Rye declined to interfere. Whatever the situation in other parts of the state, or among other Memphis officials, the spotlight was strong on Memphis and its mayor.

For all of that it was many years before there was a Crump account of exactly how the power company put the pressure on him. It was 1949 before the story was published in Crump's words, as a letter to the editor of the *Memphis Press-Scimitar*. Looking for something else in my files on Crump, I came across the extraordinarily long clipping.

The *Press-Scimitar* had called for a city audit in an editorial. On 23 August 1949 a letter from Crump almost a column long was published. Among a great many other things, Crump told of the 1901 situation when Walker Wellford, a businessman, got a City Hall audit only by hiring Kenneth McKellar (then a young lawyer who was later to become a senator) to take the demand to court. City officials resisted all the way to the Supreme Court but McKellar got a ruling that any taxpayer could see the books, and an audit was made.

Crump also told of the Haskins & Sells audit which he demanded in 1908. It showed the city books were out of balance three cents, in the city's favor. Crump also said:

> When I was mayor, the utilities and the railroads had been running the city for years, pulling the strings, grabbing franchises for a song, as the records will show. They couldn't handle me, therefore they sought to destroy me—ruin my character.
> The crowd further employed Pinkerton to trail me. After two or three months he told them there was nothing—they were wasting their money.

Crump told me that he happened to meet William Pinkerton many years after the 1915 incident when Pinkerton told him his agency had been hired to follow Crump. There was also another Haskins & Sells audit in 1915 that produced nothing damaging.

The Crump words about the public utilities seeking to destroy him stirred the wrath of Lovick P. Miles, veteran of the legal profession. He wrote a letter to the editor, more than a column long in its published form. Miles quoted from the Crump letter and also from the primary election campaign of 1948. Miles said Crump said there was "a black-jack ouster proceedings because I wanted the City of Memphis to own its own electric light plant. Had I yielded to private utilities overtures there would have been no ouster suit."

Miles then put into his letter a sweeping statement: "There is not a semblance of truth in the statement of Mr. Crump that any utility company operating in Memphis had anything whatever to do with suggesting or approving the ouster suit which brought by the State of Tennessee because of the disgusting conditions which existed in the city because of Mr. Crump's neglect of official duty. I feel it my duty to resent the statement of Mr. Crump and to defend the charges of the splendid men who directed the affairs of the public utilities."

This riled the Crump temper and he answered with a letter that used well over a column and a half. I saved it and the Miles charge when they were published because it sets out precisely the Crump account. (Several years later the Crump biographer, William D. Miller, used in his book a long quotation from the same Crump letter).

The Crump letter sets out the law partnership of Miles with General Luke E. Wright, who was at the same time attorney for the power company and a large stockholder in *The Commercial Appeal*. Other sources show that Miles was a newspaperman before he was a lawyer. Wright was vice-president of the publishing company. Miles married the daughter of the company president, W. J. Crawford. Crump wrote:

> 1915 rolled around. I was elected on a platform to build or buy an electric light plant. A bond issue had been voted. The Merchants Power Co.'s franchise expiring on January 1, 1916, simultaneously when I would take office for another term.
>
> In the spring of that year Gen. Luke E. Wright, senior in the firm representing these utilities, called on me in the Mayor's office, or rather in the office adjoining the library on the second floor, which I used as a work office. My recollection is at the same time the Electric Light Committee, composed of five members, were present—James E. Stark, C. T. Kelly and I. D. Block, deceased; Otto Metzger and Sam F. McDonald, living. Gen Wright wanted to know if I was actually going thru with the purchase of the Merchants Power Co. when their franchise expired on the first of the year, I politely but emphatically told him that would be done—that I had been elected on that platform.
>
> Gen. Wright was a large stockholder in *The Commercial Appeal*, which was controlled by an interlocking directorate. After his visit to my office and my reply on the light question, *The Commercial Appeal* came out the next morning and said Memphis was no place ro raise a family and proceeded to cartoon me.
>
> When the ouster suit was up, a very fine man, Mr. Jim Brinkley, came to my home, said he had authority to say from the president and general manger, the chief attorney of the Electric Light and Gas Co., if I would drop the light question everything would be "hunky-dory," the ouster suit would be withdrawn, no bother, no expense, no trouble, everything would be lovely and the goose would hang high. I thanked him and told him, "Never, I would go to my grave before I would desert the people who elected me on a platform to give them cheaper lights."
>
> Mr. Brinkley reminded me that the ouster filed by State Atty. Gen. Thompson was merely a tool for the crowd here . . .
>
> Mr. Brinkley further said, "Of course, you know there is no thought of law violation or reform on the part of these utilities—merely a matter of money. They don't want the city to take over the Merchant's power Co.—go in the lighting business." They didn't want anything municipally owned.

This is the Crump story of the ouster suit and the power plant which I have preserved because it is the only time I have seen it printed in detail. It shows the ouster campaign starting after Crump turned down a last chance to back down from municipal power, and turning it down before witnesses.

It is to be noticed that the direct offer to stop the ouster in exchange for stopping the municipal power program was made by Brinkley, rather than Wright. It is my opinion that Wright could have moved without letting Miles know about it. In 1915 Wright was about seventy years old and Miles forty-four. Wright was a famous man, a former prosecuting attorney of Shelby County, governor-general of the Philippines, ambassador to Japan, and a recent member of the presidential cabinet. Further, it seems to me, the top power officials could have sent Brinkley to Crump without advice from the counsel. It is at least a possibility and it is a probability that Wright could have been informed, if he was, without sharing the knowledge from Miles.

Whatever the details, the city power plant was stopped and Crump was out of the mayor's office. The city commissioner picked by Crump to take over the mayor's office let go of the municipal power plant plan. Lawyers prepared a huge stack of papers for throwing the city government into receivership and a banker told the new mayor bankruptcy of the city government would follow the move.

A few months later Crump was elected trustee (treasurer), with by far the highest pay of any city or county office at that time. In the 1923 elections Crump and *The Commercial Appeal* joined hands to defeat the Ku Klux Klan and in 1927 the entire Crump ticket of city officials was swept into office.

That was the beginning of years of monotonous winning of city-county elections, and, in alliance with Senator Kenneth McKellar, of state and federal offices. Then came the Tennessee Valley Authority opportunity to renew the municipal ownership plan. TVA was formed in 1933 and it took a struggle that went on until 1939 to get the power company out of town. But Crump in person took a hand in the final bout and had great satisfaction in reversing the outcome of 1915.

The "Red" Threat

It is more than forty years since *The Commercial Appeal* published its Centennial Edition. There were 318 pages so filled with historical items that the Cossitt Library staff made a special index to save time in answering inquiries. Standard news of the day was published as usual, except for a return to the old fashion in headlines on page one. The biggest Memphis event reported at the top of the page, 1 January 1940, was the return of E. H. Crump to the title of mayor.

It was the fourth time he had taken the oath. He had announced as a proxy for Walter Chandler, who remained in Congress to cast the decisive vote on a bill to prepare for war. Crump said he would serve one day and resign so the City Council could make Chandler mayor. Crump said he would do exactly one thing as mayor—notify John L. Lewis that the City of Memphis's invitation for the annual convention of the American Newspaper Guild was withdrawn.

He only served as mayor about 30 minutes. When the year was a few minutes old he stood on the observation platform of the Panama Limited at Central Station, while dozens of men and women in the political organization stood in the snow cheering, and was sworn in.

The message telling the president of the Congress of Industrial Organizations (CIO) that the guild convention was unwelcome had been written in advance. He spoke to the New Year's Eve crowd of celebrating, snowball-throwing well wishers, the only time I ever heard him speak in public. Then he handed his resignation as mayor to the city attorney, went into the train, and departed for the Sugar Bowl game.

Extraordinary as the whole situation was, for Crump to speak may have been the most unusual of all. He had a great deal to say on many subjects over the years but he said it in advertisements or carefully written statements. He wrote it out, reworded it and when he was satisfied, asked the opinions of several close associates, rejected all suggestions for alterations, and then handed it to newspapermen. The organization had several men with golden voices or long platform experience to do the orating. It is most unlikely that a Crump speech was part of the plans for the railroad station demonstration. He seemed to be speaking spontaneously, goaded by a young man who said *The Commercial Appeal* wanted a statement.

Crump attacked me by name. I had said nothing to him and was standing back in the crowd, just in case something newsworthy happened. Of course his real objective was to keep CIO unions out of Memphis. The guild was a small young union of newspapermen, and the Crump understanding of my importance to the Memphis local was exaggerated. Nevertheless some researcher may come across my name in the report of this event and its background is an interesting sidelight on Crump.

Crump had demanded that I resign from the guild. Memphis newspapermen were in general conservative and twice had drawn back after considering the new union when its membership was largely in Cleveland, Washington, and New York. In 1936 there was a third consideration in Memphis and the guild venture was made. *The Commercial Appeal* had been sold, as was learned one morning when

Tom Fauntleroy moved out to the command desk in the city room. He fired five reporters, some of our best men, without notice. Captain Fauntleroy had been righthand man to C. P. J. Mooney, but had been shunted to one side during the years since Mooney died. Fauntleroy disapproved of new methods and especially of the larger staff.

All experienced reporters and desk men had friends among printers on the floor above, where the International Typographical Union could appeal firings and often reverse them, where pay was double or more what it was for the newsgathers, and where the pay cuts of Depression days were only a fraction of what they were on the editorial department payroll.

The union idea suddenly looked good to the newsmen when five of them were so abruptly thrown out on the sidewalk. Almost as suddenly *The Commercial Appeal* had enough members of the news staff to face the hazards of union membership in the South and form the Newspaper Guild of Memphis. Bolder men made the preliminary moves in secret and were elected the first officers. But I was a charter member and within a few weeks became secretary-treasurer, which I was for several years. I was one of the Memphis delegates to the annual convention in San Francisco in 1939.

The Memphis guild was almost three years old then and the national organization had moved out of the American Federation of Labor (AFL) to the CIO. Businessmen, especially in the South, had braced themselves against John L. Lewis and the CIO. Part of the public had become alarmed about possibilities of the Communist Party taking over the United States through CIO unions.

In the Memphis guild there was strong objection to the way "Reds" and "Pinkos" had taken over the national offices of the guild, combined with resentment of domination by the huge New York guild. The national staff wanted to take stands on such things as the Spanish Civil War and the Harry Bridges strikes on Pacific waterfronts, instead of putting more strength into organizing guilds in other Southern cities.

At the Toronto convention of the guild in 1938, three Memphis delegates, Harry Martin, W. A. Copeland, and Malcolm Adams had put together the framework of a group of anti-Red, anti-New York members throughout the country. The result of agitation, mostly by mail, was that delegates the next year were split, although New York still held control.

I was put on the convention finance committee and when we met we found a New Yorker had assumed the chairmanship. That session was brief. We opposition committee members withdrew for lunch on Fisherman's Wharf, decided who we wanted as committee officials, went back to the convention and took over the committee. (I escaped responsibilities of chairmanship by the toss of a coin at lunch.) We made some other gains at the convention and Memphis's bid for the 1940 convention was accepted. We seemed to be gaining national support of newspapermen in the guild for a replacement of union officers.

But there I was, a few months after the San Francisco convention, face to face with a demand from the most powerful man in Tennessee politics that I get out of the guild. I had felt the full thunderstorm of the Crump wrath before this incident, and would feel it again later. But this was different. It was more like an evangelist wrestling for the soul of a sinner. Crump could be persuasive in direct confrontation—most persuasive. That time there were just the two of us, except for a secretary in another part of the outer office. He had left some conferences in his main office to come out and point me to the straight and narrow path.

There was tenseness and there were firm words, without abusive language, but with total conviction that I was foolishly misguided unless I did what he said. Neither was there even a suggestion from him that I was a "Red." I had been told sometime before, when the CIO was new in Memphis, that my name had been turned in to the Federal Bureau of Investigation by Will Lee, police chief, as a possible Communist. Perhaps the "K" in my name misled him although anyone could have quickly found my ancestors in the Philadelphia area long before the Revolution, and in England. It is unlikely the FBI looked that deep into my background but whatever investigation was made it resulted in a report that I was clean. It also resulted in an inside joke about guild officials that, regardless of suspicions about others, at least Coppock was "certified pure" by the FBI.

Over the years that I had talked to him daily, Crump had gradually accepted me as "fair," meaning willing to write both sides of disputes. He was simply sure that he knew more about Communists and labor unions than I did and that I must accept his guidance. He considered himself a friend of union labor. This was based especially on a streetcar motorman's strike, when a committee of leading businessmen had called on him to force the men back on the cars they had abandoned on Main Street. He said he told committeemen they had come to the wrong office. If they wanted the streetcars to move again they would have to call on the company to yield reasonable demands to the union. That was done.

The communism situation in Memphis was, to him, a matter of

simple (but false) logic. Crump was against communism, therefore anyone against Crump was for communism. And I was told to take the Crump side on communism in unions. My first reaction was a great feeling of freedom. Neither Crump nor any of his associates had any kind of a handle on me. I had turned down offers of favors that would have become obligations. But I kept that declaration of independence to myself. What I said to Crump was that I intended to stay in the Guild in order to drive out the Reds. I said that would be far more beneficial to the public than for those who felt like I did to abandon the union and let the Reds have it.

Next day Crump renewed his verbal attack. But I had considered it overnight and renewed my stand. So that was the way it was when Crump made public announcement of his planned action against the guild as mayor.

In my opinion the Crump message to John L. Lewis would have been all there was to the story except for an unexpected circumstance. *The Commercial Appeal* had a young advertising man who wanted to be a reporter. He kept asking for a trial assignment until it seemed the only way to quiet him was let him do a story. On the last day of the year he was told that he could go to the station and try for a Crump statement. I was doing the page one story and was told nothing about the possibility of a side story from a novice.

The novice, his dream almost within reach after long effort, found himself in need of liquid reinforcements for the great test and showed up with slurred words to say *The Commercial Appeal* wanted a statement, and then to say it again and again as he was brushed off. No one in the Crump party knew him. They all knew me and I was in plain sight, having turned in the main story and the Crump statement. I was just standing ready in case something unexpected turned up. The unexpected was Crump's observation-platform attack on CIO newspapermen and on me by name. And that is how my name came to be part of the main political story of the Centennial Edition.

Let the record also show that the Guild held its 1940 convention here, that every reddish official was removed from New York headquarters, and that the new era was marked by Martin of Memphis as president, and Copeland of Memphis as an executive committee member.

Spectacular Reform

A fundamental change in government in the United States arrived in 1962. The Supreme Court announced that when a man lived in the city and found his state legislature stacked against him by men who lived in counties or farms he could get correction from the federal courts. Until then, the voice of Shelby County, which had more people than any other county in Tennessee and paid far more state taxes, was muffled on the day legislators were elected. In Moore County (Lynchburg), it took only 2,158 people to have a member in the House at Nashville, while it took 37,666 to have a spokesman for Hamilton County (Chattanooga).

In 1961, counties with forty percent of the population had sixty-six members of the House, and the counties with sixty percent of the people had thirty-three. In the Senate, counties with thirty-seven percent of the people had twenty senators, while the counties with sixty-three percent of the people had thirteen. Those were the days when Shelby County (Memphis) had eleven legislators, House and Senate. After the high-court ruling of 1962 and other associated cases, Shelby had twenty-five.

Results were spectacular, especially in passing out the taxes largely collected in the cities. State funds had flowed into the schools of Pickett County (Byrdstown) at the rate of $237 for each pupil, while for Shelby County schoolchildren the rate had been $111 a year.

This injustice accumulated for years. The Tennessee Constitution requires the legislative seats to be reassigned every ten years according to changing population. The General Assembly, in the firm control of the farm counties, simply refused. There was a reapportionment in 1901. After that there were attempts in each session of the legislature, and there were lawsuits, lots of them, but the rural politicians had the power and stood pat.

They were supported by an ancient bit of folklore in which virtue grows on the farm while vice thrives in the city. Most states had similar situations. In the North, there was fear of ignorant immigrants and in the South a distrust of blacks. Big-city politicians, here and elsewhere, became somewhat adjusted to the imbalance of power, made some deals with the country men and turned their attention to more practical changes, rather than another attempt to get representative government back into state business.

Then came the ruling in *Baker* v. *Carr* in 1962, sometimes referred to more briefly as simply "Baker." The "Baker" in question was and is

David N. Harsh (from *The Commercial Appeal* files).

Charles W. Baker of Millington. His name is as firmly imbedded in the history of the United States as Dred Scott or William Marbury. Baker has a splendid record as a public official. He was a member of the County Court for twenty-eight years, ending in 1978, when his doctor insisted on retirement. There never was an opposition candidate. He was chairman twenty-one years, including the year the famous suit was filed.

But any assumption that his name on the lawsuit indicates he was a prime mover is an error. The suit was filed by a group of citizens of Tennessee and by their city governments. The Baker name leads simply because they are arranged alphabetically. The ''Carr'' against whom it was filed was Joe C. Carr, Tennessee Secretary of State. His name also has prominence only because of the alphabet. There was a group of defendants.

Date of the filing of *Baker* v. *Carr* may have some significance, however, It was 18 May 1959. Ed Crump had died in 1954. Frank Rice, the generalissimo of Shelby County operations in Nashville, had been gone since 1938. E. W. Hale had retired as 1955 ended, after thirty-two years as chairman of the Shelby County Commission, the three-man body that administered county affairs and, unofficially, made policy too. All had been reformers and idealists in their younger years but had found more useful pursuits than chasing the will-o-the-wisp of a just division of legislative seats. After all, the U.S. Supreme Court as recently as 1946 had turned back one more legal effort, refusing to "enter this political jungle."

In 1959 new forces were astir in Tennessee politics and some younger men were ready to try again, although the public saw only another of the long list of attempts in the courts and in the legislature. In Shelby County there seemed to be more interest in another reform, unification of city and county governments. Then came the *Baker* v. *Carr* decision that federal courts could review claims of discrimination against voters by legislative apportionment. It was a six to two decision. It received a flood of newspaper space, but it took another lawsuit and many defiant moves by the rural forces throughout the country to establish the one-man-one-vote principle. Eventually, more than half of the states had to reform their legislatures to give full voice to city dwellers.

Earl Warren, chief justice of the court that made the drastic change, said after his retirement that he considered it the most important case during all his years as justice and chief justice. Thomas P. Turley, Jr., former district attorney, made the meaning clearer when he said, "This is the federal government saying to state governments, 'You've got to comply with the Constitution of the United States. Period and paragraph, and we're going to decide whether you have or not.' "

It was an abrupt change and yet it took so long for other legal cases and adjustments by legislatures to bring in the new day that little attention was paid by the public to the movers and pushers who brought it about. Among them, however, there was frequent attention to the role of Walter Chandler, the lawyer who filed *Baker* v. *Carr*.

Chandler had firsthand knowledge of the undemocratic choking of the votes of little men in the cities ever since he had gone to the legislature as a member in 1917. He had been mayor of Memphis, a member of the U.S. House, city attorney, and otherwise notable as a leader of Memphis opinion. In contrast to the younger men who were taking part, he was about seventy-five. *One Man One Vote: Baker v. Carr and the American Levellers* by Gene Graham is a book about the case, published in 1973, which says Chandler "put a brilliant legal mind, years of experience and extraordinary organizational and leadership skills to work in what was his last, and certainly his most important, reform."

Yet behind Chandler was another figure, David N. Harsh, who followed Hale as County Commission chairman. He was photographed at least once with Chandler—a pair of men deeply involved in *Baker* v. *Carr*. But when the Harsh career was reviewed in his obituary several years later, the famous lawsuit was omitted.

Perhaps it is too late now for credit to catch up with him, but historians might take note of the fact that Baker once said it was Harsh who originated the idea of this suit that overwhelmed the legal defenses at last. There had been a time when Chandler was pessimistic about getting a Supreme Court hearing but Harsh was undismayed. Further, Harsh was able to get County Commission money for the considerable expense of continuing the legal fight. Historians also can learn that Rudolph Jones, a county commissioner at the time, tells of Chandler saying: "Dave Harsh preserved democracy in America."

9

Good New Days

On 28 November 1977 a dinner program given by The West Tennessee Historical Society was announced as "An Evening with Paul R. Coppock," The center of attention was told it would be unnecessary for him to speak, but for fear of being caught off balance, he carried some notes in a pocket and was able to respond to the testimonials. This article was written from those notes and is an approximation of what he said. It also is, in a rough way, a summary of his attitudes, and it has been published as a "Mid-South Memoir."

The phrase "good old days," is of little use to me. I have found that the old days were often bad, all things considered. Health conditions alone were enough to take away the "good" label from old times. Yellow fever killed members of older generations by the thousands. So did cholera. Malaria killed many and did a great deal more damage by weakening the old, the working generation, and the youngsters, impairing their abilities for years. Pellagra was a scourge in this part of the country.

There is a feeling of luxurious living by wealthy families in the occasional account of elaborate dinners with a servant standing behind each chair to keep a fly whisk moving over the food. But the words about lush times of the past leave out the rather essential fact that the servant-at-each-chair days were also the days before screens, when every one who could afford it had a stable behind the house with a horse or two, and almost always with a cow or two.

For in those days the ordinary family had a cow and the poor family had a goat to avoid the milkman, who came down the street with a can in his cart and a dipper to be used in the dusty open air. Besides, some milkmen were suspected of getting part of their "milk" out of the barnyard water pump.

Memories of pleasant persons we have known are good; but it is something else to remember the kid sister who died of typhoid under old sanitary standards. There are a few oldsters still around from the days before the electrocardiograph was invented, when the death certificates of many a father killed by a heart attack showed the cause of death as "acute indigestion," because knowledge of the heart as so slim. Numerous persons have vivid memories of "infantile paralysis," an affliction which now can be prevented if everyone would take the "shot."

We have a great advantage over those who lived—and died—in the "good old days" because doctors in hospitals and in experimental laboratories are learning more about protecting health with each passing month, and in Memphis we have acres of buildings and thousands of men and women devoted to that purpose. I write first of medicine, partly because it shows one of the greatest contrasts between the old and the new, and partly because of my personal interest. Modern medicine has given me twenty-one years of "borrowed time."

In other portions of life, the "old" would be rejected by this generation if there was a choice. Consider schools. We used to have some fine academies but there were some shoddy institutions of instruction at the same time. Possession of knowledge and the ability to plant it in young minds are distinct from each other. Some of these teachers of the old times were youngsters in their late teens without the slightest idea of how to catch the interest of children. And some of them neither knew how to teach, nor had they absorbed into their own minds much knowledge for transplanting. Worse than that, these academies were only for the children of families with money for the fees. It took money at the front door. In many families the cash ran out when the boys had been cared for. The girls had to stay home.

As to education, there has been a far more fundamental change, almost ignored in modern writing. That is the income that allows most families to get along without the labor of adolescent offspring. The muscles of growing children, or a few dollars from outside jobs, were needed to keep bread on the table for a huge proportion of families in the old days. Even in the household with a fairly good income the almost grown children were needed, except during a few weeks of bad weather when work in the fields had to stop. We have new campuses filled with new buildings where new teachers perform the chores of college. They would have been useless surplus a hundred years ago, for many "students" of today would have been "geeing" and "hawing" a mule yesterday whether their skins were brown or white. Against such a backdrop, pupils privileged to sit in the glow of gifted teachers in the good academies were entitled to all the distinction they had, but they were uncharacteristic of their contemporaries.

Then there was the subject of transportation in the old days, back when leg muscles of horses or men were the most common power of motion. Steamboats that could move upstream on the Mississippi are only a little more than 150 years old. Steam trains that could run on days when the water was too low for boats, or the mud was too deep for wagons, are even younger. The boats are a colorful part of life in this region, often described by gifted writers and painted by artists. But they were slow compared to trains or automobiles. They frequently were stopped by low water, ice, boiler explosions, and fires or stabbed below the waterline by snags.

Sometimes the boats were stopped by a lack of the freight that paid the bills of a business for which passengers were only a sideline. Sometimes when the advertised schedule called for departure at 5 P.M., there would be a great tooting of whistles and ringing of bells to cause merchants to rush drays to the waterfront. But if the drays stayed away the boat might stay tied up until another day. Sometimes there was a chorus of deck-hands singing in the moonlight—as long as coins showered down from rails of the upper deck. But sometimes the winter winds sweeping across miles of water forced everyone to look for protection from frigid air. Many staterooms were over boilers and, in the summer, were too hot for sleep. Sometimes soot fell on the decks from the stacks like black snow.

Any fear that I may do a detailed examination of pimples on the face of the packet boat is groundless. I share in the fascination of sidewheeler glory and paddlewheel excitement. I ride a boat at every opportunity. I know every boat picture interests at least five persons for every one curious about the engraving of an old man with a full beard. I am even a "son and daughter," that is, a member of "The Sons and Daughters of

Pioneer Rivermen'' (by election). But it seems to be time to let anyone interested know that I have seen the smoky side of boats.

So, surely at least there were "good old days" in politics, when James K. Polk, a future president, was governor; when Wm. R. Moore, a Republican merchant, was elected to Congress from Memphis; or when Kenneth McKellar, master of the levers of senatorial power, was on his way up as the representative of Memphis. But it should be remembered that a résumé of splendid performances in public offices can be compressed into one book, or one chapter, that gives a false impression of time, overlooking the years and the decades of plain men in office, between the starring roles.

Or we might add another word to speak of the "good old lazy days" when many voters could, and often did, just leave it to the judgment of Ed Crump as to who should fill the offices and what priorities there should be in public affairs, knowing that anything that would raise the tax rate would probably have to wait.

But let us look. In the early 1900s we had an election in which a reform ticket won the city election. But one big gambling house kept on running after the reformers took their oaths. Eventually public curiosity forced a police raid. Immediately the mayor got a message from the gambler saying that if he was ever bothered again he would go to court and have them all extracted from office. They had been elected by fraudulent votes. The annoyed gambler had been a "reformer" and he still had 200 of the premarked ballots which had been an unneeded surplus on election day—and he would be happy to let the public see the fake ballots in court. That was only a short time after a raid on another gambler, when pistols were taken away from the raiding officers and two deputy sheriffs were killed.

In the 1890s we have a primary for Congress in which, the House was told much later, there were thirty-eight voters in Ward 2 but 238 ballots were turned in. In Ward 4 there were fifty-nine voters, but they marked 417 ballots. In Ward 8 the number of voters was ninety-seven, but the number of ballots was 408. Ward 10 got an honest count that night, almost. Poll watchers had filed into the saloon and announced themselves early in the day. They counted thirty-three voters and there were only forty-five ballots.

Readers should be cautious about filling in the names of men involved in these peccadillos. The only persons who would have the names would be specialists in local history, who are very few, or those whose great-grandfathers took part in the incidents, and they are even fewer. Or perhaps we should go even farther back, when the original Memphis voters were unable to vote for mayors. All they could do was elect seven aldermen, who chose one of themselves to take charge.

The plain fact is that some of the "good old days" in Memphis were pretty bad. This town went to war on the losing side. It lost thousands of citizens to diseases, and to the terror of diseases that caused residents to flee to other cities. There have been floods that covered surrounding areas. Crops have failed and prices fallen.

But Memphis has climbed over its troubles, to grow in numbers and in strength. It has fine air, rail, barge, and highway transportation. It has abundant and pure water, and so on through the municipal advantages comparison. Whenever someone sings the downhearted blues I think of some of the long ago doubts and look forward to another upturn.

In addition to physical facts, Memphis has had for many years some most resourceful personalities. For instance, one of my favorites among the numerous characters of the region is Dr. Frank McGavock, of Mississippi County (Blytheville), Arkansas. Just after the Civil War farm help was scarce. For many newly freed slaves "freedom" included freedom from work, especially while gifts from the North and help from the Freedman's Bureau was available.

But Dr. McGavock was determined to make a crop, and he did, with a good profit. He went to New York and signed up newly arrived immigrant girls from Ireland, seventy-five of them, as young as fifteen and as old as forty-five. He housed them, provided a mess hall, and a priest and, most important of all, he provided a barrel of whiskey. The girls were given a drink of two drams, three times a day. He had put several ounces of quinine into the barrel and the malaria that knocked out so many field hands stayed away from the McGavock fields. The girls had a tendency to get married, but the clever doctor went back to New York and got some more. This is the kind of originality that has shown up again and again hereabouts.

A few weeks ago the Friends of the Memphis and Shelby County Libraries presented a Book and Author Dinner, with four visiting writers of recent books. Since Friends are the publishers of my book, *Memphis Sketches,* I was seated on the dais. Nearest me was William Armstrong, author of *Sounder.* We exchanged a little small talk, without either of us mentioning my book. But someone did a fine selling job on him.

For as soon as he got home to Kent, Connecticut, he wrote the Friends for a book and asked them to get me to autograph it. He went beyond buying my book. He read it, and he wrote a second letter commenting on something near the end. Then he said: "Memphis must be a delightful place to live." That a stranger here for a day, learning about our town from my book came to the conclusion that this is a delightful place to live was hardly accidental. I intended for it to be that way.

Fifty years ago this fall I saw Memphis for the first time, a stranger looking for a job. I have found it to be a delightful place to live, as well as an interesting town to write about. It is, I believe, a better city than it was in the so-called good old days.

Index

Illustrations are indexed in boldface type. This index was compiled under the direction of Mary Davant.